Manhood Enslaved

Gender and Race in American History

Alison Parker, The College at Brockport, State University of New York
Carol Faulkner, Syracuse University

ISSN: 2152-6400

Manhood Enslaved

Bondmen in Eighteenth- and Early Nineteenth-Century New Jersey

Kenneth E. Marshall

UNIVERSITY OF ROCHESTER PRESS

First published 2011. Reprinted in paperback and transferred to digital printing 2012.

University of Rochester Press
668 Mt. Hope Avenue, Rochester, NY 14620, USA
www.urpress.com
and Boydell & Brewer Limited
PO Box 9, Woodbridge, Suffolk IP12 3DF, UK
www.boydellandbrewer.com

ISSN: 2152-6400
Hardcover ISBN: 978-1-58046-393-5
Paperback ISBN: 978-1-58046-435-2

Library of Congress Cataloging-in-Publication Data
Marshall, Kenneth E. (Kenneth Edward)
   Manhood enslaved : bondmen in eighteenth- and early nineteenth-century New Jersey / Kenneth E. Marshall.
      p. cm. — (Gender and race in American history, ISSN 2152-6400 ; v. 2)
   Includes bibliographical references and index.
   ISBN 978-1-58046-393-5 (hardcover : alk. paper) 1. Slavery—New Jersey—History. 2. Slaves—New Jersey—Biography. 3. Slavery in literature. 4. Melick, Yombo, b. ca. 1739. 5. Melick, Dick, b. 1749. 6. Buccau, Quamino, 1762–1850. 7. Allinson, William J., 1810-1874. Memoir of Quamino Buccau, a pious Methodist. 8. Mellick, Andrew D., 1844-1895. Story of an old farm. I. Title.
   E445.N54M37 2011
   306.3'6209749—dc23   2011020885

A catalogue record for this title is available from the British Library.

This publication is printed on acid-free paper. Printed in the United States of America.

An earlier version of chapter 2 was published as "Powerful and Righteous: The Transatlantic Survival and Cultural Resistance of an Enslaved African Family in Eighteenth-Century New Jersey," *Journal of American Ethnic History* 23, no. 2 (2004): 23–49. © 2004 by the Immigration and Ethnic History Society. Used with permission.

An earlier version of chapter 3 was published as "'His Disposition Was Not in Any Sense Agreeable': The Making of an Eighteenth-Century Malcontent Northern Slave, 'Old Yombo,'" *Contours: A Journal of the African Diaspora* 3, no. 1 (2005): 1–26. © 2005 by the Board of Trustees of the University of Illinois. Used with permission of the University of Illinois Press.

An earlier version of chapter 4 was published as "Threat of a Bondman: Political Self-Fashioning and Christian Empowerment in the *Memoir of Quamino Buccau, A Pious Methodist*," *Slavery and Abolition* 29, no. 3 (2008): 361–88. © 2008 by Frank Cass & Co. Used with permission.

An earlier version of chapter 5 was published as "Work, Family and Day-to-Day Survival on an Old Farm: Nance Melick, a Rural Late Eighteenth- and Early Nineteenth-Century New Jersey Slave Woman," *Slavery and Abolition* 19, no. 3 (1998): 22–45. © 1998 by Frank Cass & Co. Used with permission.

   Cover art: Colorized frontispiece of William J. Allinson's *Memoir of Quamino Buccau, A Pious Methodist* (1851). Drawing by "Mason & Maas."

For Meri, whose love makes all things possible.

The slave knows, however his master may be deluded on this point, that he is called a slave because his manhood has been, or can be, or will be taken from him. To be a slave means that one's manhood is engaged in a dubious battle indeed, and this stony fact is not altered by whatever devotion some masters and some slaves may have arrived at in relation to each other. In the case of American slavery, the black man's right to his women, as well as his children, was simply taken from him.

—James Baldwin, *No Name in the Street*

Contents

Illustrations

Acknowledgments

For all my hard work, I could not have completed this book by myself. First of all, it rests on the shoulders of numerous scholars and historians who have come before me, who made it possible for me to write this kind of book. The structure and content of *Manhood Enslaved*, however, owes a particular debt to three pioneering historians: John Blassingame, Gerald (Michael) Mullin, and Deborah Gray White. I am equally grateful to the anonymous reviewers for providing me with many useful comments and suggestions that I have incorporated into the book. Their insights undoubtedly made this project much stronger. I thank *Slavery and Abolition, Contours*, and the *Journal of American Ethnic History* for not only publishing my earlier work, but also for allowing me to publish portions of these articles in *Manhood Enslaved*. I also owe a sincere word of thanks to the Gender and Race in American History Series at the University of Rochester Press—Alison Parker, Carol Faulkner, Suzanne Guiod, Tracey Engel, and Ryan Peterson. My book was published by a rather supportive, professional, and enthusiastic series and press.

I first became interested in the topic of New Jersey slavery while an undergraduate at Rider College (now University). I took a history class with Roderick McDonald, whose passion and insight ultimately led me to Clement Price's documentary history on blacks in New Jersey. What I read in Price's book stunned me: not only were black people once enslaved in New Jersey, but they also resisted slavery under an oppressive system. I felt embarrassed and angry that, as an "educated" black male, I was totally ignorant about the black presence in my state's past. Though I could recite from memory Ernest Lawrence Thayer's famous baseball poem, "Casey at the Bat" (a feat I first accomplished in my seventh-grade English class), I had no idea that slavery existed in my hometown of Trenton. To my young and impressionable mind, United States slavery was strictly a Southern phenomenon. As a result of my harsh awakening in Roderick's class, I changed my major from communications to history. I want to thank Roderick for helping me to find my calling in life.

I took my deep commitment to learning more about early black life in New Jersey with me to graduate school at Michigan State University. Though none of my professors in the history department were necessarily experts on the subject, they nonetheless indulged my intellectual curiosity, allowing me to write research papers that did not always fall within the scope of their seminars. I would particularly like to thank David Bailey and

David Barry Gaspar for turning me loose (so to speak), for these experiences enabled me to further develop my ideas on slave resistance and day-to-day survival. *Manhood Enslaved* was born directly from my dissertation, supervised by Harry Reed. In addition to Harry, I wish to extend heartfelt thanks to the other members of my dissertation committee for their positive feedback and encouragement: Darlene Clark Hine, Laurent Dubois, Stephen Esquith, and David Bailey. They perhaps have no idea of how good it felt to hear that the dissertation was not far from being a "good book."

Though she never served on any of my graduate committees, Susan Klepp played a critical role in my professional development. I avoided her while she was teaching in the history department at Rider (she had a reputation as a ruthless grader), but she later gave me an arduous year-long tutorial on how to get my work published. These long-distance writing sessions resulted in an article in *Slavery and Abolition*. (I had yet to complete my comprehensive exams.) More than any other scholar in the profession, Susan has championed my work and career. I will never be able to repay her for all she has done for me. All I can say—with the utmost sincerity—is thank you.

Words also cannot adequately express my gratitude to New Jersey genealogist Fred Sisser III. Besides providing me with source materials I never would have found on my own, he made a critical observation regarding one of my enslaved subjects. While we were both conducting research at the New Jersey State Archives, I was struggling to corroborate the name of Quamino's "Buccau" owner, mentioned in the former's memoir. Sensing my exasperation, Fred took off his glasses, stared at the name, and grumbled, "That's not Buccau, that's Brokaw." Thereafter, I was able to make better sense of Quamino's obscured life under slavery.

Many thanks, moreover, to William "Buzzy" Hundley for sharing his resources with me; and the curators at the New Jersey State Archives, Alexander Library at Rutgers University, Burlington County Historical Society, David Library of the American Revolution, Magill Library at Haverford College, New Jersey Historical Society, Hunterdon County Historical Society, and Clements Library at the University of Michigan. I met some incredibly nice and helpful people at these places who made my research less of a chore.

It helps to have good friends and colleagues, and I have been fortunate in this respect as well. Kristin Waters and her daughter, Jiaqi O'Reilly, welcomed a distraught man into their happy home, providing me with clean linen, gourmet meals, and companionship at the coffee shop. Ruth Haber also saved me from the streets, and even gave me a (temporary) car to drive. I received similar valued support over the years from Eric and Jody Duke, Donald Bray, Jason Rogers, Frank Spooner, Gloria Hall, Marc Wallace, Kelly McKithen, Geoffrey Hale, and my students at Worcester State

College and SUNY Oswego (who allowed me to be myself in the class-room). Pero Dagbovie and Doug Deal, two very different but fine histori-ans, closely read the manuscript. Pero reminded me, among other things, that it takes creativity to write about the Middle Passage. Though I did not always agree with him, Doug forced me to hone my arguments and make more judicious speculations. Thank you all for being there for me.

I also owe special thanks to my family, which was particularly gracious during this process. My mother, Peggie Bellamy, has been a constant source of kindness and encouragement since my days at Rider. One of my fondest research trips was when she drove my wife, Meredith, and me to Haverford College so that I could conduct research there. My in-laws, Ronald and Cecilia Roman, demonstrated kindnesses too innumerable to recount here. They always made trips to New Jersey enjoyable experiences. Their home has become my home over the years, making my research and writing (not to mention my married life) even more enjoyable. The Brant-ley, Cook, Englehart, Kaufmann, Kuldoshes, and Quinn families provided much needed solace and good cheer.

Above all, this book would not be possible without the love, support, and encouragement of my wife, Meredith Roman. She did it all—listened to me doubt myself, read the manuscript numerous times in its many forms, typed parts of it (including the index), and constantly reinforced to me that I would get it done because Yombo, Dick, and Quamino (my principal subjects) deserved to have their stories told. For some ten years, she patiently endured as I walked and talked with these slaves. Thank you, Meri, for doing all that for me. This project stands as testimony that her love makes all things possible in my life.

Lastly, I would like to acknowledge Yombo, Dick, and Quamino for enduring a brutal experience that requires much more research. How they appear to have (to borrow the phrase from Earth, Wind, and Fire) kept their heads "to the sky" has humbled me over the years, instilling me with incentive to do the same.

Introduction

"Ain't No Account"

By 1800 New Jersey boasted the second largest enslaved population in the northeastern United States.[1] Yet, because of the paucity of useful published sources in which African Americans discuss their lives under New Jersey bondage—an undeniably brutal, as well as important economic and social system—former enslaved blacks there are virtually mute. Consequently, when Silvia Dubois (1788/89–1889), a former central New Jersey slave, was asked by a certain white man, in 1883, if he could publish her life story, which was part of local legend, the free black woman bluntly retorted, "Most of folks think that niggers ain't no account, but if you think what I tell you is worth publishing, I will be glad if you do it. 'T won't do me no good, but maybe 't will somebody else. I've lived a good while, and have seen a good deal, and if I should tell you all I've seen, it would make the hair stand up all over your head."[2]

Manhood Enslaved reconstructs the lives of three of Dubois's male slave compatriots, and brings greater intellectual and historical clarity to the muted lives of enslaved peoples in eighteenth- and early nineteenth-century New Jersey, where blacks were held in bondage for roughly two centuries.[3] This study contributes to the evolving body of historical scholarship that argues that the lives of the enslaved in America were shaped not only by the powerful forces of racial oppression, but also by these people's own notions of gender—of what constituted a man and a woman.[4] In addition, the present work uses previously understudied, white-authored nineteenth-century literature about New Jersey slaves as a point of departure. Reading beyond the racist assumptions of the authors, it contends that the precarious day-to-day existence of the three protagonists—Yombo Melick, Dick Melick, and Quamino Buccau (Smock)—reveals the various elements of "slave manhood" that gave real meaning to their oppressed lives. *Manhood Enslaved* connects the gendered lives of eighteenth-century enslaved Northern peoples to Northern white thought over the eighteenth and nineteenth centuries, revealing shared assumptions and divergent views regarding race and gender in the new nation.

Un-Muting Black Voices

Out of fear of creating discontent among enslaved blacks, Southern whites deliberately denied most of them literacy by enacting stringent state laws and local ordinances that forbade their instruction in reading and writing. Many Northern whites, lacking such legislative weaponry but equally aware that literacy stimulated black ambition, also deprived the enslaved of education.[5] Black people in freedom from the revolutionary through the antebellum periods confronted two devastating modes of white paranoia and domination: institutionalized segregation and discrimination. These obstacles likewise inhibited many blacks from receiving an education and, consequently, denied them the ability to "account" for their lives under slavery.[6]

Even so, blacks are not completely silent about the slavery experience in America. Indeed, while exploring and reconstructing the lives of enslaved black Southerners, historians have frequently and creatively utilized the seemingly countless autobiographies of former slaves (slave narratives) published during the ante- and postbellum eras, and the even more numerous interviews of ex-bondmen and bondwomen conducted by the Federal Writer's Project during the 1930s. Though invaluable, these sources are also problematic in that they are tainted by degrees of racism, distortion, and personal bias. Without them, however, historians would have even greater difficulty trying to understand the minds of enslaved men and women.[7] By contrast, there exists a greater paucity of useful published sources in which African Americans discuss their lives in the context of Northern bondage.[8] Historians have thus relied upon eighteenth-century white records, often with very limited information pertaining to persons under slavery. These include wills and deeds, newspaper advertisements for the sale of slaves and recapture of fugitives, census reports, law books, tax records, slave manifests, writings of observers, and court and manumission records. But the possibility of using these records collectively may yield only a shadowy sketch of the enslaved north of the Mason-Dixon line. In a sense, historical analysis of the interior lives of enslaved Northern blacks, particularly those in rural areas such as central New Jersey, the Somerset County area—where our three protagonists were enslaved, for the most part—requires an even higher degree of scholarly flexibility and creativity.[9]

Accordingly, *Manhood Enslaved* is framed through two obscure yet provocative pieces of nineteenth-century literature that typify how elite written texts elide the agency of oppressed groups: *Memoir of Quamino Buccau, A Pious Methodist* (1851), and *The Story of an Old Farm; or, Life in New Jersey in the Eighteenth Century* (1889).[10] The former was written by William J. Allinson (1810–74), a noted New Jersey Quaker abolitionist who composed the short, thirty-page biography of Quamino Smock (1762–1850) as a romantic racialist tract.[11] George Fredrickson, exploring the black image in the

minds of white Americans, posits that many leading white abolitionists during the mid nineteenth century were proponents of romantic racialism,
which maintained that blacks were naturally moral, religious, affectionate,
forgiving, and, most of all, docile. As freed people, therefore, they posed
no threat to white public safety. This racist, one-dimensional composite of
blacks, Fredrickson contends, expressed romantic racialists' disillusion-
ment with slavery, geographical expansionism in the name of "manifest
destiny," and the unbridled materialism of the time. In other words, white
social reformers of the 1840s and 1850s extolled the idealized black person
as "a symbol of something . . . tragically lacking" in materialistic, warlike,
and dominant white American civilization.[12] Not surprisingly, then, William Allinson rendered Quamino's life story as "the struggle for survival
and ultimate redemption of a black saint in a hostile white world." To Allinson, Quamino represented "the downtrodden, meek, and poor who, unlike
the rich and powerful, would 'inherit the kingdom of heaven.'"[13] But, as
demonstrated in this study, we can interpret Quamino's life differently. It
allows us to envision, for example, how Christianity served as a source both
of personal defense and of masculine empowerment for enslaved Northern males as they took on the perilous yet equally empowering roles of
fathers, husbands, and protectors.

   The Story of an Old Farm, dictated by Andrew D. Mellick Jr. (1844–95),
who was rendered paralyzed in the prime of his life, also sheds important
light on the gendered identities of enslaved males in the rural North. While
Mellick's book encapsulates the entrenched local dogma that deemed
blacks as inferior, exotic, and the wards of merciful and beneficent whites,
it presents us with two rather intriguing constructions of slave manhood.[14]
Yombo (b. circa 1739) represents a form of manhood grounded in obstinacy and pride in one's African ancestry, whereas Dick (b. circa 1749) represents a passive type of manhood exercised mainly through one's family
relations.[15] To put it differently, Mellick portrays Yombo as the "bad nigger" version of black manhood, and Dick as the "house nigger" version. In
African American culture, the "bad nigger" is a heroic person who refuses
to act in a docile manner and rejects the social norms imposed by the dominant culture. The "house nigger," by contrast, is the reprehensible person
who has extensive contact with whites, and *seems* more loyal to them than
to his or her compatriots.[16] Mellick's depiction of Dick as a "house nigger"
obscures how the bondman was highly self-controlled and, by implication,
highly deceptive. One might argue, in fact, that, because of the climate of
racial hostility in eighteenth-century New Jersey, and Dick's imposing and
hence threatening body, the bondman engaged in acts of dissimulation
that enabled him not only to express his humanity and creativity, but also
to preserve his tenuous family relations, which, unprotected by law, faced
possible dissolution.[17] To dissemble, then, did not necessarily reduce Dick

to an obsequious "house nigger" with little or no integrity. On the contrary, it suggests that he was as much a survivor as his openly defiant counterpart Yombo, who lived apart from his enslaved wife and could, therefore, take more risks to express his displeasure with bondage.

Of the two works under discussion, *The Story of an Old Farm* is by far the best known. Not only did Andrew Mellick's book achieve international acclaim, but writers often used it in attempting to demonstrate, in varying degrees, the paternalistic nature of New Jersey slavery. In particular, frequent mention is made of Dick and his wife Nance's joyous experiences during the Christmas season, when they did little work, and General Training, a holiday event centered on the drilling of the local militia.[18] The importance of *The Story of an Old Farm* was not lost on historian Clement Price, who has called it "a personal account which provides some interesting insights into black life under slavery in eighteenth-century New Jersey."[19] Historians James and Lois Horton are more specific in their assessment, explaining that the lives of Dick and Nance—their relatively benevolent circumstances aside—point to how "vulnerability" in the lives of Northern bondpeoples "existed even in the best situations."[20] This study uses Mellick's eleven-page discussion of his ancestor's "Negroes" to illuminate how some enslaved blacks in New Jersey may have attempted to construct themselves as men and women, notwithstanding their vulnerable circumstances.

Similarly, the *Memoir of Quamino Buccau* has largely escaped the attention of historians. Only Arthur Zilversmit's important 1967 investigation of Northern slavery and abolition, and Earnest Lyght's detailed 1978 study of blacks in Burlington County, New Jersey, have employed it to any real extent. Zilversmit uses the narrative briefly as supplementary documentation about the harsh realities of Northern bondage, and to stress the ebullience of newly emancipated African Americans. For Lyght, it serves merely as "an interesting story in the history of manumissions."[21] Neither author seems to consider that one of the narrative's greatest attributes is its range of complex human emotions—sorrow, contrition, tears of gratitude, righteous indignation—that allow us to begin to probe into the hidden thoughts of enslaved males in the eighteenth-century rural North. Moreover, it challenges the popular belief propagated by such prominent historians as Zilversmit, W. E. B. Du Bois, Lorenzo Greene, Winthrop Jordan, Ira Berlin, Gary Nash, and William Piersen that Northern slavery, in comparison to the institution below Mason and Dixon's line, was mild or benign.[22] At the same time, it strongly supports the more recent work of Gary Nash and Jean Soderlund, Shane White, Susan Klepp, Graham Hodges, Kenneth Marshall, Leslie Harris, and Berlin (who changed his position), which stress how Northern slavery was not only a heinously cruel system, but in terms of black family life was probably more oppressive than its Southern counterpart.[23] As we might expect, Quamino bore the scars of slavery well into old age. For example, the elderly free black man never forgot the image of a "nice" bondman who was publicly burned at the stake for retaliating against his owner's offense.[24] As a noted literary historian points out, "Reconstructing their past lives required many ex-slaves to . . . relive the most psychically charged moments of [their] past and to be reminded of thoughts and deeds about which [they] had come to feel very ambivalent."[25] In the end, William Allinson's romantic racialist account of Quamino reads as a subtle yet powerful indictment of an institution that brought great harm to black peoples and greatly challenged the ability of the enslaved to see themselves as fully human, much less as persons with masculine and feminine sensibilities worthy of respect from their owners.

Significantly, this seldom used account, and the study overall, complements the excellent monographs that Graham Hodges has written. In *Slavery and Freedom in the Rural North* (1997), a nuanced micro-study of African Americans in Monmouth County, New Jersey, Hodges explores a range of important topics pertaining to enslaved blacks, including their tenuous family life, adoption of Christianity, various labor roles, levels of autonomy, forms of resistance, and subjugation to physical brutality. These themes are expounded upon in *Root and Branch* (1999), in which he convincingly argues that the resistance and cultural lives of the enslaved in New York City and its rural environs, including central New Jersey, were inextricably linked.[26] Much of the same ground is covered in *Manhood Enslaved* but within the context of slave manhood, which Hodges explores primarily in terms of overt resistance. As this study demonstrates, Yombo, Dick, and Quamino—who appear not to have engaged in open, violent warfare with whites—enhance our understanding of how the enslaved resisted and survived in and around eighteenth-century New York.

Enslaved Manhood in (Scholarly) Literature and Society

Manhood Enslaved is informed by a range of scholarly inquiry as it interrogates the obstacles facing enslaved males of African origin and descent, and the ways in which they responded to their oppression. It has profited greatly, for instance, from the wealth of cross-disciplinary literature focusing on the historical dilemmas of black males in America. This literature addresses, specifically, how the experience of slavery altered the role of black men in Africa and how powerful social forces, including poverty, crime, joblessness, and disparate rates of prison incarceration, continued to affect the black man's role and, consequently, shaped his behavior in contemporary urban environments.[27] According to Richard Majors and Janet Billson, some African American males in urban areas have adopted a coping strategy they refer to as the "cool pose." This strategy, which Majors and Billson contend is rooted in ancient African culture, adds particular insight to Yombo's hostile disposition. Similar to contemporary black urban males, Yombo created a defiant (mean) persona that conveyed strength and pride while perhaps also hiding his vulnerabilities as a black male slave.[28] As the cool pose and such other perspectives on black males suggest, Yombo and his eighteenth-century rural Northern counterparts (like their enslaved Southern brethren) persistently fought their white oppressors for physical and psychic survival.

Without question, this study owes an even greater debt to the rich historiography that examines various aspects of the gendered lives of enslaved men in America. The scholarly interest in enslaved men was spawned by Stanley Elkins's controversial 1959 book *Slavery: A Problem in American Institutional and Intellectual Life*. Elkins argued that the especially repressive system of US slavery created a "Sambo" personality in blacks. Specifically, the total authority that slaveholders possessed negated alternative social bases and standards for enslaved blacks, thereby reducing them to a state of childlike dependency. Elkins depicted this all-embracing, personality-deforming bondage as emasculating black men.[29] During the 1970s when black studies programs were emerging at colleges and universities across the United States, a coterie of now-distinguished historians countered Elkins, both directly and indirectly, by demonstrating that enslaved Southern men exercised their manhood in courtship, work, providing for and protecting enslaved women and children, naming offspring, and in overt and subtle forms of resistance.[30] This groundbreaking and, moreover, highly politicized scholarly literature (which, admittedly, portrayed men's lives as the normative experience under slavery) laid the foundation for conceptualizing enslaved males as the possessors of manhood.

More recent scholarly studies have conceptualized American bondmen as impotent yet dedicated fathers, husbands, and warriors; as freedom fighters in the young Republic; as violent revolutionists with previous military experience in Africa; as proponents of situational self-assertion; and as vital community caretakers on the southwestern frontier.[31] *Manhood Enslaved* furthers this burgeoning discourse, demonstrating that, like those enslaved males who assumed the roles of father, husband, protector, and caretaker seriously, despite the risks thereof, Yombo, Dick, and Quamino—in divergent and intriguing ways—were strong and resilient individuals who advocated for their loved ones. They reaffirm that slave manhood was multifaceted and complex, and rooted in the willingness of bondmen to survive and resist oppression by any means necessary, including compromising their principles for the sake of their families' well-being. That is to say, they conceived of manhood in neither monolithic nor static terms. Rather, their definitions were necessarily fluid and included elements of power, self-determination, self-respect, self-control, and familial responsibility.[32]

The ways in which Yombo, Dick, and Quamino conceived of themselves as men did not occur in a socio-cultural vacuum. They were approximately thirty-seven, twenty-seven, and fourteen years old, respectively, during the outbreak of the American Revolution, when American white men, the reputed sons of Great Britain, sought to liberate themselves from the despotic English father. Regardless of a white male's occupation or station—be it gentleman, artisan, or farmer—manhood in the late eighteenth century meant having control of a person's own life, liberty, and property. In short, for the revolutionary-era generation of white men, manhood was associated with independence. Slavery and servitude, in turn, were the main symbols of dependence. References to dependence and independence thus permeated American culture and society, including personal and family relationships, political and literary works, and personal and business debts. Dependence was seen as the antithesis of manliness and was measured against women, children, and slaves, who were deemed as lacking the virtue, self-control, independence, and responsibility found in manly adulthood in the young Republic. According to the (white) Sons of Liberty, Yombo, Dick, Quamino, and their male compatriots were forever "boys"; they were permanently emasculated and infantilized as white males had once been by father England. In the eyes of whites, blacks as a whole were feminized.[33]

It goes without saying, however, that enslaved males, Northern and Southern, saw themselves differently. If anything, the freeing of the white sons from the despotic English father served only to bolster the desire of bondmen, whose African roots were steeped largely in patriarchal authority, for their own manly independence.[34] It has been argued, for example, that Venture Smith, the well-known African-born New England slave who bought himself as well as various family and friends out of bondage, "resisted tyranny with a mixture of force and appeals to rights."[35] Certainly, Dick's strong desire to exercise patriarchy, Yombo's hostile disposition, and Quamino's steadfast faith in God and determination to protect his family were partly influenced by the ubiquitous white male quest for "freedom" and manhood during the revolutionary era. But because they were deemed "boys" and required to acquiesce continually to whites, the protagonists' conceptions of manhood were constructed on rather shaky ground in central New Jersey, where the institution of slavery was of great importance.

The Importance of Slavery in Central New Jersey

The significance and endurance of slavery in central New Jersey warrants an analysis of the institution centered on the lives of Yombo, Dick, and Quamino. This study focuses mainly on the late eighteenth century, and in 1790 Somerset County ranked second only to Bergen County (northern

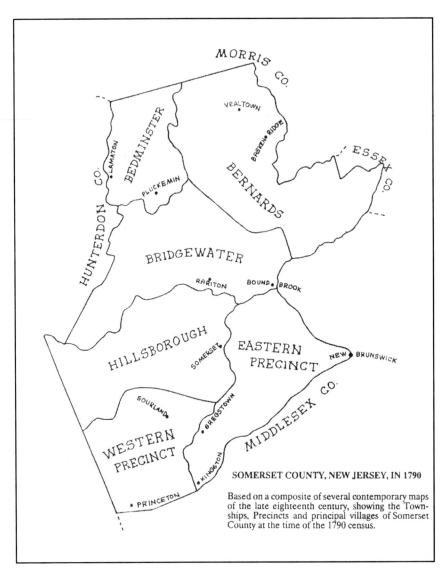

MORRIS CO.

BEDMINSTER

VEALTOWN

BROKEN RIDGE

BERNARDS

ESSEX CO.

HUNTERDON CO.

LAMATON

PLUCKEMIN

BRIDGEWATER

RARITON

BOUND BROOK

HILLSBOROUGH

SOMERSET

EASTERN PRECINCT

NEW BRUNSWICK

SOURLAND

GREGSTOWN

MIDDLESEX CO.

WESTERN PRECINCT

KINGSTON

PRINCETON

SOMERSET COUNTY, NEW JERSEY, IN 1790

Based on a composite of several contemporary maps of the late eighteenth century, showing the Townships, Precincts and principal villages of Somerset County at the time of the 1790 census.

Figure 1. Map of Somerset County, showing its townships, precincts, and principal villages at the time of the 1790 census. Frontispiece of *Somerset County Genealogical Quarterly* 7 (June 1990). Drawing by Fred Sisser III. Courtesy of the artist.

New Jersey) in both the total number of slaves (1,810) and the percentage of the total population they comprised (15.9 percent). Somerset is bounded on the east by Middlesex County and on the west by Hunterdon County, which ranked fourth and fifth, with 1,318 and 1,301 total slaves, respectively.[36] In 1800 when New Jersey had 12,422 total slaves, an all-time high for the state, Somerset again was second in enslaved population (1,863), Middlesex again fourth (1,564), and Hunterdon now sixth (1,220). Moreover, Somerset again ranked second behind Bergen in terms of the percentage of the enslaved population to the total population (15.9 percent).[37]

A major reason why slavery flourished in the Somerset County area was the county's prime location in the fertile Raritan River Valley region. While much of New Jersey's geographical diversity comes together in Somerset, the county itself and the surrounding area lies mainly in the Piedmont, a physiographic region characterized by rolling hills, such as Sourland Mountain (839 feet in height), and ubiquitous waterways, the largest of which was the Raritan River (more than one hundred miles in length).[38] The Raritan Indians (a subgroup of the Lenni Lenape Indians) were the original inhabitants of the Raritan Valley, having settled there by the 1650s. Yet, owing to a host of debilitating factors—their exposure to European diseases, violence, and alcohol; their differing interpretation of European land purchases; and the hostility they encountered from other Native Americans—the Raritan Indians had basically disappeared from the region by the mid 1700s.[39] Their gradual demise was owed, in no small part, to the pelt-hungry and profit-seeking Dutch, who probably settled, along with their slaves, in the Raritan Valley in the 1680s, by way of New York and especially Long Island, which became a major Dutch settlement. Indeed, though a diversity of white Europeans held blacks in bondage, a preponderance of slaveowners in the region and throughout the state were of "Dutch" descent.[40] In Somerset proper, the Dutch, the principal landowners in the 1800s, resided mainly in the central and southern part of the county composed of Bridgewater and Hillsborough townships and the Eastern and Western precincts (present-day Franklin and Montgomery townships, respectively). Many owned large farms between a hundred and three hundred acres, and thus depended on slave labor to cultivate their fields and tend their livestock.[41]

Correspondingly, a number of slaveowners in and around Somerset County possessed large retinues of slaves. For example, in Franklin Township, one of the Vliet families may have owned as many as seventeen slaves, whereas the Quick family, at one time, had fourteen slaves.[42] In 1784 Mary Middlesworth of Hillsborough Township and William Crook of Bridgewater Township owned twenty and twenty-two slaves, respectively.[43] The papers of Andrew Mellick mention that his Bedminster ancestors, who lived outside the center of slavery in Somerset, "had about 20 Negroes which they owned, which with a big family of boys and other employees, gave them a force to carry on a large [tanning] business."[44] This temporary— and exploited—workforce, which Mellick fails to mention in his book lauding his ancestors, mirrors the large slave gangs that were used at the iron furnaces in Hunterdon County prior to the Revolutionary War.[45] Still, like most slaveowners in the New York hinterland, the majority of those in the Somerset area kept no more than two or three slaves at a time.[46] The result of such small slaveholdings meant that blacks lived in close proximity to white scrutiny and had unstable family lives, hardships that Yombo, Dick, and Quamino faced as well.

The lives of the three bondmen also intersect with the controversial issue of black abolition in the late eighteenth century. Though many white citizens of Quaker-dominated "West Jersey" were willing to liberate their blacks, the residents of "East Jersey" (where slavery in rural areas like Somerset County was a viable institution) largely opposed uncompensated abolition. After much planning and political debate, the New Jersey state legislature passed a gradual emancipation act in 1804, making New Jersey the last Northern state to pass legislation for the immediate or gradual elimination of slavery. The 1804 law provided that any enslaved child born after July 4 of that year would serve as an apprentice to its mother's owner until that child reached the age of twenty-five if male and twenty-one if female. The owner was required to maintain the child for one year, after which the owner could abandon the child to the local overseer of the poor, who frequently boarded the youth with the same owner who had abandoned him or her. The state paid for this service.[47] In effect, the 1804 law made enslaved children born after July 4 neither slave nor free, and insured, as Graham Hodges points out, "that in rural societies . . . where slavery remained popular, blacks would exist in the shadow of slavery."[48] Designed to protect the property rights of slaveowners, relieve whites of the presence of thousands of newly freed blacks, and foster social stability among whites, the 1804 law relegated our three protagonists and countless other blacks born before July 4 to a lifetime of bondage.[49]

To his great fortune, however, Quamino eventually became the property of William Griffith, a prominent New Jersey abolitionist who liberated him and wife Sarah in 1805.[50] In addition to the gradual emancipation law of 1804, manumission was legalized (in 1798) in a certificate signed by two (township) overseers of the poor and two (county) justices of the peace which certified any slave brought before them in the following language: "who, on view and examination, appears to us to be sound in mind, and not under any bodily incapacity of obtaining a support, and also is not under the age of twenty-one years, nor above the age of forty."[51] Born in 1762, Quamino was forty-three years of age when interviewed in 1805, and thus technically was not eligible for manumission. William Allinson suspects that "William Griffith probably kept this fact a secret." When "this discrepancy" was brought to Quamino's attention, he reportedly "laughed heartily, and said, 'Well—well—I trust it's for the best.'"[52]

Yet this was not the case for Yombo and Dick, both of whom died under bondage. Nance, however, was among the three hundred fifty blacks who were manumitted in Somerset County between 1805 and 1844.[53] Even so, because of "the limited commitment to emancipation that prevailed in New Jersey," observes Graham Hodges, slavery or some modified version of it continued to exist in the Garden State until the outbreak of the Civil War.[54] The 1870 census finally shows no African Americans designated as slaves.[55]

Chapter Outlines

Manhood Enslaved locates Yombo, Dick, and Quamino within the context of shifting social and personal circumstances under a harsh institution which, as indicated above, was of great importance to whites in central New Jersey. Thematically arranged, the chapters are designed to provide instructive (though not definitive) answers to the difficult questions raised about manhood, gender, and the inner lives of New Jersey bondmen as they struggled to survive the psychologically subversive and destructive ramifications of slavery. Chapter 1 takes the position that, in order to analyze effectively the lives of Yombo, Dick, and Quamino, it is imperative to also interrogate the lives and works of the men who brought the three bondmen to our attention. The chapter begins by examining William Allinson's account of Quamino, and situates it within the context of Allinson's antislavery Quaker heritage; his social activism against slavery; his antislavery poetry, which called for abolitionists to enlighten slaveholders; and his paternalistic relationship with Quamino. All these factors, chapter 1 argues, shaped how Allinson wrote the *Memoir of Quamino Buccau* as a romantic racialist tract that gave expression to his own sense of manhood as a pacifist Quaker abolitionist who saw free and enslaved blacks ultimately as victims in dire need of white (male) protection and guidance. In its analysis of Andrew Mellick, chapter 1 discusses how this once rugged businessman projected his pride, privilege, and racial dominance as a white man in late nineteenth-century America into the writing of *The Story of an Old Farm*. The chapter shows that Mellick's widely acclaimed history of his Somerset County ancestors was representative of racist/racialist literature written during the "nadir" of the black experience in America (1877–1915), a period characterized by the consolidation of "Jim Crow" racial segregation, unprecedented racial violence, and the vicious (literary) assault upon black people's character.

In a rather novel way, chapter 2 further sets the stage for an examination of the malcontent Yombo. But instead of turning to either William Allinson or Andrew Mellick for contextualization, the chapter deconstructs part of a speech given by a contemporary of Mellick's, the Reverend John Bodine Thompson. In 1894 Thompson discussed a joint suicide of an enslaved couple from West Africa, explaining that they were held in bondage by one of Mellick's ancestors, who had also for a number of years been Yombo's owner. Chapter 2 uses the once prestigious couple—who, it speculates, were Yombo's mother and father—to explore how enslaved Africans possibly survived and resisted aboard slave ships, and continued to resist once they arrived in colonial New Jersey. A political statement apparently sanctioned by the African couple's religious beliefs, the suicide had a great affect on Yombo and fueled his own resistance, which Mellick downplays.

Yombo is also the subject of chapter 3, which more fully considers the factors that contributed to his obstinate or mean persona. The chapter places him in the context of the socially and racially turbulent Revolutionary War era, and argues that his inability to escape slavery permanently (he had a clubfoot) compelled him to develop strategies that enabled him to contest his owners' incessant appropriation of his "time," a critical means of white control. The chapter contends, in other words, that Yombo's unpleasant disposition was a result of his inability to challenge the hegemony of his owners more satisfactorily. In sum, chapter 3 politicizes his meanness, demonstrating that it made him a powerful force that brought constant discomfiture to the lives of his oppressors. In viewing Yombo as a political agent who had, in a sense, terrorized whites, chapter 3 broadens the discourse on day-to-day slave resistance.

The fourth chapter analyzes Quamino's transition from docile to religiously empowered slave. In contrast to Yombo, he appears not to have been empowered by the Revolution. Rented as a young boy to a man who eventually relocated to upstate New York, Quamino was forced to live in this distant land with the possibility of never again seeing his family and friends. His sense of terror was heightened by the wartime chaos and his owner's demand that he witness the public execution of fellow slaves. Upon his return to New Jersey some seven years later, Quamino was no longer the "young cub" favored by his (original) elderly owner, but rather a young man who, as this chapters claims, developed an acute awareness of the significance of his adult (black) body. Thus, Quamino initially perceived Christianity as a means of presenting himself to whites as a trustworthy slave. This would all change, however, with his conversion experience. Christianity no longer represented just a means of political survival, but had emerged as a real and empowering force in his life. Endowed with the "gift" of God's grace, Quamino threatened the hegemony of his owners, thereby making his existence all the more treacherous.

Chapter 5 revisits Andrew Mellick's *The Story of an Old Farm* and focuses on the enslaved couple Dick and Nance. In addition to reminding us of how difficult it was for enslaved couples in the rural North to establish a meaningful social life with other blacks and keep their families intact, Dick and Nance also put into perspective the onerous labor responsibilities forced upon the enslaved, particularly enslaved women. Yet if Nance endured more as a beast of domestic burden under constant white supervision, then Dick faced certain scrutiny as a big, "dark" male. As suggested here, the strategically quiet bondman perhaps cut a more conspicuous and, hence, more threatening physical presence than either Yombo or Quamino. This set of circumstances had serious implications for his devoted wife. Specifically, Nance's oppression appears to have stemmed not only from the fact that she was black and female, but also from how Dick persistently had his manhood undercut by the dictates of race. With so few available opportunities to engage in "manly" endeavors with other males (black and white), Dick attempted to maximize those opportunities that did exist, opportunities that tended to manifest through his tenuous family relations.

The epilogue is framed through an obscure incident of male slave rage that further underscores the precarious nature of male slave life in the rural North. It proposes that, whether a slave acted deferentially like Dick and Quamino or rebelliously like Yombo and the epilogue's protagonist, York, the issue of rage was an important element in the lives of all bondmen. Both potentially liberating and destructive, rage could have served as a unifying force among bondmen, even among those as different in temperament as Yombo and Dick. Rage confirmed the humanity of enslaved peoples. In making this point, the epilogue emphasizes that historical writing is a process informed, to varying degrees, by personal experience and the time in which one lives. In a sense, this study, like the two texts it examines, is a reflection of my own complex notions of race and manhood in American society. Indeed, in some ways, the two authors and I are more similar than we are different. Thus, as the epilogue is clear in stating, it is imperative to weigh carefully what both they and I have to say about Yombo, Dick, and Quamino.

All said, *Manhood Enslaved* is an extended and, at times, contentious historical conversation with two fascinating works about three fascinating bondmen (who were held in bondage, collectively, from the 1740s to the 1810s). The only way to realize fully the potential of these works, as well as similar pieces of nineteenth-century literature, is to scrutinize and challenge them. In doing so, I use alternative scholarly discourses that can help us understand their hidden agendas. The "truth" is not always forthcoming in the documents; it often requires extraction from them. In short, a study such as this requires the willingness to read between the lines and make many (informed) speculations that, in the end, bring its subjects into sharper relief.

Though Yombo, Dick, and Quamino are the main focus of this study, they are in no way its only important figures. A host of other intriguing characters who appear throughout the text are vital to the telling of their forgotten stories. Foremost among these secondary black personages is Silvia Dubois, whose 1883 colloquy with Dr. Cornelius Wilson Larison (1837–1910) provides a wealth of useful information about slave life in rural New Jersey and Pennsylvania during the late eighteenth and early nineteenth centuries. Her white-authored *Biografy*, albeit highly racist in its own right, gives greater context to the insights made in the *Memoir of Quamino Buccau* and *The Story of an Old Farm*, as do advertisements for runaway slaves, which are extensively employed here. These and other invaluable sources make it possible to reconstruct many of the complex issues surrounding our three protagonists.

Still, Silvia Dubois and other black personages are only invited guests in *Manhood Enslaved*. The real stars are Yombo, Dick, and Quamino, who help to dispel the notion that Northern slavery is a closed subject with nothing new and exciting for us to contemplate. They powerfully refute the widespread belief during Dubois's time (and even the present) "that niggers ain't no account," that black people enslaved north of the Mason-Dixon line were passive zeros absent from the historical record. To the contrary, these intriguing personalities tell us a great deal about how black men and women saw themselves as more than chattel.

Despite their importance, Yombo, Dick, and Quamino represent a mere glimpse of masculine or gendered possibilities that have implications for the past and present. In his 1997 book, *Thirteen Ways of Looking at a Black Man*, Henry Louis Gates Jr. assessed what it means to live as a black man in twentieth-century America. Through eight intriguing essays focusing on a diversity of prominent African American men, Gates dismisses the notion that black males are a monolithic group who approach their blackness in exactly the same ways.[56] Yet Gates's illuminating insight is not a total revelation; it is rooted in a much more volatile era when black males labored and, more importantly, survived and resisted as despised slaves. That is to say, enslaved black males—our three protagonists among them—were the harbingers of contemporary black male dynamism. Though the three bondmen faced many of the same trials and tribulations under central New Jersey slavery, they are fascinating characters in their own right, each with their own unique (masculine) identity and strategies for dealing with slavery. Overall, then, *Manhood Enslaved* uses Yombo, Dick, and Quamino to enrich our understanding of an invisible segment of the American population, without furnishing more stereotypes.

Chapter I

Black Images in White Minds

This study of slave manhood in the rural North begins with an analysis of William Allinson's and Andrew Mellick's racialized accounts of our three male protagonists. The purpose here is to situate their respective works, the *Memoir of Quamino Buccau* (1851) and *The Story of an Old Farm* (1889), within broader ideological and literary contexts, that is, within the larger Western (white) mind of the mid to late nineteenth century. Once contextualized, the works will comprise part of the greater hegemonic discourse on black peoples.

Indeed, Allinson and Mellick represent white authors in the nineteenth century, the majority of whom were male, and who constituted the conduits of power through which "Negro" slaves and other "subaltern" subjects appear in the historical record.[1] Although Allinson's romantic racialist tract and Mellick's paternalistic account of his ancestors' slaves are very different in terms of their politics, in the end they both dehumanize their black personages by failing to portray them as real or complex individuals having multiple dimensions. Specifically, Allinson depicts his protagonist, Quamino Buccau (Smock), as a good (righteous) slave turned safe and redemptive free black because of his remarkable religious devotion, whereas Mellick portrays Yombo Melick as the troublesome slave, and Dick Melick as the likeable slave, on his benevolent great grandfather's farmstead. The authors, in other words, characterize Yombo, Dick, and Quamino not as real historical actors but as static and exotic objects largely acted upon by whites, including the authors themselves. In doing so, they reveal how their conceptions of manhood were forged partly through the oppressed condition of black peoples.

In no way is this chapter an effort simply to indict the white male authors' skewed portrayals of the three bondmen, which would serve as a senseless and unproductive exercise. The overall success of this study is largely dependent upon the *Memoir of Quamino Buccau* and *The Story of an Old Farm* yielding critical insight regarding the lives and self-concepts of rural Northern slaves, which they both do rather brilliantly. Yet this does not protect them from scholarly criticism. Only by thoroughly scrutinizing these two important works can we understand fully their potential in terms of historical analysis.

Quaker-Abolitionist Heritage

To appreciate the politics of the *Memoir of Quamino Buccau*, it is necessary to discuss William Allinson's family background and emergent politicization. Quamino's neighbor and biographer was a descendent of the highly respected Allinson family of Burlington County, Quakers who were known as "rigid members of the Religious Society of Friends," as well as devoted abolitionists.[2] Since the late seventeenth century, individual Quakers (Friends) argued that racial bondage violated the belief that all humans are equal in the sight of God. Although there were non-Friends in colonial American society who condemned the institution of slavery, Quakers were the only (white) group to advocate black emancipation prior to the outbreak of the American Revolution. This does not mean that Quakers failed to invest in the buying, trading, and owning of black peoples. On the contrary, Quakers as a group were deeply involved in all aspects of the business of slavery prior to the Revolution, when they finally concluded that participation in the institution was incompatible with their religious beliefs.[3]

William Allinson's grandfather, Samuel Allinson (1739–91), was an influential lawyer and highly respected abolitionist Friend in the Delaware Valley region.[4] In fact, he played an active role in an antislavery network that stretched from the Delaware Valley across the Atlantic to England.[5] An obviously strong proponent of the Golden Rule, that is, to do unto others as you want them to do unto you (Luke 6:31), the elder Allinson took great interest in Friends who invested in slave labor.[6] In 1772, for example, he offered a Friend to help mediate in "the two negro cases which came before the last Y[early] M[eeting] & seemed so much to divide you," and pledged his services if "it would not be thought officious in a young man to urge his elder brethren to works of justice, peace & love."[7] Moreover, in 1773, Allinson argued "in favor of a New Jersey law eliminating the required surety bond for manumission, that free blacks would lead peaceful and productive lives under the law."[8]

Allinson's gadfly role in promoting black abolition appears to have taken on an even greater sense of urgency during the Revolution, which forced colonists to confront the paradox of espousing the equality of men while most blacks were held in bondage.[9] To illustrate, in 1778, the Quaker wrote an impassioned letter to New Jersey governor William Livingston, urging him to take the lead in the struggle for abolition in the colony. "I fear," he wrote, "America never can or will prosper in a right manner; or receive & enjoy true peace & its delightful fruits; until she 'proclaims Liberty to the captives, & Let's [*sic*] the oppressed go free.'"[10] Livingston responded promptly in a letter explaining that not only did he share Allinson's sentiments, but he had also sent a message to the New Jersey General Assembly to provide for the manumission of slaves.

The House of Representatives, however, determined that his message was delivered at "too critical" a time and asked him privately to withdraw it. Though he complied with this request, the governor promised Allinson that he would continue to use his influence to eradicate slavery in their state, which he believed was "utterly inconsistent, both with the principles of Christianity & Humanity."[11]

Very few people could rival Samuel Allinson's commitment to black abolition. Yet it is important to bear in mind that Allinson and his fellow Quaker spokesmen were not "liberals" who stressed individualism, social mobility, and equal opportunity for freed blacks. Rather, they simply held that ex-slaves would lead peaceful and productive lives—lives that these paternalists closely monitored through their local Committees on Free Negroes.[12] Indeed, Allinson viewed slavery as a degrading institution that deprived blacks of "the common advantage of education or example to correct their bad habits," shortcomings that the Committees on Free Negroes sought to correct.[13] Although they professed that all people were equal in the sight of God, this belief did not, for abolitionist Friends, fit easily into the colonial hierarchical structure of "gentlemen" (at the top), the yeoman or middling classes, and the "lower sort" (at the bottom).[14] In the end, Quaker egalitarianism did not extend to social relations. Blacks, for instance, were often segregated from whites in, of all places, Quaker meetinghouses.[15] Typical of their class, Quakers advocated a social order that was stable, hierarchical, and consciously elitist. Such a social order, to quote James Oakes, "assumes an inherent inequality of men: some are born to rule, others to obey."[16]

This paternalist, as opposed to liberal, assumption was evident in Quaker visits with free blacks, whereby the former gave the latter advice that was not always well received.[17] Significantly, one of these Quaker visits took place in Burlington County in 1805. It involved William Allinson (1766–1841)—the oldest of Samuel Allinson's nine children—and a free black resident who undoubtedly was Quamino Smock.[18] In his journal that year, William Allinson wrote that he and a companion had "visited 4 Families of Bl[ac]k People, in one of which was a young man who has [perhaps] 12 or 14 yrs. much afflicted with [swelling] by which he is quite a cripple yet"; however, "when well enough he attends the Methodist Meetings on his crutches, [and] has joined that Society."[19] (According to the *Memoir*, Quamino used crutches and was a member of the Methodist Episcopal Society in Burlington.)[20] With a palpable bitterness to which we will return later, the crippled black man told his white visitors "that he did not expect much enjoyment in this World but was placing his hopes of Happiness in another, and that the exercise of his religious Duties and Contemplation on Divine Things was his richest source of consolation." Still, Allinson ended the entry by stating that "good seemed sensibly near this family and we were well paid in satisfaction of the visit."[21] In another journal entry in 1805, Allinson explained that, with his mind "more at liberty than usual of late," he went alone to visit with two other black families "previously noticed" by fellow Quakers. Again satisfied with these visits, "I thought I had the [company] of the Sure Friend of this Poor Oppressed People."[22]

Despite his concern for the welfare of free black families, the tone of Allinson's journal is undeniably elitist and paternalistic. For not only did he and fellow Quakers basically drop in on black families discovered by the Society of Friends, but they left when they were satisfied that the families had complied with their expectations. The phrase "this Poor Oppressed People" suggests that Allinson (like his father) viewed free blacks as in dire need of guidance and direction, which he and his associates were more than willing and able to provide properly. Certainly, these meetings between Quakers and free blacks, where the former exercised greater power, functioned as sites of white masculine dominance. In a revealing 1804 journal entry, Allinson asked the "Almighty Helper" to "preserve me, I am indeed as a Woman—my frailties are innumerable."[23] Yet his sense of manhood was probably redeemed or reaffirmed when meeting with and advocating for socially, economically, and physically afflicted free blacks. We may assume that this was also the case when intervening on the behalf of slaves. Allinson mentions that, in 1806, he and William Newcomb went to Monmouth County to negotiate with William Haight for the manumission of the bondwomen Patty and Fanny and their children, which, as he proudly states, "we affected to a good degree of [our] Satisfaction."[24]

Certainly, Allinson's religiosity was largely the driving force behind his antislavery activities.[25] But, similar to William Lloyd Garrison—the foremost white, pacifist, and national abolitionist leader of the antebellum era—his sense of himself as a man also played a vital role. "Garrison's conception of manhood, characterized by intellectual achievement, personal dignity, and moral responsibility, was shared by many abolitionists, whose underlying antislavery motivation was religious," state James and Lois Horton.[26] Like Garrison, Allinson's conception of manhood was a complex meshing of elements, not the least of which was his belief that he had a "moral responsibility" to assist oppressed black people.

Scholars identify two important ideals of middle-class manhood in the nineteenth century: the "masculine achiever" and the "Christian gentleman." The masculine achiever—active, dynamic, and aggressive—was linked closely to the emerging American market economy of the nineteenth century. A ruthless and rugged individualist, his competitive nature manifested in the bustling arena of commercial capitalism. He stood in stark contrast to the Christian gentleman, who eschewed self-seeking behavior and the obsession with competition, and placed emphasis instead on self-restraint, Christian morality, and humanitarian endeavors. A product of the religious revival known as the Second Great Awakening that flourished in the early nineteenth century, this gentler ideal of manhood did not necessarily translate into passive behavior. On the contrary, the Christian gentleman was an aggressive and dynamic man of action but in the name of the principles previously noted.[27]

Clearly, Samuel Allinson and his male descendents had constructed themselves as men in a manner very similar to the Christian gentleman. For example, an 1884 memorial to Allinson's grandson, also named Samuel (1808–83), explains that he led a "kind, modest, self-sacrificing, philanthropic and beautiful Christian life." This statement seems to apply to other males in his family, who, like him, greatly opposed "oppression, cruelty and injustice among men, without distinction of nationality, race or color."[28] Yet it perhaps best describes Samuel's younger brother William, Quamino's biographer, with whom Samuel was extremely close. An anonymous and equally effusive memorial to William declares, "The poor, the destitute, and the afflicted had in him ever a true friend; and his kindly ministrations to the needs of a common humanity were cordially valued, alike in the smitten abodes of opulence or of poverty, his facile mind devising modes of relief, or presenting Christian consolation."[29]

As it appears, Allinson men historically forged their manhood (in part) by finding, assisting, and advising free and enslaved blacks. In this way, the Allinsons and other Quaker abolitionist males served as the proxies of black manhood in the eighteenth and nineteenth centuries.[30] Their willingness to do so was not merely a reflection of the virtues associated with the Christian gentleman. It apparently also stemmed from the fact that male Friends (owing to their pacifism and rejection of compulsory military service) had, by the time of the Revolution, relinquished political power, public office, and the commercial benefits of slaveholding—important spheres of white masculinity.[31] Male Friends, as a result, had relatively fewer opportunities to assert white masculine authority in the eighteenth and nineteenth centuries. Their interactions with oppressed blacks thus served as a critical means of masculine empowerment.

Maintaining the Family (Quaker) Tradition

Notwithstanding their racism, paternalism, and apparent anxieties related to manhood, Friends were fiercely committed to black abolition. Such devotion characterized the lives of Samuel Allinson's grandsons, the brothers Samuel and William Allinson. The conservative moral persuasion of their grandfather with respect to black abolition presaged the brothers' more assertive strategies. The prominence of the Allinson brothers, it has been stated, "in temperance and anti-slavery movements brought them

Figure 2. Photograph of William J. Allinson (c. 1870). Courtesy of Special Collections, Magill Library, Haverford College, Haverford, PA.

and others in Burlington," particularly Samuel, under intense public scrutiny "regarding those measures of reform."[32] Evidently, Samuel, a noted philanthropist and prison reformer who staunchly opposed products made from slave labor, was the more aggressive or outspoken activist.[33] Yet William, a druggist, poet, author, editor, and educator, may well have been the more institutionally engaged reformer.[34] In 1845, for example, he and five other Quaker men, not including his older brother, organized the Free Produce Association of Friends of Philadelphia Yearly Meeting, later known as the Philadelphia Free Produce Association of Friends (PFPAF). Combining evangelistic faith with an urgent desire to reform the world, the PFPAF planned to utilize the boycott of all slave-produced goods as a primary tactic in the fight against slavery.[35]

Two years later, in 1847, the PFPAF created the *Friends' Review* in opposition to the old orthodox Quaker journal the *Friend* and the many other literary organs that it contended were "constituted of matter which can contribute little to the advancement of their readers." Founded under the editorship of Enoch Lewis, this new journal denied devotion "to any single object of discussion or enquiry," but mentioned that it would address two particular topics in later editions: slavery and war, "evils which disgrace our age and nation, and retard the progress of civilization."[36]

The *Friends' Review* was also a venue for the expression of romantic racialist propaganda and aggressive Christian manhood in the name of oppressed blacks. This agenda is perhaps best exemplified in the article written by "E. L." (Enoch Lewis), "An Old Slave Set Free," published in the journal's October 1847 issue. Less than two full columns, the piece focuses on the abolitionist piety of Friend Isaac Jackson of New Garden, Pennsylvania. The moral of the story, however, is that black freedom was no cause for racial warfare because of blacks' utter loyalty to their former owners.[37]

The article opens by noting that Jackson was representative of "Friends who were zealously engaged, eighty or ninety years ago, in laboring upon their fellow professors to emancipate their slaves." While Jackson was traveling one day with fellow Friends in the name of "this righteous cause, he was informed of one [a Friend] who held a single slave, about seventy years of age, who was kindly treated, and sufficiently furnished with the necessities of life." Though the slave lived comfortably, Jackson began to ponder whether he desired freedom "at his time in life," and if "freedom would not be an injury rather than a favour." The thoughtful abolitionist had "adopt[ed] the Christian principle to judge of the feelings of another by considering what his own would be"—specifically, what would he think if he were the old slave? Jackson naturally concluded he would chose freedom. Notwithstanding the owner's residence "was several miles distant" and his associates "did not fully share his feelings on the subject," Jackson decided to visit "the house where the slave was held" that evening. Within a short time, Jackson was able to convince the owner to liberate his captive, who later was "brought in" and informed of the momentous decision. In the spirit of the romantic racialist Negro, "as soon as the old man was made to comprehend the situation, he gave vent to the most rapturous indications of joy." Fully expecting to die in bondage, he allegedly rejoiced, "*But now . . . I am free.*"[38]

Following his emotional outburst, Jackson asked the bondman if he had a "good master," to which "he readily answered in the affirmative." Read from an abolitionist perspective, Jackson was unconcerned with how the "old man" felt about his owner. Rather, he was attempting to appeal to the sensibilities of pro-slavery Southerners, for whom the piece was intended. Had the story described the relationship between owner and slave in terms of racial warfare, which was perhaps closer to the truth than racial amicability, it would have undermined the argument that black abolition was a positive and safe endeavor. Hence, when Jackson queried the bondman about what he would do as a free man, he paused for a short while before responding, "Master will want work done yet, and I will stay and work with him." While the protagonist of this tale did not exemplify the simple but unique religious piety that characterized Quamino and other romantic racialist Negroes, he possessed other prototypical characteristics: he was childlike, loyal, docile, and, given that his owner needed persuading to free him, forgiving. Far from a threat to the status quo, he served as evidence that freed blacks would prove themselves as valuable assets to white society. As the story concludes, "If any of our southern brethren, who insist that the emancipation of their slaves would necessarily lead to a war [between the] races, which must terminate in the extirpation of one of them, had been present to witness this scene, we should suppose they must have been convinced that in this case at least, the life of the *quondam master* was in no great danger from his manumitted slave."[39]

"An Old Slave Set Free" advances the Quaker agenda in at least two ways. First of all, it demonstrates that Friends were largely dutiful and principled men dedicated to protecting the interests of the enslaved. Isaac Jackson was representative of aggressive yet righteous Christian manhood. Secondly, it demonstrates that both the *quondam master* and the "Negro" could possibly coexist because black men would remain loyal to their former benefactors. In the end, the piece promoted a peaceful but hierarchical world in which Friends of Jackson's enlightened and humane masculine sensibilities would play a critical role in promoting racial harmony.

The image of Quaker males as aggressive advocates of blacks was also conveyed in the *Non-Slaveholder*, another periodical created by the PFPAF, in 1846, to further promote the free-produce idea. The editors of this publication stated unequivocally their opposition to slavery, and pledged to "overthrow" the institution "by all just and peaceful means." Despite their intention not to neglect "any of the just modes for the slave's liberation, the doctrine of abstinence from the productions of his toil will be prominently held up to view." They "regard[ed] it necessary to give proper force to all proper modes for accomplishing that purpose."[40]

Accordingly, the *Non-Slaveholder* denounced the Fugitive Slave Act of 1850, which allowed slaveholders and their representatives to enter the Northern (free) states and apprehend runaways. By contrast, the *Friend*, while deploring the Compromise made by the North with the South, applauded the "peace" and "harmony" that it said had ensued. The *Non-Slaveholder* argued that this conciliatory position dishonored the (heroic) legacy of those Quaker forefathers who had risked their lives for black liberation. But neither was the *Non-Slaveholder* beyond reproach. "Since, as a Quaker publication," observes Thomas Drake, the *Non-Slaveholder* could not advocate violence "to liberate the slaves, it had to fall back on the weapons of peaceful persuasion and quiet boycott." He quips: "No wonder this journal of but a single idea, and that a self-denying one, suspended publication after the nation accepted the Compromise!"[41] In reality, then, the *Non-Slaveholder* was as moderate as the *Friend* on the slavery issue, albeit more forthright in its condemnation of American politics. The *Non-Slaveholder* suspended publication in 1850, but was revived briefly under the editorship of William Allinson from 1853 until its total demise in 1854, "when the difficulty of obtaining free-labor goods, and the increasing tensions over Kansas made the free-produce method seem hopeless."[42]

The PFPAF was not the only vehicle through which Allinson expressed his antislavery sentiment. He also did so through his poetry, such as in the piece entitled "A Plea for Liberty," published prior to 1873. In the first stanza he writes,

> The injured, outraged slave to hope shall cling,
> And stay his vengeful hand, consoled to know
> That human breasts commiserate his woe.
> Cheered by the thought, that thousands feel his
> wrong,
> He *bides his time*, in faith that they, made strong
> By Him, the God of Freedom, Truth, and Right,
> Will on the oppressor's [sic] hearts pour floods of light,
> Till Tyranny, made hideous in its blaze,
> Disperse, like noxious mists at morning's rays.
> Speak trumpet-tongued—your shout shall save the land . . .[43]

According to Allinson, although the bondman's anger is justified, what prevents him from acting upon it is the hope that abolitionists, such as himself, with the help of God, will ultimately enlighten slaveholders. This perspective corresponds with the notion that Quaker abolitionists viewed themselves as the proxies of black manhood. Yet the issue does not end here. Bruce Dorsey, examining the activity of men and women reformers in the antebellum North, argues that, owing to their own fears, middle-class moralists of the era were rather critical of self-interested, aggressive expressions of masculinity. Such masculine expressions, charged abolitionists, were bereft of human feelings and compassion, and typified Southern men. In associating Southern men with utterly callous behavior, including sexual abuse and the fragmentation of enslaved families, abolitionists had rendered them inhuman and thus devoid of true manhood. As Dorsey summarizes, "attacking southern white masculinity became one of the means of establishing the abolitionists' superior vision of gender."[44]

In view of this insightful analysis, "A Plea for Liberty" was hardly a mere rhetorical flourish. It speaks to an ideal of manhood grounded in the expression of feelings and sympathy and moral suasion, and thereby was superior to that ideal which callously kept black men in bondage. It implies that the abolitionists' gentler ideal of manhood would eventually win out against the tyrannous manhood of slaveholders, but the "outraged slave" needed to exercise patience while the abolitionists did his bidding. Hence, the poem is probably as much a statement on William Allinson's own vision of true manhood as it is about the sufferings of angry bondmen, gender politics that are also played out in his portrayal of Quamino as a passive and safe black Christian.

Construction of a Romantic Racialist Negro

Underlying Allinson's rendition of Quamino's life story—at the expense of our learning about his family and heritage—is the struggle for survival and ultimate redemption of a black saint in a hostile white world. On the *Memoir*'s first page, Allinson establishes Quamino as a blind, poor, and crippled man who had been chosen by God to receive the "Divine gift" (God's glory). Rather than attributing Quamino's former enslavement and economic distress as a free man to some curse or disfavor of God, Allinson cites numerous New Testament passages to prove that this "good old man" had been blessed as a result of these unfavorable circumstances. Slavery and poverty had allowed Quamino to focus his attention on "things above" and gain "treasure in heaven."[45] Allinson even closes the narrative on this theme, comparing Quamino to the poor man Lazarus in the Book of Luke (16:19–31), who was "carried by angels into Abraham's bosom."[46]

As Allinson portrays it, Quamino's life, in the tradition of holy men, begins only when he experiences his religious epiphany, that is, when "he had been called out of darkness into [God's] marvelous light."[47] Thus, although Quamino was known in his later years by the surname "Smock,"

Allinson refers to him in the title of the *Memoir* by the surname "Buccau." This was the alleged surname of the owner under whom Quamino experienced his transformative conversion.[48] By changing Quamino's last name, Allinson asserts control over his illiterate subject's identity and molds him into an image by which he could further his own political agenda. In addition to Allinson's use of racial and professional hegemony to alter Quamino's identity, this seemingly benign construction entailed other pernicious implications. As pointed out by Joanne Melish in *Disowning Slavery*, whereas George Fredrickson refers to such representations of blacks as "'anomalous' and 'benevolent' in intent," they are in fact "consistent with other forms of symbolic displacement and rather more malevolent than not." In other words, the remarkable piety of Quamino and other black "saints" eliminated, symbolically, the vast majority of black peoples "who so manifestly did not and could not behave like [saints]."[49] Ironically, Allinson's construction of his black neighbor speaks to his own discomfort about the presence of "free" blacks in antebellum American society; it indicates his doubts over the ability of blacks to live peaceably with the *quondam master* in a society dominated by white men.

In light of all this, it comes as no surprise that we learn little about Quamino's inner life. Significantly, the name "Quamino" closely approximates the West African day-names "Kwame" or "Kwamina," which mean, among Twi- and Fante-speaking peoples in Ghana, Togo, and Dahomey, "a male born on Saturday."[50] Hence, it is probable that not only was Quamino born on this particular day, but that his anonymous enslaved parents, one or both of whom had roots in West Africa, had named him.[51] Their son's name would have been a matter of great importance to the enslaved couple. The renowned religious philosopher John Mbiti emphasizes that almost "all African names have a meaning. The naming of children is therefore an important occasion which is often marked by ceremonies in many [African] societies."[52] As such, Quamino's name likely had significant personal meaning which instilled in him a sense of "two-ness" as an African and American.[53]

This and other personal aspects of Quamino's life, including the fact that he had three sisters and a brother whose names are unknown, were of no real interest to William Allinson. With regard to Quamino's life as a free man in the city of Burlington, Allinson bluntly maintains that he has no intention of recording "the details of his meridian life."[54] Allinson was uninterested in delineating Quamino as a complex person whose African roots helped shape his identity. Rather, he looked upon Quamino as a symbol to help ease the anxiety of Southern slaveowners over black freedom and, conversely, to stimulate feelings of sympathy, compassion, and indignation among Northern whites who read what Bruce Dorsey calls "sentimentalist literature." Mid nineteenth-century sentimentalist literature, as he writes, "fixed its gaze on themes of suffering, enslavement, freedom, family, and the control of sexual passion." As was typical of abolitionists, Allinson created an image "that was largely an abstraction and that targeted a sentimental reading public" in the North.[55]

The romantic racialist/sentimentalist literary tradition received its greatest expression in Harriet Beecher Stowe's famous novel *Uncle Tom's Cabin*, published in 1852. A melodramatic indictment of the horrors of Southern slavery, *Uncle Tom's Cabin* also glorifies black people's putatively childlike Christian uniqueness, as manifested in the obsequious character Uncle Tom—an immensely popular figure among white liberals in both America and England that some black abolitionists found troubling.[56] On the one hand, Uncle Tom, as George Fredrickson indicates, was "a spokesman for the evangelical 'religion of the heart' which Harriet Beecher Stowe was recommending as the only path to salvation for those [whites] whose cultivation and intellectuality led them to doubt the redeeming power of Christ." But, on the other hand, he embodied "the perfect 'gentleness' and 'facility of forgiveness' which are supposedly latent in the Negro and which will come to flower under favorable circumstances"—that is, in freedom.[57]

William Allinson's account of Quamino fits neatly within the romantic racialist paradigm; it demasculinizes Quamino, rendering him highly susceptible to his emotions and attributes to him nearly feminine language. That is, Allinson refers to his subject as "tender-spirited Quamino," depicts him as crying and weeping on at least two occasions while enslaved, and mentions that the bondman exclaimed, "Oh dear! oh dear!" after he was rebuked by Dr. Griffith for asking the owner to free him upon his death.[58] By describing Quamino as highly emotional, Allinson ascribes to him behavior that antislavery writers "clearly understood in that culture to be feminine," effectively diffusing his ability to demonstrate masculine authority. Bruce Dorsey, conversely, identifies "slave narratives of African American men, such as Frederick Douglass and Solomon Northup," as exhibiting "an ever-present struggle of resistance" that proved the manliness of bondmen.[59] Allinson obviously believed it imprudent to confer such masculine agency upon Quamino; he thus constructed his subject as a safe and gentle Uncle Tom character whom whites—either Northern sentimentalists or proslavery Southerners—could more easily embrace. But by appealing to the intuitively racist consciences of his white audiences, Allinson perpetuated white racist ideology that deemed black peoples hopelessly emotional and childlike.

The Real Quamino?

Allinson's concern with not offending his white readership manifests itself in the glaring omission from the *Memoir* of any real discussion of Quamino's

MEMOIR

OF

QUAMINO BUCCAU,

A PIOUS METHODIST.

BY

WILLIAM J. ALLINSON.

"But the righteous live forevermore — their reward also is with the Lord, and the care of them is with the Most High."—WISDOM OF SOLOMON.

PHILADELPHIA:
HENRY LONGSTRETH, 347 MARKET ST.
LONDON:—CHARLES GILPIN.
1851.

Figure 3. Frontispiece of William J. Allinson's *Memoir of Quamino Buccau, A Pious Methodist* (1851). Epigraph reads: "But the righteous live forevermore—their reward also is with the Lord, and the care of them is with the Most High" (from the Wisdom of Solomon). Drawing by "Mason & Maas."

physical appearance. Biographical works typically provide a description of the subject's appearance or physicality to enhance his or her human quality. Allinson, however, simply describes Quamino as "an aged coloured man, with a luxuriant growth of snowy hair," who was also "blind, and supported by two crutches," a figure that clearly reinforced the benign image of the romantic racialist Negro.[60] A generic profile sketch of Quamino's head and upper shoulder also appears on the frontispiece of the *Memoir*. The image reveals an elderly black man with a gentle, humble, and friendly countenance, hardly someone whom antebellum whites needed to fear, who was well past his prime in terms of exercising masculine authority.[61] One can imagine how Quamino, especially in his later years, was in fact gentle, humble, and friendly. But were these attributes the only dimensions of his personality? This nonthreatening black man was the same individual who had expressed bitterness to William Allinson's uncle in 1805; told his wife shortly after their emancipation that "such things" in life as the luxury of strawberries "were not 'for the likes of them'"; and experienced racism in his church. This was the same person, moreover, who "listened with much interest to the narrative of Paul Cuffee, whom he remembered with much affection and respect, and spoke of his meeting with the coloured people of Burlington, which resulted in the formation of a highly beneficial society among them."[62] Cuffee, a black Quaker sea captain, lent his support to black colonization in Liberia in the early 1800s, because he was convinced that black people would never find real equality as citizens in America. The narrative in question is Cuffee's *A Brief Account of the Settlement and Present Situation of the Colony of Sierra Leone in Africa* (1812), which, as James Sidbury writes, was "an opening salvo in his public campaign to build a movement in the United States." Cuffee visited port cities such as Burlington asking the local blacks "to form voluntary organizations devoted to his African cause."[63] Thus, beneath William Allinson's benign construction of Quamino was a broken and embittered man who contemplated the notion of marginalized black peoples participating in Africa's redemption, and who may well have struggled with the difficult paradox of living as a "Negro" in America.

If Quamino was indeed a contemplative and at times angry person whose conduct disproved the romantic racialist Negro image, how then was Allinson able to use him to help promote it? The two men formed a lasting friendship based on their respective Christian faiths and Allinson's concern for the black underclass. Allinson, who inherited his uncle's home on High Street where Quamino resided, had basically continued his uncle's interest in the former slave, who emerged as a religious leader within the Methodist Episcopal Society.[64] Allinson himself comprised part of Quamino's interracial world, in which the illiterate former slave interacted relatively freely with white clergymen and reformers, who apparently treated him as a near equal. "During his latter years, he was often visited by pious individuals, who were led to his abode to derive instruction, and to impart encouragement, and sometimes pecuniary aid," Allinson wrote. "Many strangers of this description," the abolitionist continued, "on entering his apartment, found him to be 'as unknown, yet well known.'"[65]

In retrospect, Quamino became a kind of black religious curiosity in Burlington, an identity that seemingly was partly his own invention. He realized how his religiosity—accentuated by his emotionalism and incoherent language, which Allinson refers to as "so beautiful"—intrigued if not fascinated his white benefactors, who were also put at ease and convinced of their own superiority.[66] It is probable, then, that romantic racialism was partly substantiated by the very same persons it described, by persons who spoke and acted in ways that confirmed what many whites already believed, or wanted to believe, about black people's inherently quiescent character. For survival's sake, poor and vulnerable free blacks such as Quamino surrendered themselves to the interrogating, racialist pens of white abolitionists in search of material that appeased white sensibilities, and validated their role as the defenders of "Poor Oppressed" black people. Though Quamino referred to Allinson as his "dear friend" (and even hugged him as he left his home for the final time), Allinson was still his intellectual and social superior, a reality that doubtlessly shaped their relationship and, hence, Allinson's writing of the *Memoir*.[67] Arguably, the two Christians exploited each other: Quamino needed Allinson to help him survive in a racist society (particularly after the death of his wife, Sarah, in 1842), and Allinson needed Quamino to help articulate his ideas about how black people possessed the "unrestrained enthusiasm of an artless and overjoyed child," as he described Quamino during their last meeting.[68]

Fallen Manhood

Unlike William Allinson, Andrew Mellick did not personally know his black subjects in *The Story of an Old Farm*. His eleven-page discussion of his ancestor's slaves was based entirely on the account that William P. Sutphen provided him in 1887. Much of what Sutphen's "sketch" conveyed about the slaves and their owner, Aaron Malick (Mellick's great grandfather), was learned years earlier from Charlotte Van Dayton, who "lived . . . in Aaron Malick's time." According to Sutphen, "she was a good talker and delighted in talking of the old time." A religiously devout woman, she "had great faith in [the slaves] Dick and Nance," who were churchgoing Christians.[69]

Andrew Mellick did not intend to write a book of more than seven hundred pages about his family heritage that included his ancestor's slaves. Whereas William Allinson wrote Quamino's *Memoir* to promote his antislavery politics, *The Story of an Old Farm* served an entirely different function for Mellick: it helped to fill the empty spaces in an otherwise dreary life befallen by tragedy. The author of this widely acclaimed local family history was a complete invalid who suffered an unexpected spinal injury that gradually took his life over the course of thirteen years. Prior to his debilitating paralysis, however, Mellick had lived a rather active, intense, and accomplished life.

Born in New York City, Mellick received only a common school education and, at the age of sixteen, went to work for his father, who, by this time, had turned to real estate. For more than twenty years thereafter, Mellick was an extremely energetic and determined businessman. In 1870, at age twenty-six, he established a real estate firm with his brother, James: A. D. Mellick, Jr. & Brother. It was perhaps the most widely known real

Figure 4. Photograph of Andrew D. Mellick Jr. following his spinal injury
(c. 1880). Frontispiece of *Somerset County Historical Quarterly* (1912).

estate firm in central New Jersey, owing in part to liberal and aggressive adver-
tising. Indeed, Mellick was the embodiment of the masculine achiever model
of nineteenth-century manhood described earlier. An obviously rugged and
competitive individualist, Mellick equated manhood with succeeding in the
world of commercial capitalism. But, despite his efforts, within two short
years he became victim to the economic depression of the early 1870s. Sad-
dled with an abundance of once valuable and saleable New Jersey property,
the economic crisis wrecked him and his brother financially.[70] The depression, which was a recurring phenomenon through the late 1890s, had drastic
consequences for Mellick and other middle-class men who dreamt of manly
independent entrepreneurship. Gail Bederman, in her engaging study on
race and gender at the turn of the twentieth century, remarks that, "under
these conditions, the sons of the middle class faced the real possibility that
traditional sources of male power and status would remain closed to them forever—that they would become failures instead of self-made men."[71] Unable to
accept such failure, Mellick "patiently went to rebuild his fortunes."[72]

It was then, we are told, "that the true manliness and honor of Mr. Mellick shone forth in gratifying colors." That is, "he deliberately sat down
to the hardest kind of toil—in the real estate business by himself—and
endeavored to pay off the claims against the firm, in the meantime making
frugality and the strictest economy his guiding principles."[73] By this statement, Mellick, in the manner of many middle-class men of the nineteenth
century, sought to "rebuild his fortunes" on what Gail Bederman calls
"high-minded self-restraint." This may explain why Mellick never wed. As

Bederman writes, "celebrations of manly self-restraint encouraged young men to postpone marriage until they could support a family in proper middle-class style, to work hard and live abstemiously so that they could amass the capital to go into business for themselves." Mellick, it is possible to conjecture, had imbibed fully the Victorian masculine discourse that, by century's end, Bederman avers, stressed "self-mastery and restraint," and "expressed and shaped middle-class identity."[74]

Victorian codes of manly self-restraint, active membership in the New York State National Guard, and the pursuit of a law degree occupied Mellick's time until he accepted a position with the well-known law offices of Coudert Brothers in 1878. Based in New York City, the firm was interested in lands in the American West. Subsequently, Mellick made several trips to the region, where he investigated and reported on certain grants of land. A trip in 1880, however, had fatal consequences. That year, while investigating a large tract of land near Las Vegas, New Mexico, Mellick was thrown violently from a pony. Not only was he badly injured, but the incident appears to have exacerbated a disease that had already manifested in his system. A physician in Colorado later diagnosed Mellick's condition as the incurable spinal disease locomotor ataxia. Over time, the gradual paralysis rendered him totally helpless, eventually taking his life in 1895.

Mellick reportedly accepted his fate, confirmed by a New York specialist, with equanimity. Though he soon gave up work, he was determined to maintain his general health, keep his mind engaged, and live a full and useful life. Thus, in 1882 he made a trip to Europe (his second), visiting France, England, and Holland. The two-month journey stimulated Mellick's intellectual curiosity but did nothing to improve his health. In fact, he returned home a confirmed invalid, without hope of final recovery. He was unable to leave the house except for an occasional drive in a carriage and could not stand, sit erect, or hold a pen. From 1873 to 1885, Mellick resided in New York City with a relative, until he relocated with the family to Plainfield, New Jersey, where he lived in excruciating pain for the remainder of his life.[75]

Far from living his life in full pursuit of manly independence through competitive capitalism, Mellick was confined either to an invalid's couch or to his bed. Having essentially failed at his endeavor to gain independence, and forced to rely on the help of others for his daily survival, Andrew Mellick may well have gone to the invalid's couch in great despair over his masculine identity.

Writing during the Black Nadir

Abraham Van Doren Honeyman, who served as principal editor of the historically illuminating *Somerset County Historical Quarterly*, was a close friend of Mellick's. Honeyman wrote a lengthy editorial about his deceased comrade, whom he portrayed as a veritable saint: "Take him as a man or as a friend, his was . . . the most beautiful character I ever met. His morality was irreproachable. His thoughts, like his words, were choice, elevated, dignified, sweet, chaste." He then waxes: "His ambition was to be of use to the world and to build up, where others would destroy."[76] Perhaps Mellick did possess such noble attributes, but the fact remains that he was also rather racist, a reality confirmed in *The Story of an Old Farm*,[77] in which he uses disparaging terms such as "necessarily savage," "barbarians," "sable merchants," and "dusky toilers" to describe enslaved blacks, and refers to Indians as "redmen," "savages," and "dusky Indians."[78] As implied in Mellick's borrowed account of his ancestor's slaves, Dick and Nance were nothing more than passive and smiling Sambos, and Yombo a mere brute.[79]

The racist sentiments Mellick espoused were indicative of the marked increase in white supremacist sentiment during the last quarter of the nineteenth century, a period when, according to Rayford Logan, African Americans experienced their nadir. The resurgence of racism, in the North and South, Logan forcefully posits, was a result of several critical factors, including the collapse of Reconstruction, the emergence of Social Darwinism, and the Scramble for Africa.[80] These events and the negative images of blacks in various literary forums greatly influenced white public opinion with regard to African Americans. Accounts of Mellick describe him as "an omnivorous reader. There was little in the general range of human knowledge about which he did not possess some information. He liked philosophy. He cared in his later years little for poetry, except of the finest."[81] We are thus led to speculate that Mellick, like many white Northerners, was familiar with the racist works about African Americans produced by the pens of influential Southern white writers such as Thomas Nelson Page and Joel Chandler Harris. These writers, Logan contends, developed seven harmful stereotypes of blacks: "The Contented Slave, The Wretched Freedman, The Comic Negro, The Brute Negro, The Tragic Mulatto, The Local Color Negro, and the Exotic Primitive." Though a reputed advocate of blacks, Harris ascribed these stereotypical words to Uncle Remus: "Hit's [education is] de ruinashun er dis country. . . . Put a spellin'-book in a nigger's han's, an right den dar' you loozes a plow-hand." Page, in his *Red Rock* (1898), acidly described the black character Moses as "a hyena in a cage," "a reptile," "a species of worm," and a "wild beast."[82] Even more disturbing, in 1892, Page envisaged the extinction of African Americans.[83]

Late nineteenth-century Northern newspapers and magazines also sanctioned the groundswell of white supremacist sentiment, and the racism advanced in Andrew Mellick's book. While they rarely identified white criminals by racial descriptors, Northern newspapers frequently used the terms "colored" or "negro" to refer to black law breakers, and employed hostile appellations such as "burly negro," "negro ruffian," "African Annie," "a Wild Western Negro," and even "colored cannibal" to condemn their actions. The adjectives "coon," "darky," "uncle," "picka-ninny," and "nigger" or "niggah" were the nomenclature of comics, cartoons, and short stories about blacks that appeared in the *New York Times* and other newspapers.[84] Leading Northern literary magazines, including *Harper's New Monthly Magazine, Scribner's* (later renamed *Century*), *North American Review*, and *Atlantic Monthly* regularly published fictional pieces, cartoons, and poetry (some of which was the work of noted white Southern writers) that gave credence to the widespread belief that African Americans were comic, inferior, and dishonest.[85]

Before his death, Andrew Mellick contributed numerous articles to the *Newark Daily Advertiser, New York Times*, and other newspapers (and magazines) about the places he visited, including Cuba, Europe, and the American West.[86] Given his close association with Northern newspapers and magazines, it is no wonder that his commentary on blacks in *The Story of an Old Farm* mirrors the racist diatribes common in these publications. Presumably, moreover, Mellick was familiar with *Silvia Dubois, A Biografy of the Slav Who Whipt Her Mistres and Gand Her Fredom*, written and published (in 1883) by Cornelius Larison, a doctor, educator, and publisher of Hunterdon County.[87] The narrative represents a rare account of a former central New Jersey slave, and was printed in Larison's odd phonetic spelling with diacritical marks.[88] Surely, a locally based narrative that stages, as one scholar phrases it, "the great hegemonic divide between an unlettered black woman and a professional white man," and was printed in a kind of code, would not have escaped the attention of someone as intellectually precocious as Mellick.[89]

Reflective of nineteenth-century colonial literature, Larison describes his sojourn to interview Silvia Dubois at her daughter's impoverished "hut" on snowy Sourland Mountain as leaving his civilized white world for the backwards, dark world of this once physically large and powerful woman who drank, cursed (even during the interview), and engaged in fist fights. Upon his arrival, the doctor immediately racializes the fabled old woman, whom he found sleeping while sitting upright, as "a dusky form." "Her head," he mocks, "tied up with a handkerchief, after the usual manner of colored ladies, was bowed forward, so that the chin rested upon her fleshy chest." As if to indulge further the racist sensibilities of his white readership, Larison reports, "Her apparel was not Parisian, yet it was reasonably whole and not dirty. There seemed to be enough of it and adjusted entirely in accordance with the genius of the African race."[90] This initial image of Dubois as a "fleshy" or sensuous black exotic pervades Larison's narrative, revealing how the doctor was very much a product of his age.

Figure 5. Photograph of Silvia Dubois (right) and her daughter, Elizabeth Alexander (1883). Courtesy of Hunterdon County Historical Society, Flemington, NJ.

Again, it is difficult to imagine how such a unique and provocative (racist) book—which spoke powerfully to local history, the Southern plantation tradition, and the colonial project—could have eluded Andrew Mellick. Indeed, both Larison and Mellick wrote books that perpetuated the hegemonic divide found not only in the literature of the United States but also in Europe. By the end of the nineteenth century, the tendency among whites on both sides of the Atlantic to racialize and essentialize non-Western subjects was standard currency in everyday discourse.[91] This would explain, then, why Mellick was such "a great admirer" of the Scottish novelist Robert Louis Stevenson, who supposedly sent a "pleasant letter" to Mellick while he was living on the island of Samoa.[92] Stevenson, as Judith Walkowitz convincingly demonstrates, depicted his East London subjects as a kind of racialized other.[93] Mellick, as we shall see in the ensuing chapters, portrayed Yombo, Dick, and Nance in a similar fashion.

In the end, a host of important factors in the late 1800s—the failure to turn Southern blacks into the political equals of whites, the theories of biological racism, the colonial (European) conquest of dark races, and the proliferation of hegemonic literature written in America and Europe— facilitated the acceptance by most American whites, including Mellick, of blacks' inherent inferiority and of whites' inherent superiority. If it is true that Mellick's "ambition was to be of use to the world and to build up, where others would destroy," then his flagrantly racist commentary in *The Story of an Old Farm* suggests an entirely different desire: to help maintain the racial status quo of white over black.

Redemption of Manhood and Northern Slavery

The Story of an Old Farm did more than allow Mellick to help maintain the status quo; it also provided him with a critical means of masculine empowerment, if not redemption. The book, he told a friend in Iowa after its publication, "was undertaken to enliven what would have otherwise been dreary hours." "It has brought to a sick man that best of all medicine—content; satisfied vague longings for emotion and excitement, and has been an incentive for him to gladly welcome each day," he professed. Unable to experience the "excitement" of manhood through the competitive market economy, exotic foreign travel, voluntary military service, and prolonged academic study, Mellick began, in 1887, to gather facts concerning his German ancestors—the Moelich family—with the much-needed assistance of his family and friends. Mellick candidly explained his travails in writing the book to this same friend:

> During the entire time the writing of the book was under way no visits could be made to localities, libraries, the rooms of historical societies, or to individuals. Information not obtained from books was only to be had by extensive and prolonged correspondence, necessitating the dictating of over two thousand letters. In addition, not only did the body of the work grow by dictation, but the copious notes, covering two thousand folio pages, made from reading the books enumerated in the bibliography in the appendix, were preserved

in like manner. This was the more difficult because of it never being possible to foretell what special pains or ailments each day would claim for its own.[94]

The production of *The Story of an Old Farm* represented the great adventure in Mellick's once dreary life, providing him with some semblance of his previous existence as an energetic man who had goals to accomplish.

The publication of the large octavo book made Mellick an instant minor celebrity. It was praised in the *Saturday Review* of London, the *New York Tribune*, the *Evening Post*, the *Mail and Express*, the *Magazine of American History*, the *Philadelphia Ledger*, and even the highly prestigious London *Athenaeum*. Within a short time, Mellick received a deluge of letters offering effusive praise and sincere gratitude not only for the book's historical fullness but for its unique style. The letters came primarily, if not exclusively, from a range of white males, including historians, writers, public officials, lawyers, a college president, and a bishop.[95] William McDowell was among those moved by Mellick's book. In 1889 the Plainfield resident wrote to Mellick to express, "As a son of Somerset Co., and Bedminster Township, I feel a debt of gratitude to you for your work, beyond my ability or the ability of the English language to express."[96] In the words of another male reader in 1890, the book "would be always very interesting to every Jerseyman who is interested in the early history of the colony and state."[97] These and other correspondents applauded Mellick in part because he, perhaps more dramatically than any other New Jersey writer of the nineteenth century, had captured the story of white masculine struggle and achievement in the province from the colonial through the revolutionary era. Abraham Van Doren Honeyman, who proofread his friend's magnum opus, confessed, "On every page, not the faults but the virtues of our ancestors are brought out in pleasing pictures . . . who made American Independence possible and American Christianity a certainty."[98] In dramatic fashion, Mellick walked and talked with his brave, noble, and pious German American ancestors as he wrote them—and their local white compatriots—into history.

Since he lived vicariously through his ancestors, it is hardly surprising that Mellick described New Jersey slavery as an essentially benevolent institution. He claims that "in Somerset County, especially, the slaves soon fell under the sway of kindly influences, and became almost portions of their owners' families." The slaves, he further alleges, "were comfortably clad; when sick, well cared for; and even to this day old residents tell pleasant tales of the affection existing between our forefathers and the old-time family and farm servants." Mellick was equally defensive about his slaveholding ancestors, insisting that "slavery on the 'Old Farm' was not altogether an unmitigated evil. For a number of years much happiness in their mutual relations came to both bond and free."[99]

In a novel way, Mellick's paternalistic portrayal of slavery promotes the colonial project of the late nineteenth century. Like the European imperialists who ruled over allegedly heathenish African peoples, slaveholding whites in New Jersey, he informs his readership, had "advanced and civilized the blacks."[100] Readers are told that the captives "were chiefly gathered from points in the far interior of the dark continent," a statement that invokes the image of Africa as a land steeped in barbarism.[101] The implication here is that "the dark continent" was in desperate need of white colonization, which, as Bruce Dorsey explains, was "associated with masculine prowess."[102] Indirectly, then, *The Story of an Old Farm* articulates the historic "burden" of white men; it is a not-so-subtle expression of eighteenth- and nineteenth-century masculine civilization.

Mellick's position on slavery echoed that of numerous other nineteenth-century Northern whites, many of whom assumed the superiority of the North over the South, particularly with respect to race relations, and experienced an acute sense of guilt (over black oppression) and racial amnesia.[103] A work that surely influenced Mellick's account was Abraham Messler's *Centennial History of Somerset County*, published in 1878, which celebrates the greatest among Somerset's white male citizens. In Messler's words, "For intelligence, culture and refinement, its inhabitants are excelled nowhere. It has given the State and Nation some of their noblest men, at the bar, on the bench and in the pulpit. Society is nowhere better ordered, properly more secure, or comfort and happiness more generally diffused."[104] Accordingly, in his slim and impressionistic chapter on slavery in Somerset, Messler argues that while owners and slaves did not eat, sleep, or work together, frequent the same places of amusement, or wear the same grade of clothing, "it would not be true to state that both were not comfortable in every essential particular necessary to the well being of the individual man." The end result, he boasts, "was a great deal of harmony of action between them; even in the most instances, a mutual and zealous cooperation in business and in social necessities in all the important matters of life, and also so much amity and attachment in all actions, that serious collisions seldom occurred." He provides as partial evidence the "few" captives who escaped to the British during the Revolution.[105]

This interpretation of Somerset slavery as a benign institution was most forcefully articulated in obituaries of and short articles on former captives in central New Jersey during the latter half of the nineteenth century. These overlooked sources (which often testify to the high turnover rate among New Jersey slaveholders) form a composite of extremely old blacks who were devout Christians, well-respected by the local whites, able to live comfortably because of the charity of their former owners, still deeply interested in white family affairs, and apathetic to the Emancipation Proclamation.[106] The image of former slaves—a number of whom were reputed centenarians—that emerges from these accounts affirms the paternalistic ideology espoused by Abraham Messler, Andrew Mellick, and other writers. Only slaves who were favorably treated could have lived such long and healthy lives. Local newspapers rendered them exotic curiosities of sorts. Consider, for example, the former Somerset slave, Bob. According to a newspaper story published around 1868, Bob, age seventy-five, was "considered rather a curiosity for the oddity of his remarks and his quaint, original remarks." The article contends that he "lives 'happy as a king,' unmindful of the Emancipation Proclamation or the great revolution we are passing through in regard to his race."[107]

Among the most representative of these accounts is the 1887 obituary of Mary C. Jackson. Born in Lebanon Township, Hunterdon County, in 1789, Jackson was "given, at the age of 15, as a wedding present to her master's daughter in 1804, by whom she was taught to read and write." Her owner's 1860 will stipulated that, on his death, "she should be kept by his four surviving children in turn"; hence, "she changed her home every year." Jackson typified enslaved blacks in that she was perceived as movable property. But rather than make this important point, her obituary emphasizes that she was privileged to receive an education and have several homes. It also says that, upon the abolition of US slavery in 1865, "Aunt Mary refused to accept her freedom, saying she was too old to bother about such nonsense." In the piece's estimation, "she undoubtedly chose wisely, as she had the best homes among the children, who all used her very kindly and allowed her to do about as she wished."[108]

Though Jackson may have chosen "wisely," this was not necessarily because of her former owners' benevolence. That is to say, like many of her indigent free black compatriots in central New Jersey where work was not always forthcoming, it would have been extremely difficult for her to survive without the economic assistance of whites. As an example, in 1885, Silvia Dubois was reported to have been on a "begging tour" in Somerset County with her daughter.[109] In addition, many old and physically infirm blacks were dependent upon the support of the poor houses of their respective townships.[110] This struggle for day-to-day survival must have greatly affected black behavior. Following the death of her second husband, alleged centenarian Nancy Van Pelt was forced to work "around the neighborhood" of Harlingen in Montgomery Township. A local newspaper reporter visited the "old lady," who was cleaning kitchen closets at the time. She reportedly said to the interviewer, "Here I am, boss, now look at me. I'm a little busy to-day, but come in." This remark speaks not to a well-preserved ex-slave who "might live 20 years more," as the story concluded, but instead to a free black woman who lived a precarious existence and adopted the language of modesty and submission to help her survive.[111]

As we can see, Andrew Mellick wrote *The Story of an Old Farm* within the context of an entrenched local (and transatlantic) dogma that deemed blacks inferior, exotic, and the wards of merciful whites. And yet, he seemed conflicted over the institution of slavery. He acknowledges, for example, both the horrors associated with the transatlantic slave trade— referring to it as "the devil's work"—and the fact that the captives were "stolen" from Africa and brought to a strange land where "much cruelty was inflicted through fears of risings and rebellions." The eventual fragmentation of Dick and Nance's family also distressed him, though there was "a silver lining": the children were sold to men known to the family and the aged parents got to remain on the Old Farm.[112] And probably most revealing of all, as indicated in the introduction, he fails to mention in his book that his ancestors once owned about twenty slaves. Thus, notwithstanding his ancestors' rugged determination, the family fortune was built partly on the coerced labor of blacks. In her childhood reminiscences in Mapleton, Middlesex County, Margaret Nevius Van Dyke Malcolm (1824–1916) further testifies to white guilt over slavery. Her grandfather, she laments, "was a righteous man—unless his owning [of] slaves was charged against him in the 'Book of Life'—we have many unconscious sins to answer for, in the day of reckoning." Yet she added, "But, as I remember, he was very good to them."[113] Such conflicting comments, to cite Joanne Melish, are reflective of a kind of white (historical) amnesia that seeks to erase or greatly minimize the brutality and centrality of slavery's legacy in white people's history.[114] Because slavery, an inherently violent institution that typically ruptured black family ties, was such an important part of white people's history, it seemed only logical to them that blacks, an inferior people with ties to the "dark continent," benefitted as much from the institution as they did.

Conclusion

The works of William Allinson and Andrew Mellick are written from clear ideological perspectives that obscure the gendered identities of Yombo, Dick, and Quamino. Indicative of abolitionist literature in the mid 1800s, Allinson's objective in Quamino's *Memoir* was to frame his subject as a suffering and ultimately triumphant black saint who would appeal to the consciences of pro-slavery Southerners and sentimental Northerners. Mellick, conversely, uses his ancestor's slaves in *The Story of an Old Farm* to demonstrate further the paternalistic nature of slavery in Somerset County and promote the white hegemonic project of the late 1800s. Both of their agendas rendered it impossible for them to delineate their black subjects as gendered persons with the same range of human complexity as white people.

Interpreting the writings of others is always a risky and vexatious task, especially when the author is a proud descendant of slave owners, or the self-appointed protector of a degraded people. Imbedded therein are layers of truth and fiction that are not always easily discernible, and produce a certain anxiety that may dissuade historians from engaging these writings seriously as scholarly sources. This problem is exacerbated, of course, by the gaps and omissions that normally exist in such works. But rather than focus on what these writings fail to say, it is important to concentrate on what they appear to tell us. In other words, it is important to see the "silences" as strengths and not as weaknesses. In sum, what Andrew Mellick and William Allinson do not say about their black subjects is just as important as what they do say about them.[115]

This especially applies with respect to Allinson, who not only knew Quamino personally, but also established a brotherhood of sorts with him that was based upon their respective religious faiths. Yet, in the *Memoir*, Allinson, perhaps in part because he did know Quamino so intimately, omits numerous important details about his bondage, including the first names of his owners and the exact places of his captivity. If Allinson was so negligent in covering such basic details, then it stands to reason that his one-dimensional rendition of Quamino as a "tender spirited" Christian is vastly incomplete, and serves as a platform for his manhood as an aggressive abolitionist Christian.

Interestingly enough, William Griffith, an abolitionist who emancipated Quamino and his wife, Sarah, is the only slaveholder whose full identity is revealed in the *Memoir*.[116] Allinson shows how Griffith stands apart from those callous persons who hire out, buy, abuse, interrogate, and refuse to liberate Quamino. Griffith represented that segment of white men who truly sympathized with purportedly defenseless and dependent blacks, a point that resonates in a "Plea for Liberty." Yet, paradoxically, in the 1850s African Americans had grown increasingly frustrated with both the prominence of white males in the abolitionist movement and the passive, half-hearted tactics employed by pacifists such as Allinson to eradicate slavery. Many black abolitionists, to the great disproval of their paternalistic counterparts, advocated the violent overthrow of the institution. Thus it is not difficult to see how the vulnerable, emotional, and docile Quamino was also a trope that validated the "peer relationship" within the abolitionist movement, that substantiated the "'father knows best attitude' of white abolitionists."[117] The trope in turn obscures how Quamino possibly saw himself as a man.

Anxieties related to manhood are also evident in Andrew Mellick's book. Indeed, Mellick was in a sense obsessed with manhood, which had been taken away from him in the prime of his life. He poignantly described his once promising and active life as "horizoned by the walls of an invalid's room."[118] Small wonder, then, that women, children, Indians, and slaves are peripheral to his grand narrative of white masculine struggle and achievement. Mellick essentially redeems himself as a man through his male ancestors and their compatriots, whom he credits with transforming the Bedminster community from wilderness to settled countryside, and who subsequently triumphed with General George Washington during the destructive Revolutionary War. He thus had little interest in blacks aside from what whites had supposedly done for them. This perspective hindered his ability to view slaves seriously as men and women.

Despite their glaring shortcomings, Mellick's and Allinson's works have provided the skeleton necessary for us to unravel some of the experiences of three enslaved males otherwise buried in historical obscurity. Antiquated treatments like theirs provide insights that neither current historical scholarship nor traditional source materials can. The key, then, as the following chapters demonstrate, is to use these different sources together with critical reading, in such a way that allows us to reconstruct the hidden lives and obscured gendered identities of Yombo, Dick, and Quamino.

Chapter 2

Powerful and Righteous

Andrew Mellick's *The Story of an Old Farm* is a thoroughly researched book that tells us a great deal about how enslaved blacks resisted against and survived their oppression in eighteenth-century central New Jersey.[1] And yet it fails to mention or discuss a rather sensational incident of slave resistance in the area that had great implications for Yombo's life in bondage. Reverend John Bodine Thompson made this intriguing remark in his 1894 address commemorating the 175th anniversary of the Reformed Dutch Church of Readington Township, Hunterdon County:

> Those [slaves] who came [to New Jersey] from the coast of Guinea [i.e., southern West Africa] were regarded as the most valuable because of their superior endowments, both mental and physical. "Guinea Negroes" brought more on the open market. Among these were a man who had been the chief of his tribe, with his wife, who now shared his slavery as she shared his rule in the land of their fathers. These became the property of Jacob Kline.... [Slavery] is bitter at the best, and it is no wonder that these Africans were fearfully homesick. Every endeavor was made to cheer and comfort them— save, of course, that of setting them free, which, probably, was never thought of. The result was, that when all hope was gone, they sought and found together the only freedom possible for them. The spot is still pointed out, on Kline's brook, a mile directly north of this place, where stood the cedar tree upon which, one morning, the master found only the lifeless bodies of those who refused to remain as slaves in a strange land.

Thompson's speech, focusing on the Hunterdon church's "members of African descent," was printed a week later in a local newspaper and is important because it provides a rare glimpse of native West Africans who lived and died under bondage in New Jersey.[2] At the same time, the minister left several critical questions unanswered: What was the ethnicity of this presumably noble West African couple? Where exactly in "Guinea" did they rule? What factors led to their enslavement? How were they able to survive their wrenching voyage to the New World, and when did they arrive in New Jersey? And finally, why did they choose to take their own lives in such a horrific manner?

This chapter makes an effort to explore these inquiries and thereby bring into sharper relief the two captives' ambiguous lives and, moreover, the dimensions of the nebulous manifestation of West African thought—

namely, religious beliefs—in central New Jersey during the eighteenth century. The couple's suicide suggests strongly the ideological conflict between
enslaved West Africans' concepts of the supernatural and the white hegemony that ruled them. In a way, this argument is an extension of the one
that William Piersen made in his seminal 1977 article on slave suicide, in
which he maintained that "in certain instances, West Africans considered
suicide an admirable act" sanctioned by their religiosity.[3] This chapter also
seeks to provide clues as to the husband and wife's survival of the elusive
experience of the Middle Passage which, it proposes, was linked to their
Sierra Leonian origins. In another sense, then, it complicates Michael
Gomez's discussion on this topic, found in his path-breaking 1998 book on
early African American identity in the South. Gomez describes the Middle
Passage as a brutal rite of passage that encouraged captives to form bonds
based on mutual suffering that cut across ethnic lines, and forced them to
rethink who and what constituted community.[4] African religion, it is contended here, was equally critical to their survival of this life-altering ordeal.

Reverend Thompson's thought-provoking commentary on "Readington Negroes" has an important dual function. On the one hand, it is a
vital piece of slavery-related local history that omits valuable information
about the Guinea blacks acquired by Jacob Kline. On the other hand, it
serves as a counterpart to Andrew Mellick's family narrative of Somerset
County, which verifies indirectly that the African couple was Yombo's parents. Both Thompson's speech and Mellick's book downplays the often
antagonistic relationship between owners and slaves, yet forms a unique
late nineteenth-century window into the transcontinental saga of this prestigious African family turned common New Jersey slaves. Moreover, these
two literary works (and hence this chapter) build upon Graham Hodges's
probing 1999 analysis of slave culture in the New York area. In *Root and
Branch*, Hodges shows that African religious practice both legitimized and
strengthened resistance to bondage, as evidenced in insurrections and
other instances of black militancy in the colonial era, when Kline's two captives appear to have killed themselves.[5] Yombo and his parents deepen our
knowledge about the cultural resistance and sense of identity of enslaved
peoples in colonial New Jersey.

Assessing the Middle Passage: The Value of African Religions

Of no small consequence, our three subjects were survivors of the African
enslavement process that brought them to the New World. This brutal
method of human displacement typically occurred in three distinct stages:
(1) the capture of Africans, usually by other Africans involved in the slave
trade; (2) the forced migration of the captives to the West African coast,

and their subsequent confinement in barracoons, or slave factories, so that European merchants could evaluate, purchase, and consign them by branding; and (3) the journey of the black cargos across the Atlantic, known as the Middle Passage, which frequently included a brief stopover in the West Indies, where they were "seasoned" or initiated into racial bondage. Perhaps the most traumatic leg of the coerced exodus, these voyages (generally eight weeks long) to the North American colonies (and the Caribbean archipelago) severed African peoples completely from the complex system of customs, relationships, taboos, and religious ceremonies that had ordered their lives. Viewed by their European adversaries as inherently libidinous and savage, the naked prisoners were often raped, beaten, and whipped. Moreover, they were relegated to cramped quarters in filthy vessels and ravaged by infectious diseases that claimed numerous black lives—repulsive conditions exacerbated by lengthy delays in the transoceanic journey because of storms and calms. Even under the most favorable circumstances, the Middle Passage was a horrifying experience that former slaves never forgot completely.[6]

Consider, for example, Phillis, the daughter of an African king who, during her youth, was kidnapped in Africa and purchased from a slave vessel by Cornelius DeHart (d. 1769) of Six-Mile Run in present-day Franklin Township. She remembered distinctly "that on the voyage to America she was often terribly frightened by some of the crew attempting to feel her hands, she supposing that it was done for the purpose of ascertaining whether she was in good condition for slaughtering, and her carcass to be eaten, as the neighboring tribes of cannibals did in Africa, to avoid which she fasted to cause leanness, so as to disappoint them in their expectations, and thereby preserve her life."[7] Phillis's briefly described ordeal, one of the few commentaries about the Middle Passage left by a black woman, reminds us not only of African females' fear of callous and sexually depraved white crewmen recruited from the margins of European society, but also of Africans' general anxiety as to white cannibalism, a belief particularly prevalent in the interior of Africa.[8]

While historians have debated intensely the number of Africans brought to the Americas, they have given comparatively little attention to how the captives endured the Middle Passage.[9] Cedric Robinson avers that the human cargos aboard slave ships "contained African cultures, critical mixes and admixtures of language and thought, of cosmology and metaphysics, of habits, beliefs, and morality"; in other words, the captives were real human beings and not "intellectual isolates or deculturated Blacks—men, women, and children separated from their previous universe."[10] Correspondingly, there can be little doubt that religious faith played a prominent role in many West Africans' survival of their voyages to the North American colonies. Religion was, and still remains, immensely important in the lives of most West African peoples. It explained their place in the universe and their kinship with nature; it regulated their sexual relationships, marital responsibilities, and ceremonies of passage through puberty; and it dictated the roles of women, men, and children in the community and society at large. For the majority of ethnic groups in West Africa, religion symbolized a system of social control, a source of therapy, a reliable mode of organization, and a means of protection. In short, religion there, as elsewhere, was not simply an intellectual abstraction, but was crucial to everyday life.[11] Thus, the ability of Jacob Kline's bondpeople to withstand the Middle Passage probably was aided by their strong religious faith—namely, belief in a supreme being, spiritual ancestors, and life after death.[12] Religion may have continued to bolster their self-esteem and courage, served as their defense against personal degradation, and helped to keep alive their desire for freedom in the "strange" and racially oppressive New Jersey colony.

Religious or spiritual linkages in the long, fascinating history of African American spatial movement justify a further analysis of the Middle Passage in the context of West African religious beliefs and practices. A salient commonality of the major occurrences of black geographical mobility is that the participants—whether slaves escaping because of the Revolutionary and Civil wars, millenarian-minded Southern "Exodusters" fleeing to Kansas after Reconstruction, or poor and disfranchised Southern tenant farmers (sharecroppers) quitting "Jim Crow" for the industrial North during and after World War I—often believed in some form of an all-powerful and protective God.[13] Therefore, exploring the utility of African religions aboard slave ships not only has methodological value, but also facilitates understanding of the bridge of African American spiritual consciousness from slavery through the twentieth century.

Prior to the publication of Michael Gomez's *Exchanging Our Country Marks*, where he argues that the horrific nature of the Middle Passage helped to undermine the ethnic separateness of captive Africans, scholars of American slavery, especially those focusing on Northern bondage, generally had failed to allot serious attention to the transatlantic component of the enslavement process. The two notable exceptions are John Blassingame and Nathan Huggins. Blassingame, in his 1972 book *The Slave Community*, was among the first historians to discuss the Middle Passage as a tragic ordeal in enslaved Southern blacks' long struggle against white oppression. Although Blassingame readily acknowledges that Africans brought some of their "cultural baggage" to the New World and that it assisted greatly in their acculturation, he, like Gomez, does not explain explicitly the utility of African religious beliefs as they pertain to black survival aboard slave ships.[14] Huggins's eloquent 1977 work, *Black Odyssey*, analyzes the captives on shipboard from a psychological perspective, concluding that they were fatalists who believed they had been abandoned by the spirits that had made their lives whole. Huggins was unwilling to concede the importance of African religious beliefs during the Middle Passage, and dismissed them as a source of mere "emotional suppleness" (as one historian puts it) for black peoples.[15] Stephanie Smallwood, in her recent provocative study on the "saltwater" or transatlantic dimensions of the enslavement experience, is equally skeptical of the utility of African religious beliefs at sea. In her estimation, "the very habitat of the ship—the open sea—challenged African cosmographies, for the landless realm of the deep ocean did not figure in precolonial West African societies as a domain of human (as opposed to divine) activity—just as it had not figured as such in medieval European systems of knowledge." Thus, she declares, "The ship under sail was a world unto itself, where the passengers had to rely only on the expertise of the sailors—and on whatever spiritual power they might be able to summon."[16] It would seem that Smallwood underestimates the ability of a fundamentally religious people to summon "spiritual power" during these terrifying journeys, and assigns too much credit (in terms of their survival) to the "expertise" of oppressive crewmen.

The Middle Passage has received relatively scant attention in American slavery historiography, primarily because it is difficult to analyze. For the most part, white seamen and not the African captives themselves discussed (in print) the Middle Passage's horrific and temporal natures. Not only has the credibility of the principal African testifier, Olaudah Equiano, been called into question, but rarely if ever was commentary by black women recorded (Phillis's account is one of the few exceptions).[17] Equally problematic "records of slave ships [which] mention points of embarkation" are usually vague regarding "the original homelands of the human cargo. On this side of the Atlantic, the ethnic names supplied by slave merchants and owners to newly arrived Africans were confused and inexact."[18] As a result, these muted African personages, the vanguard of African American culture, do not possess easily recoverable historical identities. By examining black survival of the Middle Passage in relation to African religions, however, we are able to look in meaningful human terms at the bondpeople who belonged to Jacob Kline and other slaves.

Ambiguous Lives

The anonymity of our adult African subjects requires us to verify their enslavement in the Somerset County area. In *The Story of an Old Farm*, Andrew Mellick explains that, prior to 1786, his great grandfather Aaron Malick (1725–1809), of Bedminster Township, had never owned blacks because of his Quaker wife's antislavery disposition. But that year he purchased an African-born bondman from his brother-in-law, Johan Jacob

Klein or Jacob Kline (1714–89), of adjacent New Germantown, Hunterdon County, to work on his farm and in his tannery. The name of Malick's African purchase was Yombo, who, as Malick's great grandson writes, was "a Guinea Negro, having been brought from Africa when a boy, where, as he claimed, his father was a 'big man.'"[19] No doubt Yombo's father—whom Malick's record book refers to as a "negro king"—was the very same former African "chief" who hanged himself on "Kline's brook" along with his wife, Yombo's mother.[20]

Why, then, did Andrew Mellick fail to mention or discuss the suicide in his book? One might assume that Mellick simply was unfamiliar with the suicide, and thus we cannot hold him responsible for information that was unbeknownst to him. Yet his ignorance on this matter seems highly improbable when considering the substantial amount of research (as pointed out in chapter 1) that went into the writing of *The Story of an Old Farm*. Notwithstanding Mellick's paralysis, there was little that he did not know about the history of his ancestors; indeed, he was more likely to know about the suicide than Reverend Thompson. The admission, however, that an ancestor of his was directly responsible contradicts his paternalistic portrayal of New Jersey slavery. Though Mellick could write about the widespread "savagery" or rebelliousness of enslaved blacks in eighteenth-century New Jersey, it was another matter altogether to associate their discontent with the slaves of his "kindly" ancestors.[21] For this reason, even if he had been aware of the suicide, he would never have included it in *The Story of an Old Farm*.

Mellick's sentimentalism is also reflected in Reverend Thompson's church address, which essentially presents Jacob Kline as a thoughtless man who had failed to truly realize, if at all, the full scope of his African servants' longing for freedom. In doing so, Thompson absolves Kline of any real culpability for the suicide, and reinforces the benign interpretation of slavery in late nineteenth-century central New Jersey. Indeed, Thompson contrasts the suicide victims with "Readington Negroes" such as Dick and Rose and Sam and Kate, couples who occasionally visited their former mistress and were "loaded with gifts" upon their happy departure.[22] Thompson's address, like Mellick's book, encapsulated the entrenched local dogma that, as shown in chapter 1, deemed blacks as the wards of benevolent whites. The tensions imbedded in these two accounts would indicate that Yombo and the suicide were much more complicated than what the writers actually convey.

Yombo was seventy years old upon Aaron Malick's death in 1809, and hence the captive was born in Guinea around the year 1739.[23] Yombo's vague contention that he was a "boy" when taken from Africa sheds little light, however, on the year he and his parents were brought to New Jersey. Conversely, his ambiguous reference to his nameless father as a "big man" in the vast territory of Guinea suggests that he was rather young, per-

haps no older than age ten, during their momentous journey. Also suggestive of this point is that Andrew Mellick, who vividly describes Yombo as
"stout, coal black, club-footed, and very bow-legged" with "rings [hanging]
from his ears," does not mention whether the "perverse" and "treacherous" bondman had any bodily mutilations such as "tribal marks" (Mellick's
words), which in many West African societies symbolize the transition from
childhood to adulthood. The attentive and racist author would not have
missed the opportunity to comment on an aspect of African culture with
which he was familiar (although not knowledgeable) and thereby enhance
further Yombo's "coal black" or exotic presence on Malick's homestead.[24]
As indicated in chapter 1, Mellick wrote his book at a time (c. 1880–1914)
when whites in both America and Europe tended to racialize and essentialize non-Western subjects. We may assume, then, that the African family landed in New Jersey around the period 1744–49, when Yombo was
between five and ten years old.

The family's mid eighteenth-century North American arrival corresponds with the influx of African and West Indian captives to New Jersey to
help satisfy the colony's desire for workers, which had been left unfulfilled
by natural black reproduction. The slave labor force was boosted by both
the Spanish government's decision in 1714 to allow English slave traders
access to its Caribbean colonies, and by the ensuing rapid expansion of
their slave-trading operations on the west coast of Africa. This increased
trade in humans made more captives, including our subjects, available to
whites in and around New Jersey. Interestingly, more than six hundred
captives from Africa and the West Indies were recorded (in an incomplete
and thus inaccurate importation schedule) to have landed at Perth Amboy,
Middlesex County, the principal slave port in the colony, between 1718 and
1757.[25] This figure appears to represent only a portion of the total number
of captives brought to Perth Amboy within this period. Again, Yombo and
his parents likely would have come to New Jersey about 1744–49, during
the time that the colonials had an insatiable demand for slave labor power
that the black population was unable to accommodate.

By 1750, when the Africans had landed in the Jersey colony, Jacob
Kline and his business partner, Johannes Moelich (Aaron Malick's
father), together owned a large farm and tannery in Readington Township that consisted of several hundred acres, which seemingly required
them to seek extra help. Many years passed before Kline's five sons—
John William (b. 1750), Jacob (b. 1751), Aaron (b. 1760), Peter (b.
1771), and David (birth date unknown)—were able to assist their father
in running the vast business enterprises carried on by the Kline family
for more than seven decades. In addition to his roles as father, husband, tanner, currier, and agriculturist, Jacob Kline was a public official
in Hunterdon County, and as early as 1749 a trustee of Zion Lutheran

Church in New Germantown.[26] Like many New Jersey farmers during the colonial period, the ever-busy Kline purchased Yombo's family to address the pressing labor needs both inside and outside of his burgeoning homestead.[27] Here the new captives appeared to have lived isolated from other blacks. The 1745 census indicates that Hunterdon County's "slave" population consisted of 244 males and 216 females, and constituted 5.2 percent of its population. The next census, taken in 1772 (after the couple had apparently taken their lives), reported a "Negro" population of 586 males and 509 females, accounting for 7.5 percent of the local population.[28] The data is clear in saying that the Kline captives had to work and ultimately survive without an extensive black support system, a condition exacerbated by their precarious family life and the racial violence in their midst.

Where did Kline purchase the Africans? According to Andrew Mellick, Johannes Moelich made a special trip in 1752 to Perth Amboy to retrieve a possible letter "from the old country." During Moelich's visit, Mellick explains, he probably took notice of the New Jersey capital's diverse population of "the expatriated Irish, Dutch, Germans, and English," "the sturdy yeomanry," "the gentry, richly dressed in all the magnificence of the times," and lastly, "the Negroes," many of whom "were freshly imported, bearing their tribal marks, and exhibiting their native characteristics, as if still inhabiting the wilds of Guinea." If Moelich had witnessed this human spectacle—namely, the stolen Africans—then so did his business partner, Jacob Kline, who, as a justice of the peace in Hunterdon County, was required to attend the annual gathering of state officials in Perth Amboy known as "court days."[29] In short, Kline may have gone to the slave barracks on the corner of Smith and Water streets to buy his Africans.[30]

In all likelihood, the captives entered New Jersey through Perth Amboy. But because of the faceless nature of the city's Customs House records on black imports during the period 1718–57, we will never know the exact ship that brought them to the colony, from which we might gain greater insight into their lives. Even so, twenty-one of the reported twenty-seven slave ships which docked there at this time had come directly from the Caribbean, suggesting that both Andrew Mellick and Reverend Thompson failed to mention that our three protagonists may have been held briefly in the West Indies prior to arriving in New Jersey. Significantly, blacks who were shipped to colonial New York and New Jersey from the Caribbean did not experience this leg of the Middle Passage with numerous other captives in the cramped conditions typically associated with the voyage. Rather, they came either individually or in small groups, a situation which could perhaps help keep a small family intact.[31]

Yombo's first name provides important clues regarding the specific area in "Guinea" (which, in the eighteenth century, encompassed the vast region roughly between the Senegal River and Angola) where the enslaved family originally lived.[32] Yombo closely resembles the name "Yamboo," which has been identified among the Mende, Bobangi, and Hausa peoples. The fact that both the Hausa and Bobangi were located outside of Guinea proper in present-day northern Nigeria/southern Niger and central Zaire, respectively, eliminates the possibility of the family's belonging to either ethnic group. Therefore, our "Yombo" probably is kindred to the Mende "Yamboo," pronounced "yambu," "yambo," "lambo," and "jambo."[33] Another point to consider is that, in Mende society, women oftentimes were rulers as well as holders of high offices and less authoritative political positions.[34] As Michael Gomez writes, Sierra Leonians "came to North America from small-scale polities with egalitarian tendencies as far as gender was concerned, in contrast to the large, centralized Gold Coast states, where women were not as prominent."[35] The implication here, inspired by Reverend Thompson's speech, is that Yombo's anonymous mother was or could have been politically powerful. According to this suggestive body of evidence, the Africans enslaved under Jacob Kline were probably Mande-speaking Mendes who resided in Sierra Leone. During the 1700s, this region was a key supplier of Africans for the slave trade, owing to the "inter-group hostilities [that] were motivated by and oriented towards" this nascent enterprise.[36]

Indeed, numerous captives brought to New York and New Jersey were refugees from the political turmoil in eighteenth-century Africa precipitated by the expanding frontier of slavery.[37] In her journal, kept from 1810 to 1811, Rachel Van Dyke of New Brunswick, New Jersey, wrote that the old family slave "remember[ed] that the people were all fighting and the town was on fire when she was carried away" from Guinea as a youth. There was "one black man she will never forget. He tore all her gold ornaments from her and when she cried boxed her ears."[38]

Rebels and Survivors aboard Ship

Andrew Mellick contends that the Africans who were "stolen" and forcibly shipped to New Jersey "were physically powerful and good workers, but without much power of reasoning or of controlling their undisciplined imaginations."[39] Notwithstanding Mellick's trite racism, his comment is important because it testifies indirectly to newly arrived Africans' ability to maintain their sense of humanity despite having been subjected to the harrowing Atlantic slave trade. Mellick's insight begs the question: Why were Yombo's parents and many of their compatriots not demoralized completely by the Middle Passage? Consideration of West African religious beliefs and customs sheds light on this elusive issue. The discussion that follows is neither exhaustively researched nor definitively argued; it merely seeks to make a contribution to the all-important debate on black transatlantic survival.

Any analysis of the thought processes of Africans aboard slave ships requires not only imagination, but also some general understanding of how they were confined with regard to gender. The captain and personnel of "Yankee" slavers (and others) made the captives' existence practically unbearable. Once brought on shipboard, crewmen coerced these emotionally traumatized individuals, who despaired of ever seeing their homeland again, into hot and poorly ventilated holds only a few feet high between decks. This was to prevent them—namely, adult males who initially had been chained together in twos and then stowed "spoon fashion"—from seizing the vessel. Women and children, conversely, typically remained unfettered yet separated from the men, and therefore from their protection and influence, by deliberately constructed partitions. Shipboard security was often based on the chauvinistic belief that the physically weaker females represented little if any real threat to the armed crew's safety. Captain William Snelgrave, for example, writing in 1727, explained that, "when we purchase the Negroes, we couple the sturdy Men together with Irons; but we suffer the Women and Children to go freely about: And soon after we have sail'd from the Coast, we undo all the Mens [sic] Irons." Some paranoid skippers, however, kept the men shackled the entire voyage. Despite their possession of pistols, knives, and cutlasses, whites feared greatly the angry and despondent African males in these incommodious compartments, who were lying naked, thirsty, hungry, and diseased on bare wooden planks and subjected to violent motions of the rolling ship that caused skin to rub off prominent parts of their bodies.[40] (Although conditions on slavers carrying blacks from the West Indies to New York and New Jersey may not have reflected this degree of security and suffering, we can scarcely imagine that the captives on this leg of the journey, who again were transported individually or in small groups, experienced no trauma.)

Surely, then, the stolen Africans (whether they were transported with many or a few compatriots) had a great need for divine intervention and consolation. In numerous traditional or precolonial West African societies, men comprised the priesthood and were reputed to possess magical and other such powers. As among the Mende, the religious life of society typically was placed under the aegis of the group, namely, the eldest or family patriarch who often performed the ceremonies to communicate with the spiritual ancestors that explained the destiny of man. This role was usually passed down to the eldest son. According to the creeds of many West African religious systems, man, while not the king of all creation, was placed in the center of the world by God, a position symbolic of his strength and marriage to the divinity.[41] Would such "big" and spiritually endowed men have descended into the frightening hold, which many captives possibly perceived as entering "a world of bad spirits," without the cosmologies that defined their sacred place in the universe?[42]

While many Western observers (that is, people of white European descent) were well aware of the religious devotion of African males living on the Guinea coast, they frequently dismissed it as "fetishism." A misnomer, as pointed out by several scholars of religion in West Africa, the term is of Portuguese origin meaning an object with magical, protective powers. It was used widely by Western encroachers to describe religion and worship on the African continent. That is to say, Westerners often wrongly perceived the charms, amulets, and incantations utilized by African peoples—similar to those of the Portuguese themselves—as constituting the whole of West African belief systems.[43] For example, William Smith, who surveyed the Guinea coast in 1726–27 for the Royal African Company (a slave-trading firm in England), referred to the largest sect in Gambia as "Pagans" who had "no Religion at all," but instead worshipped a "Fittish" ("a Lion's tail . . . a Bird's Feather"), which they believed would "defend them from all Danger's." In Smith's Eurocentric opinion, this kind of adoration was completely nonsensical.[44]

Significantly, John Newton, in his 1750–54 account of his participation in the Atlantic slave trade, made reference to a slave plot in which the male captives sought "to poyson the water in the scuttle casks upon deck . . . with their country fetishes, as they call them, or talismans." By tainting this vital resource, they hoped "to kill all who drank it." Newton, however, downplayed the rebels' plan of action, scoffing that they intended "to charm us to death."[45] Whether or not he (or William Smith) cared to admit it, these "Pagan" beliefs instilled captives with a sense of guardianship, and thereby cunning and daring, which put every white man's life in serious jeopardy. Missionary Joseph Corry, who visited the Windward Coast (Sierra Leone) from 1805 to 1806, wrote of the blacks inhabitants that not only did they place great trust in "their fetish, as an antidote against evil," but they also believed forgiveness was "incompatible with the nature of man; and [hence] a spirit of retaliation is very prevalent and hereditary [among them], descending in succession from father to son."[46]

All this does not mean that female captives (who, along with African children, "made up the majority of those transported to the Americas during the entirety of the transatlantic slave trade") were devoid of religious or spiritual sentience.[47] As with the men, a case can be made that women's hardships on shipboard, and sexual exploitation in particular, caused them to turn to their religious sources for strength and safekeeping. Jennifer Morgan, in a penetrating discussion of the Atlantic slave trade and West African gender roles, astutely remarks, "Women and men carried their belief systems on their persons, offering food and thanks and requesting blessings from a pantheon of gods before eating, stepping into a boat, or going to sleep."[48] The influence of religion in the lives of African women was truly profound. Indeed, as Dominique Zahan remarks, even though, in present-day African society, religion "is princi-pally a man's affair, its reason for being is woman, guardian of life and link between the living and the dead, between the past and the future."[49] Moreover, women, especially in West Africa, frequently were sacred spe-cialists, such as diviners and mediums (individuals who act as intermedi-aries between human beings and the supernatural worlds of ancestors, deities, rivers, and the bush), and had secret societies of their own (as among Sierra Leonians) that functioned along religious lines.[50] It has been argued that, among the Senufo in Sierra Leone, women generally assumed the roles of ritual mediators to a much larger degree than men did. Senufo women, as was the case throughout Sierra Leone, accord-ing to Michael Gomez, "were indispensable to the creation of any new Poro male society and its *sinzanga*, or sacred grove"; "the founding of the male society required a ritual involving both a man and woman."[51] In ret-rospect, similar to African men, African women boarded slavers equally endowed with a sense of religion, if not more so in many instances.

Therefore, is it a coincidence that some whites were as concerned about the women rebelling as they were the men? In his 1734 letter to Captain Samuel Rhodes, Samuel Waldo, the owner of Rhodes's ship, admonished, "For your own safety as well as mine You'll have the needful Guard over your Slaves, and putt not too much confidence in the Women nor Chil-dren least they happen to be Instrumental to your being surprised which may be fatall."[52] In 1721 an unidentified "Woman-Slave," using the free-dom of movement allowed her on the deck of the English slaver *Robert* (which was still within sight of the coast of Sierra Leone) assisted another captive known as Captain Tomba to stage a rebellion. She was to inform Tomba of the best time to attack the crew. After she had done so one night, Tomba, who was only able to convince her and another male captive to join him, murdered three crewmen with the hammer his female accom-plice provided him. The noise from the killings, however, awoke Captain Harding and the crew, who quickly suppressed the rebels. For her role in the conspiracy, the female captive was "hoisted up by the Thumbs" and then "whipp'd, and slashed . . . with Knives, before the other Slaves till she died."[53] Ottobah Cugoano recalls that, during his forced passage to the island of Grenada, "the women and boys . . . were to burn the ship, with the approbation and groans of the rest; though that was prevented, the discov-ery was likewise a cruel bloody scene."[54] As suggested by Michael Gomez's theory of African reidentification during the Middle Passage, the militant consciousness of many women stemmed in some measure from their col-lective suffering as Africans and as women.[55] Another probable factor, how-ever, was the religious disposition of African females, who believed that God ultimately was on their side. In fact, several historians have argued convincingly for the connection between religiosity and slave resistance.[56]

There can be little doubt that Africans' fear of white violence deterred many of them from overtly resisting oppression while aboard ship. According to Olaudah Equiano, the whites on his slaver behaved in a savage manner that was completely alien to him. Their barbarity seemingly influenced how he and his compatriots conducted themselves.[57] William Snelgrave attributed the passive behavior of captives to "kindly" treatment and "a good Watch" against their insurgency.[58] Snelgrave and his slave-trading contemporaries were unwilling to see the Africans as thinking, feeling human beings who realized the futility in confronting the armed and organized Westerners and instead called on their own personal resources for survival.

Still, this fails to explain fully the amenable disposition of the captives. The Middle Passage, as noted, represented a death of sorts for Africans, as it signaled their complete separation from their prior existence. So we can hardly suppose that this traumatic realization was reconciled easily or quickly, but instead involved a complex range of emotions, including denial, anger, depression, acceptance, and, most significantly, hope.[59] Arguably, much of the emotional and physical energies of future North American bondpeople were spent grappling with the reality of their symbolic deaths. Perhaps it was because of the bonds of their shared experience of suffering, and because many captives believed in a supreme being that governed all events, that they were able to endure such an ordeal and emerge from it somewhat whole, psychologically. In the words of John Matthews, a lieutenant in the Royal Navy and resident of Sierra Leone during the period 1785–87, the black inhabitants there "acknowledge and profess their belief in a God, who, they say dwells above them, and made and governs all things"; "if any circumstance of joy or distress happen they very cooly say God sent it them (unless they fancy it was caused by witchcraft)."[60] This conceptualization of God as both gracious and just offers a useful context for understanding why the future slaves of Jacob Kline were able to survive the passage, and then decide to end their lives in New Jersey upon realizing that their enslavement was permanent. To this point, it is said that the "Guinea Negroes" who were once scattered about Hunterdon County would discard their "fetich" upon realizing that a certain outcome would not occur in their favor; in other words, the fetish was thrown away when all hope was lost.[61]

Living with Indignation on the Mainland

Bonded males in North America who had been leaders or of high status in Africa often refused to work for any white person, and thus received punishment to change their resolve.[62] So Yombo's father probably made known his disapproval with regard to his degraded status under Jacob Kline. Then again, this interpretation ignores his sense of survival. Reverend Thompson's comment that the man and his wife committed suicide after "every endeavor was made to cheer and comfort them" indicates that the husband had modified any aberrant behavior on his part that might have precluded the couple from gaining any concessions and given credence to the dominant society's perception of him as extremely dangerous. Bertram Wyatt-Brown has written that enslaved males "were considered the most troublesome, and therefore on them fell the greater demands for signals of full compliance."[63]

This belief was related directly to whites' fear of black male sexuality. Black men were characterized as having a rapacious desire for white women, and therefore condemned as a direct threat to whites in general if left unrestrained.[64] This sentiment was articulated by the New Jersey General Assembly, which attempted to make the rape of a white female by a black male, as well as "fornication" between the two parties, punishable by castration in a 1704 law that the Privy Council in London quickly disallowed. Although in the 1713 slave code (created in response to the 1712 slave revolt in New York City) corporal punishment replaced castration for rape, the view that black males posed a real danger to the white populace, and white women in particular, had been espoused effectively. The 1768 decree regulating slave behavior certainly did nothing to alter this perception: it called for blacks found guilty of arson, murder, or physical assault to face execution without the benefit of clergymen.[65] This repressive legislation was linked indirectly to Europeans' negative perception of human blackness. The view that blackness connoted "evil, baseness, wretchedness, and misfortune" further justified the codification of laws designed to suppress an inherently savage people.[66]

No doubt the 1734 slave conspiracy near Somerville, Somerset County, in which a body of captives allegedly intended to murder their male owners and ravish their mistresses, furthered the early negative image that whites had of bondmen (and women) as dangerous and beast-like. Whereas Graham Hodges views this event as evidence that the slave culture in the New York area was turning more conspiratorial during the early decades of the eighteenth century, when punitive legislation (enacted following the 1712 slave revolt in New York City) restricted the presence of free blacks, it also illuminates how bondmen were perceived as threats to white society. The plot was concealed from whites until a drunken bondman, emboldened by his intoxicated condition, told a white man named Rennels how "he was as good a Man as himself, and that in a little Time he should be convinced of it." Incredulous, Rennels referred to his black antagonist as a "great Raskal," for he had breached the code of silence and consent typical of all power relations. As evident by their emphasis on the word "Man," the editors of the *New York Gazette* were similarly aghast by the bondman's display of "freedom and Independence," or sense of manhood. One white contemporary who followed the court proceedings referred acidly to the rebels in the newspaper not as men but as "these barbarous monsters." Unable to see the captives as real human beings with legitimate grievances against their servile condition, it would have been easy for him to approve the punishments meted out following the inquisitions (two of the several hundred slaves arrested were hanged, another had an ear cut off, and many others were flogged). These acts of brutality, he doubtlessly surmised, were befitting of "barbarous monsters" in need of greater surveillance. And, in fact, he urged "every Colony to make proper Laws and Ordinances for their own Security" against treacherous slaves who were "so much indulged" by their owners.[67]

The actual violent crimes that enslaved males perpetrated against whites must have also had a major impact in sustaining the notion of the former's supposed brutishness. The following examples in Somerset County are highly suggestive of this point. In 1739, a bondman belonging to Robert Hooper of Rocky Hill butchered a white child with an axe because its mother (Hooper's overseer's wife), whom he failed to kill, ordered him to build a fire.[68] He most likely was a recently arrived "new Negro" who had yet to acclimate to his degrading circumstances under bondage. "Punishments, reprimands, or corrections . . . could trigger extreme and unexpected responses" from such despondent individuals, states Alex Bontemps.[69] Moreover, in 1752, Jacob Van Neste of North Branch, which was bounded on the southwest by Readington Township, where our subjects lived, was executed by the axe of his own male captive, who was described as large, athletic, and dangerous. Subsequent to his confession, the bondman (like Hooper's) was sentenced to a public burning, which was perhaps attended by Jacob Kline's slaves. To the astonishment of the white press, "he stood the Fire with the greatest Intrepidity," shouting that "they had taken the Root but left the Branches." Not only does this man's defiance, as Graham Hodges explains, reflect a slave culture with strong African roots (to show pain in West African society was considered dishonorable), but is also suggests that there were many more black insurgents or "branches" like himself.[70]

The hostile disposition of bondmen in the Somerset County area was a microcosm of the discontent among bondmen in colonial East Jersey, of which Somerset was a part. Similarly, Perth Amboy (east of Somerset) was the scene of telling and brutal acts of black male violence. In 1729, a bondman named Prince was tried for murdering an itinerant tailor, William Cook; and in 1750 two enslaved males had conspired to murder their mistress, Obadiah Ayers. After Ayers had reprimanded the older bondman for misconduct, he procured a gun from his young compatriot ("a new negro" pining for home in Africa) and proceeded to shoot Ayers while she was sitting by a window in her home. Although the youth was induced into aiding the homicide, he was burned at the stake along with his volatile elder, who may have also been African-born and not completely reconciled to his bondage. To emphasize the point of white intolerance for black resistance, even from the hands of the young and innocent, all the blacks in the neighborhood were "summoned from their homes, and obliged to be present, in order that they might be deterred from the commission of like offences." This fateful day, we are informed, "was long remembered with awe."[71] Nevertheless, violent acts of black (male) resistance were committed throughout the colonial period, and graphically conveyed to the white populace of East Jersey "that the enslaved population was desperately angry and that some of its members were prepared to lash out fatally when provoked."[72]

Given the hostile, even brutal relationship between enslaved males and whites during the eighteenth century, Yombo's father—who perhaps was also thick-set and very dark-skinned, and hence a perceived physical threat to the safety of whites—doubtlessly moved with caution around Jacob Kline and whites in general. Alex Bontemps, who characterizes the institution of slavery as a concerted assault on bondpeople's sense of self, elucidates eloquently the dilemma each bondperson confronted: in order to survive in a hostile white world, they each had to adopt the identity of a servile "Negro" without actually turning into one. Yombo's father, we may assume, was also confronted with this "truly savage paradox."[73] By this logic, it was inevitable that he would attempt to liberate himself from bondage, that is, to reclaim his manhood, which to some degree was characterized by physical prowess and husband- and fatherhood (fundamental aspects of manhood in precolonial Africa). Under slavery, contends Daniel Black, it was nearly impossible for black males to assert themselves as warriors, husbands, and fathers, a reality that surely fueled their indignation and spurred many to retaliate against their oppressors.[74] We can only imagine that the captives who came from patriarchal societies—a fact of most precolonial West African communities—had an especially difficult time accepting the dictates and reprimands of unheralded white women.[75]

Jacob Kline's bondwoman was certainly no more reconciled to life as a slave than her husband. She serves as a compelling example of black women's rebellious consciousness, which manifested in gender-specific acts of resistance such as abortion and infanticide, and feigning pregnancy and poisoning; and in nongendered acts such as malingering, carelessness, thievery, running away, plotting insurrection, and mistreating the owner's property.[76] As implied here, the enslaved couple's suicide was a joint agreement made between relatively equal partners. Like the Somerville conspiracy, it was supposedly after several private discussions conducted away from the main house that the couple agreed to their strategy of resistance, which was "kept so private amongst themselves, that there was not the least appearance or suspicion of it," that is, until Jacob Kline found them hanging from his "cedar tree."[77] In other words, their deaths were the result of a process of intimate deliberation and preparation totally unbeknownst to Kline, who had failed to acknowledge the extent of his captives' cerebral capabilities.[78]

African Culture, the Suicide, and Yombo

Without question, to Kline the couple's premeditated death epitomized African people's innate savagery "little understood by the Jersey people."[79] He and other whites assumed that such actions on the part of their Africans (Kwa, Ewe, Fanti, Mandingoes, Fulas, Wolofs, Jolas, Aja, Yoruba, Nupe, and Hausa) were grounded in barbarism rather than in religious-oriented consciousness.[80] William Dunlap, who spent his childhood years in revolutionary Perth Amboy, often in the company of his family's slaves, believed that "all the slaves were heathen philosophers."[81] William Piersen argues that, though "suicide is a cardinal sin in Christian theology, for most African immigrants, suicide was basically a personal concern"; for blacks, suicide "was a reaffirmation of faith—a form of religious martyrdom."[82] That is to say, as Graham Hodges has shown with respect to other examples of black militancy in the New York area, African religion sanctioned suicide as a means of resistance.[83]

The ensuing two suicides in Somerset County appear instructive. In 1754, Jeane, the female captive of South Branch resident Abraham Duboys, hanged herself in her owner's barn. Two years later, Dine, a captive belonging to Daniel Hanery of Bedminster, took her own life by hanging herself from an oak tree. As the respective "Inquisitions" or court hearings tell it, the suicides of Jeane and Dine, whose names suggest their West African roots, were "instagated [sic] by the devil."[84] More likely, however, the women's self-murders were abetted by their African-centered cosmology, and not by white Christian men's conception of the devil, which, in reference to them, implies racial barbarity. Perhaps similar to other West African-born captives who committed suicide, the two bondwomen (and possibly the Kline captives) believed that at death they returned to their homeland. Spirit migration was closely associated with reincarnation, a concept which parallels the Christian notion of immortality. Suicide, then, was arguably a heroic form of slave resistance, as it allowed for possible regeneration.[85]

As indicated, "many if not most of the populations of Sierra Leone posited the existence of a high god or creator."[86] For the Mende, this entity is referred to as Ngewo, Gewo, or Leve, the architect of the universe and the all-seeing, all-knowing father-protector.[87] In their view, God "predetermines

the life of each person, and that this cannot or should not be changed."
Thus, "if God has made a person poor, that person should not desire to be
rich."[88] Certainly, our African couple did not conceive of bondage under
Jacob Kline or any white person as their predetermined fate. By refusing
to grant husband and wife the (free) status befitting their previous high
station in Africa, Kline, it would seem, had left the couple with no other
choice but to end their lives in the earthly world for the place occupied
by the righteous (which the Mende refer to as *dadagole-hun*, or heaven),
where the ancestors resided and where they could live as they did during
their natural or human existence—namely, like rulers.[89]

Evidently, the cedar tree upon which the captives hanged themselves,
together with the adjoining brook, also constituted integral components of
their cosmology. In Mende culture, "the *dyinyinga*, or jinni or nature spirits, occupy rivers, the bush, and so on."[90] Among many African peoples, all
aspects of nature are places of divine worship. This particularly applies with
respect to trees, which Africans believe represent the complete bonding of
nature (air, rain, and sun). Trees are also involved directly with time, since
they develop according to seasonal rhythms or cycles, a periodic process
similar to the concept of prolongation by which Africans understand their
own existence. Symbolic of "power, wealth, uprightness, and everlasting-
ness," trees were regarded by Africans as having supernatural powers they
could evoke through prayer and regular offerings of food.[91] So it was probably by way of the tree on Jacob Kline's property that his captives appealed
to the ancestors to deliver them from bondage. Correspondingly, Africans
associate the still water of ponds and lakes "with the origin and creation of
man and the world."[92] Hence, the couple may have perceived the brook of
their owner as a conduit to the ancestors.

The enslavement of James Albert Ukawsaw Gronniosaw supports this
analysis. In his narrative, first published in 1772, Gronniosaw explains that
he was born in the city of Bournou (located in the interior of the Gold
Coast in West Africa), and that his grandfather was the reigning king. As
fate would have it, the young prince was traded into slavery on the Gold
Coast and transported to Barbados, where he was purchased by a Mr. Vanhorn of New York City. Sometime after their arrival in New York, Vanhorn
sold Gronniosaw to a Mr. Freelandhouse, whom Graham Hodges verifies
as Reverend Theodorus Frelinghuysen of the Reformed Dutch Church in
central New Jersey's Raritan Valley. While enslaved under Frelinghuysen,
Gronniosaw recalls frequently visiting "a large remarkably fine Oak tree,
in the midst of the wood," located at a distance from his owner's home.
It was to this tree, he states, that "I used to pour out all my complaints to
the Lord." Although Frelinghuysen had instructed the bondman in Christian prayer, teaching him that God was his father and best friend, Gronniosaw continued to turn to his African heritage for solace and support.

Indeed, he refers to the tree, to which he aired his "complaints" and told his "sorrows," as his "friend."[93] This was inspired by the palm trees in his native Bournou, one of which he says served as a religious meeting place. He describes the palm trees there as "extremely large, high and majestic," adding that, "the beauty and usefulness of them are not to be described."[94] Their meaning and importance were etched indelibly into his consciousness, helping the bondman, who became confused and deeply troubled by his religious training in America, to one day find God while sitting under or near a tree. He recalled seeing a "light inexpressible dart down from heaven upon me, and shone around me for the space of a minute. I continued on my knees, and joy unspeakable took possession of my soul."[95] As they had done for the captives belonging to Jacob Kline, the power of trees, which symbolized the presence of divinity in African culture, had enabled Gronniosaw—a slave and a sinner—to liberate himself from his wretched condition.

Whereas whites viewed the Africans' suicide as an abominable crime illustrative of their inferiority, to their son, Yombo, no doubt, it exhibited their true greatness. As an adult, Yombo continued to refer to his deceased father as a "big man," an individual worthy of his respect and admiration. Such filial veneration is hardly indicative of a person who was ashamed of his father for taking his own life in a state of emotional distress. Rather, it leads us to believe that Yombo was proud that his father had controlled his own destiny. This in no way suggests, however, that Yombo, who most likely had been a boy at the time of his parents' earthly demise, was completely unaffected by it. Then, too, Yombo may not have grieved very long because, spiritually speaking, his parents had never left him.

Many ethnic groups in West Africa, including the Mende, believe firmly in the existence of dead ancestors (the living dead) who appear to them in dreams, hover around where they dwell, and serve as a general link between human beings and the supernatural world. As members of a particular family or descent group, dead ancestors retain a continuous interest in family matters and expect a share of the affection accorded older living family members.[96] Unlike faraway Ngewo, who is distant from the everyday problems of man and woman, the ancestors, it is believed, "understand the stress and strain of human life, because they themselves had experienced them." Thus, they are "the more effective agents in determining the well-being or distress which affect the tribe or the clan or the family."[97] Specifically, it is through the ancestors that people seek the desired goals in life. As slaves, Yombo's parents could provide him with little, if any, protection against the vicissitudes of bondage. As spiritual personalities, however, those "no longer confined by time and space," and perhaps contacted through propitiatory acts, they could possibly address more effectively their son's tribulations.[98] Indeed, "virtually no slave," posits Mechal Sobel, "was without contact with spirits."[99] (We are also told that the Guinea slaves of Hunterdon County "brought all their superstitions with them and retained them. They firmly believed in visitations from the dead, and that when these were wicked and died violent deaths, their spirits appeared in some outlandish shape.")[100] Yombo's belief in the continued presence of his parents in spirit form helps explain why he was such a proud bondman. He remained an African in his philosophical orientation, evidenced by his wearing of earrings and speaking his own "peculiar" language, at a time when many of his Northern and Southern compatriots had become highly acculturated by the end of the eighteenth century.[101]

When did his parents end their lives? The will of Jacob Kline, dated June 10, 1785, helps us to unravel this mystery. In his will, Kline left his "Negroe Boy and Negroe Wench," the patriarch's only bondpeople, to his wife, Fronica Gertraut.[102] Considering that Kline sold Yombo to his father-in-law, Aaron Malick, in 1785 (and not in 1786, as stated by Andrew Mellick), and that enslaved families in New Jersey frequently were broken up in this manner, the bondpeople mentioned in Kline's will apparently were Yombo's wife and son.[103] Hence, Yombo's parents committed suicide during the period 1744–85. It seems doubtful, however, that the couple endured a prolonged period of undignified scrimping and deferential behavior just to achieve racially circumscribed freedom.[104] Newly arrived African captives to the New World tended to have little interest in establishing precedents and customs to improve their servile condition, but would rather risk all to return through escape, insurrection, and suicide to the world they had lost.[105] By all indications, the former African rulers belonging to Jacob Kline hanged themselves within just a few years of their arrival in America.

Consequently, Yombo must have been left to fend for himself as a young boy, which would partly explain why he retreated into his private African world. The bondman's resolute Africanity in memory, appearance, language, and religious disposition became his primary means of survival in the rural, racially hostile, and predominantly white world of eighteenth-century New Jersey. Aaron Malick's other two adult captives, the couple Dick and Nance, were devout Christians and avid churchgoers.[106] Yombo, however, appears to have abstained from white religious services. Instead, he clung (as much as he possibly could) to his native African religion, based upon a supreme being who was not European-oriented and watchful ancestors who reminded him daily of his self-worth, and who condemned his enslavement as most Protestant sects did not.[107] This enabled him, like those Guinea slaves in Hunterdon who believed in "the demonai or evil spirit" and kept their "superstitions to themselves," to "shun the scrutiny of white men."[108] Accordingly, Yombo, an expert tanner, often attempted to steal the valuable skins from Malick with the hope of improving his fortunes at Elizabethtown in Essex County, where his slave wife lived.[109]

Yombo's thievery bespeaks his disdain for bondage, which was incongruent with his African-centered consciousness that seemingly comforted his parents during the unforgettable Middle Passage and beyond.

Conclusion

The transcontinental enslavement of Yombo and his family is a fascinating story that testifies to the need for historians to pay greater attention to nineteenth-century sources. Yombo's parents are compelling evidence that enslaved Africans in colonial New Jersey were defined not by the white hegemony that sought to render them mere economic commodities, but rather by their own cultural sensibilities, which instilled within them the pride and courage to control, albeit minimally, their own destinies. The couple's suicide was an affirmation to both Jacob Kline and Yombo of their humanity and sense of dignity—a statement deeply ingrained in the consciousness of their son. Hence, Yombo was deprived only of his parents' physical presence; their spirits forever remained with him, constantly reminding the deformed captive of both his own self-worth and the significance of his African past (though, admittedly, he probably did not remember much or any of it). In a way, Yombo's thievery and disagreeable disposition were tributes to his deceased parents, who continued to influence and guide his life. Yombo refused to act as the obsequious servant his owners desired, for the memory of his parents' heroism would not allow it.

The other significant contribution Andrew Mellick and Reverend Thompson have made is that they insinuate the ability of captured Africans to survive the unmistakably dreadful Middle Passage. Their nineteenth-century commentaries about "Negroes" from Guinea have been critical to the attempt here to examine this slippery phase of the enslavement process from the viewpoint of the captives themselves, and to the argument that African religious beliefs played a major role in fostering black consciousness or survival aboard slave ships and in transplanting this consciousness across the Atlantic. Religion consumed African peoples' very existence; Africans viewed themselves in relation to the universe and to their God, the creator and knower of all things. Is it likely, then, that the captives would have dismissed their "fetishes" and other divine resources during the frightening transatlantic journeys? Whether they were on deck or in the hold, their religious faith was often all they had to comfort them. Logically, they frequently would have evoked the presence of the almighty, an act that, in turn, would have nurtured their consciousness, their potential to endure and resist.

Admittedly, the methodological approach presented here, regarding how nameless and mute Africans were able to endure the Middle Passage, is based upon a high degree of speculation. But the prerequisite for most scholarly investigations is a mainspring of intellectual presumption. It is principally through the writings of Europeans that we learn, often negatively, about the religious devotion of African peoples living on the Guinea coast, and the heinous conditions associated with the Middle Passage. William Snelgrave and his slave-trading counterparts felt compelled to talk openly about their benevolence toward the presumably heathenish Africans, thereby justifying their involvement in such a barbarous and exploitative enterprise, the enslavement of black "human beings" for economic profit. Surely, though, there are other conceivable explanations as to why several million Africans made it to the North American mainland despite incredible odds, and were able to maintain their sense of humanity and self-respect in their new environments, where other forms of racial oppression awaited them.

Chapter 3

"His Disposition Was Not in Any Sense Agreeable"

There is much more to consider about Yombo, who is perhaps the most intriguing of the many personages, black and white, to appear in *The Story of an Old Farm*. Shortly after the death of Aaron Malick in 1809, Yombo became the property of John Hastier, who resided in Elizabethtown, and who probably, according to Andrew Mellick, "was the owner of Yombo's wife." As Mellick dramatically puts it, "Nothing more was heard of [Yombo] by the Bedminster people, excepting that several years afterwards word came from Elizabethtown—'Old Yombo is dead.'"[1] This illuminating statement testifies to the life of a slave who had made a lasting impression on the whites who encountered him. Indeed, not every slave's death elicited a message or telegram to his former owners with whom he had lost all contact. The phrase "Old Yombo is dead" connotes a sense of incredulity that this wretched slave, who had challenged incessantly the authority of whites, actually or finally had died. Correspondingly, the original account of Aaron Malick's slaves that was given to his great grandson describes Yombo "as a sample of the kind of slave that made this institution [slavery] odious."[2] Again, we are led to envision a hostile, if not brutal, relationship between Yombo and his owners, whereby he used every means possible to mitigate their power over him.

This chapter explores why the local whites remembered Yombo, and contends that his obstinate persona was a creation of his circumstances under bondage and not a manifestation of his innate, intractable nature, as Andrew Mellick implied. In part, it serves as a rebuttal to Mellick's one-dimensional account of his ancestor's slave, which reflects the nineteenth-century literary tradition of racializing or essentializing black and other subaltern peoples. Comments such as Yombo's "disposition was not in any sense agreeable" and "the darkey [Yombo] was treacherous" belong to a certain genus of writing that intentionally disempowered its subjects.[3]

And yet, *The Story of an Old Farm* forces us to think about slave resistance in alternative and exciting new ways. Most studies of American slavery do not consider the issue of slave meanness, which was as important a resistance strategy as theft, sabotage, flight, and so on.[4] The framework of subaltern studies, with its emphasis on how elite written texts tend either to disclaim or describe negatively the political consciousness of the oppressed, allows us to configure how Yombo cultivated an image that exaggerated nonconfrontational forms of resistance. Yombo's appearance in Andrew Mellick's book helps to put into perspective how a "disagreeable" disposition could serve as a buffer of sorts against the rigors of rural Northern bondage in the late 1700s.

It is also important to consider that Yombo endured bondage during the chaotic Revolutionary War era when cases of slave insolence, subterfuge, and escape in central New Jersey were particularly widespread. This emergent slave resistance was related to two important factors that have implications for Yombo's obstinacy. First, central New Jersey served as a path for both the British and Continental armies, whose presence not only turned whites against one another but also bolstered slaves' desire for freedom. Graham Hodges notes that whether New York-area farmers were Whigs or Tories depended on their proximity to either army. The counties here, he posits, "constituted a neutral zone over which the two sides battled for food, forage, and fuel. Vigilante bands on both sides conducted guerilla actions until the end of the war in late 1783."[5] As conditions worsened, proprietors left their homes and told their slaves to fend for themselves. In the end, the military upheaval created entirely new situations for restless slaves, who often attached themselves to marauding armies.[6]

Second, white central New Jerseyans unwittingly provided the captives with a militant rhetoric (made against the alleged tyranny of the British Parliament) that sanctioned their actions and gave credence to their own claims for freedom. "Slaves in the American colonies," writes Gary Nash, "were not directly affected by revenue stamps, sugar duties, or tea parties; nonetheless they were politicized by the language and modes of white protest and were quick to seize the opportunities for securing their freedom that emerged from the disruptions of a society in rebellion." As we shall see, enslaved persons in central New Jersey were no less incited by the "ideology of natural and inalienable rights[,] and fit the ringing phrases of the day to their own situation."[7] Included among them, presumably, was Yombo, whose combative temperament would seem to dismiss any notion that he was not at all affected by revolutionary occurrences. Hence, the discussion here nuances the provocative literature on black agency during the Revolution, on what Nash has referred to as "the largest slave uprising in [American] history."[8]

The pervasiveness of slave resistance in New Jersey, and in particular during the Revolution, with its emphasis on the natural rights of man, drew little comment from Andrew Mellick's generation, which, as we will recall from chapter 1, tended to write about the subject of slavery strictly through the prism of paternalism. Yet, the psychological tensions inherent in the owner-slave relationship resonate in Mellick's own carefully written family history. Yombo, he noted, quickly made his presence known under Aaron Malick, who had purchased the bondman from his brother-in-law, Jacob Kline, in 1785. In addition to initially frightening Malick's grandchildren with his clubfoot, bow-legs, and dark skin, Yombo was a thief, averred Mellick, "whose perverseness always displayed itself when he was not under the immediate eye of his owner and master." But because he was "an excellent workman his peculiarities were passed over, and for many years he was a conspicuous feature of life at the homestead." Yombo's conspicuousness and peculiarities as defined by the white world of Malick's rural domicile were largely a result of the bondman's West African "exotic" origins. Still, Mellick seemed to doubt Yombo's proud affirmation that his father was a man of importance back in his homeland, and referred to it as a "claim" made by the "Guinea negro."[9] Mellick's sense of doubt also resonated in his great grandfather's record book, where he wrote, "[Yombo] said that he was a son of a Negro king in Guinea."[10] By denying illiterate Yombo (he spoke "a mixture of poor English and a jargon peculiar to himself") a legitimate past or history, Mellick could justify his great grandfather's exploitation and subjugation of him.[11]

Consequently, Mellick downplays Yombo's discontent, which was exhibited by his petty thievery, his satisfaction in the contempt whites held for his blackness, his repudiation of white culture, and his possible truancy to seize his "time." These markers of his defiance give credence to the idea that Yombo used his unpleasant or mean persona to combat whites. Indeed, Yombo's "perverse" behavior was far more complex than Mellick cared to convey in his book.

Truancy and the Appropriation of "Time"

Although there is no hard evidence (namely, a newspaper advertisement) of Yombo's ever escaping from either Jacob Kline or Aaron Malick, this does not mean that he never broke away from them. Yombo's thievery and meanness and Andrew Mellick's provocative contention that he had "an occasional outbreak . . . which was met by a few earnest words of reproof from Aaron, who even in extreme old age retained the spirit of mastery," strongly suggest that the bondman adopted multiple strategies of resistance, including temporary flight.[12] By dismissing the greater or political implications of Yombo's outward discontent, Mellick portrays Yombo as a purely emotional person rather than as an individual whose reason constituted the basis of his actions. The author uses seemingly innocuous terminology—"an occasional outbreak"—to equate his exotic black subject's recalcitrance with natural phenomenon. This terminology is common in the historical scholarship severely criticized by subaltern scholars, which deliberately posits that the revolts of peasant masses "break out like thunder storms, heave like earthquakes, spread like wildfires, infect like epidemics"—that is to say, "when the proverbial clod of earth turns, this is a matter to be explained in terms of natural history."[13] In describing Yombo as utterly uncivilized, Mellick effectively diminishes the bondman's defiance and reinforces his generation's altruistic interpretation of the past.

This viewpoint is discredited, however, by the numerous slaves in New York and New Jersey who ran away, and whose actions forcefully conveyed to their owners that they had no right to the fugitive's person and time.[14] To be sure, this thinking was not limited just to those individuals who, unlike Yombo with his club foot (a condition so severe "that he appeared to walk on the sides of his feet instead of the bottom, which caused him to be bow legged")[15] had relatively good mobility. To illustrate, in September 1766, a slave named Bood, who had attempted to run off on three previous occasions, again escaped from Wilson Hunt of Maidenhead (Lawrenceville), Hunterdon County. In addition to describing Bood as "a remarkable stout, cunning, artful Fellow" who was "much addicted to strong Liquor, and when drunk very noisy and troublesome," Hunt noted that "his great Toes have been froze, and have only little Pieces of Nails on them."[16] Similarly, in June of that year, a slave called Cuff left Jonathan Clawson of Woodbridge Township, Middlesex County, although he "has a scar on his right great Toe and the Ends of several other of his Toes are cut off," and he absconded again in spring 1768.[17] In June 1776, Ben, whose "left leg [was] considerably larger than the other, with a scar in the same," fled General John Taylor, who was an associate of Aaron Malick's and a resident of Tewksbury Township. Ben then appears in the historical record as a slave under another Hunterdon citizen, Thomas Scott, who, the following October, in 1776, advertised Ben's escape from his Bethlehem Township home. A year later in July, Scott again reported that Ben had absconded, and made note moreover of his escape the previous June.[18] Given the dogged determination of physically challenged bondpeople to escape slavery, it is erroneous to assume automatically that Yombo had never attempted to escape from Jacob Kline and Aaron Malick, even if just momentarily to appropriate some of his own time.

Yombo's family pride, which the bondage of the enslaved woman Phillis helps us to understand better, strengthens this point. Phillis was kidnapped in Africa as a young girl and purchased by Cornelius DeHart of Somerset County, prior to 1769. Though described as a faithful servant of the DeHart family, Phillis greatly desired that one day she, a king's daughter, would gain her freedom. Phillis's wish was eventually realized. So, too, was her request that her youngest son, Thomas, experience life as a free man before her death.[19] Phillis evidently viewed her bondage as a dishonor to her noble African heritage. Did proud Yombo, whose father's image remained with him and served as a reminder of his own self-worth, believe differently? Would the bondman, the reputed son of a "king" who was never presented with the prospect of freedom, have taken this affront lightly and failed to use it as inspiration to resist bondage?

Whites' control of his body, and by implication of his time, was another likely source of Yombo's anger and defiance. An expert in refining leather, he spent much time producing valuable merchandise for Jacob Kline and Aaron Malick's personal and economic aggrandizement.[20] Besides appropriating his time through the deployment of workday schedules, the owners would have subjected him to deferential rituals (such as seeking Malick's permission to visit his wife), seasonal calendars (such as the beginning and ending of the harvest), and decrees (such as curfews).[21] In other words, Kline and Malick sought to dominate Yombo by manipulating his utilization of time, both private and public.

Silvia Dubois, who grew up under slavery, initially in Somerset County during the 1790s, lends insight into how the captives were subjected to curfews. In her account she explains that her owner "used to let me go to frolics and balls and to have good times away from home, with other black folks, whenever I wanted to. . . . But when he told me I must come home from a ball at a certain time, when the time came, the jig was out. I knew I must go; it wouldn't do to disappoint [Minna] Dubois." She also refers to how the lives of enslaved blacks were dictated by the seasonal calendars of their owners, asserting, "They didn't no more keep the date of a young nigger than they did of a calf or a colt; the young niggers were born in the Fall or in the Spring, in the Summer or in the Winter, in cabbage time or when cherries were ripe, when they were planting corn or when they were husking corn, and that's all the way they talked about a nigger's age."[22] The life of Samuel Sutphen, who, like Silvia, had been enslaved in Somerset, was also shaped by the seasonal dictates of whites. When dating certain events in his Revolutionary War narrative, he uses the phrases "the season of plant seed sowing," "hay and harvest time," "about corn planting," and "after corn planting."[23] Both he and Dubois perceived time according to white labor demands—damning evidence of whites' incessant appropriation of slaves' time. As Dubois and Sutphen's commentaries powerfully suggest, curfews and the planting and harvesting seasons were as indelibly ingrained in the minds of blacks as their own actual dates of birth (which few actually knew because of their forced illiteracy).

In sum, the conception, utilization, and manipulation of time by white people dominated the lives of enslaved blacks, a fact that, as Silvia Dubois's remarks indicate, they greatly resented. Indeed, as it related to slaveowners, time was a construct of social control. According to Mechal Sobel, writing on slavery in colonial Virginia, "use of time was at the heart of owners' criticisms of slaves: they wanted slaves to change their perception of time and work."[24]

Correspondingly, Daniel Barkelow of Somerset County cursed at "two colored boys" for taking their time in bringing him and "a colored man" some water while they were working in his meadow. Said one of the youths, "There, did you hear the minister swear!" An ashamed Barkelow apologized to his neighbors, explaining that "the black rascals stayed so long that I got so dry I could not help it. You know that niggers will be niggers, roasted or b[o]iled."[25]

Like all oppressed peoples, Yombo and his compatriots had only a few options which they could exercise to respond to seizures of their time. They could voluntarily acquiesce, and in so doing acknowledge their owners' alleged right to their time, thereby reinforcing the hegemonic order (white over black). They could consent in deed only, compelled to do so by the forcible way in which their time was seized, but not necessarily agreeing with their owners' claim to it. Or they could resist, overtly and covertly.[26] The dictates of bondage required that slaves utilize all three options for their day-to-day survival. That is, specific situations called for slaves to respond or act accordingly.[27]

Flight was perhaps the most effective means by which slaves could undermine owners' monopolization of their lives and regain some control of their own time. Fugitives deprived owners not only of labor power, which hurt owners economically, but also disrupted owners' time by causing them to worry about the successful return of their black properties, whose value had now decreased because they were runaways.[28] Hence, the mere threat of flight enabled a slave to wield power over his or her owner. In 1793 the "trusty" bondwoman Hannah of Flemington Township, Hunterdon County, boldly and with a smile told her mistress's niece, "Do go, Miss Polly, and see Mrs. Hill, but if you don't come back tomorrow, I will run away."[29]

Some captives went beyond making idle threats. David Demarest wrote that the slave Tom, who belonged to his grandfather, Peter Demarest (b. circa 1685), of Bergen County, "would run away and stay for weeks until his clothes were worn out, and he felt a longing for the comforts of his master's kitchen. Then he would return and go to work and continue in it until another *freedom-seeking fit* would overmaster him." On one occasion Peter Demarest had Tom "arrested and put in gaol in Hackensack." Afterward, old man Demarest "went to see him and greatly enjoyed his expressions of penitence and promise of good behavior in all time to come, if his Master would only let him out and take him home with him, which of course was done, it was a foregone conclusion."[30] Demarest conceded to Tom's escaping from time to time, apparently reasoning that the bondman's flirtations with freedom made him somewhat more responsive to the old man's dictates. The slaveholder had Tom incarcerated when he abused their social contract of sorts, which was similar to the understanding between Yombo and Aaron Malick, who excused his captive's need to have a "freedom-seeking fit" or "occasional outbreak" because he was a highly valued worker.

Again, if Yombo ran away at all, it most certainly was as a truant. Truants, unlike real runaways, posits Gerald Mullin, "had no intention of leaving the immediate neighborhood and attempting to permanently change their status"; they were "so common that most [holders] either did not make [them] a matter of record, or simply referred to [them] in a random manner in their correspondence." Typically, enslaved truants "hid out" in the woods and returned to the place of their bondage during the evening for food and shelter. Truancy, as Mullin has indicated, represented "inward [slave] rebelliousness: it was sporadic, and it was directed toward the plantation or quarter."[31] Owners generally refrained from punishing these runaways as severely as Peter Demarest corrected Tom, who was whipped repeatedly on his legs for going beyond the bounds of acceptable truancy. Rather, they were more likely to reprove harshly those truants who had only briefly, albeit effectively, recovered some of their own time.[32]

The connection between flight and the local topography requires further comment. Central New Jersey features rolling hills, such as Sourland Mountain, and ubiquitous waterways, in particular the Raritan River.[33] The best contemporary descriptions of the region's landscape during the 1700s appear in advertisements for the sale or lease of land. Sellers attempted to enhance the attraction or value of the advertised properties by emphasizing such features as their dense forestry, lush meadows, and close proximity to important roads and navigable waterways. In 1773, for example, Roluff Vandine (Van Dike) of Somerset County advertised the sale of his "very well watered and timbered" plantation, located "about four miles from New Brunswick [the hub of central Jersey, and a major site of deep river navigation], up Raritan river, two miles above Raritan landing." The house on this property, he added, "stands on a small hill, not far from Raritan river, [and] the King's road [which] leads between the river and house."[34] Interestingly, three years earlier, Van Dike had advertised the escape of his slave Arch, and "imagined he is gone some back way to Albany [New York], to meet some yellow free Negroes, which went by water at about the same time, or else try to get aboard some vessel, as he attempted about 3 years ago below Philadelphia, but was taken." Van Dike realized that confident and intelligent Arch—described as a man "about 30 years of age" who "walks very upright" and "read the bible very well"—was cognizant of his physical surroundings, which in turn put the slaveholder at a real disadvantage.[35] The local topography, especially during the warmer months when most slaves escaped, effectively served as a "weapon of the weak," even among those slaves who, like Yombo, were physically maimed.[36]

The knowledge that slaves, and men in particular, had of the local and surrounding geography was relatively extensive. It derived partly from the high turnover rate among New York-area slaveholders, and partly from their work experience, which put them in intimate contact with the physical landscape.[37] Consider, for example, Peter, who was enslaved in Amwell Township, Hunterdon County, and absconded in September 1761. The fact that he was a "cunning Fellow" who "walks very upright, and speaks good English" testifies to Peter's sense of self-confidence. His determination, as well as ability, to escape stemmed in some measure from his knowledge of sailing "in small craft," an invaluable experience that provided him with a degree of mobility and the opportunity to survey the landscape. The fugitive ended up "within a few Miles of Philadelphia, enquiring whether there were any Privateers fitting out."[38] Another bondman, Cato, left Raritan Landing near New Brunswick in October 1763, a decision that also appears to have been inspired partly by his work experience. According to Cato's owner, Cornelius Low, "He is an extream [sic] handy fellow at any common work, especially with horses, and carriages of almost any sort, having been bred to it from a little boy, and to the loading and unloading of boats, a good deal used to a farm, can do all sorts of house work, and very fit to wait upon a gentleman." Though only about twenty years of age, Cato was a versatile bondman who spoke three different languages (English, Dutch, and High Dutch), was "noted for his sense," and apparently understood how the local topography could help assist his escape. Low assumed that "he will endeavour to pass for a freeman, and get away in the country, or go with some vessel to any part, so as not to be overtaken."[39]

As the above examples indicate, enslaved blacks with extensive knowledge of the local topography had a better chance to abscond and avoid capture. Certainly Yombo was not as knowledgeable as Arch, Peter, and Cato about the world outside his owners' property, a factor that would have greatly impeded his ability to escape. Yet he must have had some knowledge of local topography: rivers and rolling hills virtually constituted the "geography of [his] containment."[40] His transference from Jacob Kline's tannery to Aaron Malick's via the Rockaway River, along with his visits to see his wife in Elizabethtown, would have reinforced his awareness of the physical landscape.[41] Was he, then, any less empowered by the physical landscape than his compatriots who we know actually exploited it? Implicit in Andrew Mellick's benign portrayal of New Jersey slavery was not only a discontented bondman who was susceptible to having "an occasional outbreak," but also (like many fugitives) a skilled, willful, and thinking person who was surely cognizant of the allies he had in the natural environment. Moreover, as discussed in the previous chapter, nature served a critical (divine) function in African culture and was an outlet to which despondent African captives often turned for solace, support, and regeneration in one form or another. In short, knowledge of the local and surrounding topography was perhaps an enslaved person's greatest ally when experiencing the urge to escape temporarily slavery's exploitation with regard to the mind, body, and time.

Like permanent escape attempts, truancy openly and thus radically rejected white hegemony, even of the allegedly paternalistic kind. This may have encouraged Andrew Mellick to write, "It was Aaron's custom to permit [Yombo] occasionally to visit [his wife], for that purpose putting money in his pocket and lending him a horse and chair." Yet, despite "his master's goodness the darkey was treacherous, and, when all ready to start on the journey, Aaron was always particular to look under the seat of the chair, where he not infrequently found a wallet stuffed with finely finished calf-skins, with which Yombo had hoped to improve his fortunes at Elizabethtown."[42] Mellick, as we might expect, perceived this alleged "custom" of his ancestor as evidence solely of his "goodness" as a slaveowner, rather than as a probable compromise made between him and Yombo. Such negotiations were common among owners and slaves. In the words of William Moraley, an indentured servant in New Jersey during the early 1700s, "Masters make [slaves] some amends, by suffering them to marry, which makes them easier, and often prevents their running away."[43] Significantly, evidence points to a tradition of slaves' quitting in New Jersey, whereby blacks sought to leave owners whom they found abusive or unjust. As Silvia Dubois described it, "Under the slave laws of New Jersey, when the slave thought the master too severe, and the slave and master did not get along harmoniously, the slave had the right to hunt a new master." She explained that her mother, Dorcas Compton, successfully went in search of a new owner after Minna Dubois brutally whipped the pregnant woman "with an ox-goad, because she didn't hold a hog while he yoked it."[44] Yombo was not as powerless as Mellick portrays him. According to the evidence, it was in the best interest of old man Malick to allow Yombo to see his wife periodically, and to tolerate the bondman's politically driven "outbreaks."

Then again, the original account of Aaron Malick's slaves mentions that Yombo saw his wife just once a year and not "occasionally" as Andrew Mellick reports.[45] This suggests that the hostility between owner and slave was much greater than Mellick cares to admit, and that Yombo had even greater incentive to challenge Malick's authority through periodic truancy and any other means that circumvented his power.

Black Empowerment through the Revolution

It seems equally unlikely that Jacob Kline held absolute authority over Yombo. If it is indeed true that Kline's refusal to free Yombo's parents had caused them to commit suicide, then tensions between them may well have exceeded those between Yombo and Aaron Malick. In any event, there can be little doubt that the opportunity for Yombo to challenge Kline's ownership increased during the Revolutionary War because it disturbed the social order and altered power relations between owners and slaves in central New Jersey.

As a result of the British military occupation of New York City and New Brunswick, the local inhabitants often engaged British soldiers in warfare.[46] Many others, however, felt more compelled to flee to the nearby mountains upon hearing of encroaching British soldiers. It was, for example, "the custom of the people [from the village of Rocky Hill in Somerset County] to retire behind the Sourland hills during the British raids."[47] One local, Eliza Susan Quincy, recalled that Basking Ridge, another Somerset village, was enclosed by the Long Hills, "which was a secure place from the British, and at times in the centre of the American army."[48]

Fear of the British was not limited to whites. Evidence also suggests that enslaved and free blacks alike in central New Jersey were terrified of, and ready to take on, British soldiers, who were known to pilfer blacks. As legend has it, a frightened black couple was about to take refuge from the British military invasion of Rocky Hill Village when the mother, realizing that she had forgotten her child, returned to get it. To this her husband shouted, "Hanner, never mind de chile." Hanner seems to have recouped the infant.[49] According to another local account about blacks in Readington Township, Hunterdon County, a bondwoman known as "Old Maumy" (most likely a corruption of "Old Mammy") prepared herself to deal with the British raids from New Brunswick "with pitchfork and ax and boiling water."[50] Even more revealing, a letter written around 1780 by a man in Sussex County mentioned that a band of about thirty "refugees" from New York landed at Stoney Point on the Raritan River and then proceeded to Woodbridge, where they captured eight white persons along with "two negroes."[51]

Not only did central New Jersey slaves experience the collapse of societal order, but because they occupied the same living space as whites, they were also within earshot of the ideology of natural and inalienable rights that, indirectly, spoke to their own special grievances against living in unjust bondage.[52] The meetings of Somerset County "freeholders" (landowners) powerfully illustrate the anti-Parliament sentiment of the local whites. At the freeholder meeting held on July 4, 1774, a resolution was passed in opposition to the "severe and oppressive Act of Parliament" that had shut down the port in Boston, Massachusetts (because of the Boston Tea Party). Indicative of the increasing militancy among the colonials, the May 11, 1775, meeting declared that the "British Ministry" had taken steps "to enslave the American colonies." Their opposition was not limited to the British Parliament. On July 28 of that year the freeholders resolved to take "cognizance of every person of whatsoever rank or condition, who shall, either by word or deed, endeavour to destroy our unanimity in opposing the arbitrary and cruel measures of the British Ministry."[53]

A number of the men who attended these freeholder meetings were proponents of slavery. They included Roluff Van Dike, Matthew Ten Eyck, and Gisbart Bogart, all of whom were present at the freeholder meeting held on July 28, 1775. As noted earlier, Van Dike had a bondman who escaped on two separate occasions in 1767 and 1770. In 1771 Ten Eyck owned at least three slaves (Tone, Symon, and Tom), two of whom were accused of committing criminal acts.[54] Bogart, the owner of seven slaves in 1784, was the first owner of Samuel Sutphen, who served as a Patriot soldier during the Revolution.[55] Apparently, these and other freeholders saw no real contradiction between their support of American independence and ownership of blacks. Jack Greene has argued that republican political theory sanctioned the exclusion of blacks as well as women from political equality so as long as each group was perceived as lacking the independence and civic competence necessary for public virtue.[56]

Blacks in search of freedom, however, such as the slave named Prime, were little affected by this political expediency. Prime belonged to Absalom Bainbridge, a Tory doctor who practiced medicine in Maidenhead prior to 1773, when he moved his family to Princeton in Somerset County. Bainbridge, according to a short biography, "joined the British army on the first invasion of New Jersey in 1776 and his house served as the headquarters of the Commander-in-chief, Sir William Howe." Consequently, "he was declared guilty of high treason against the State and his considerable property," the four-hundred-acre Princeton plantation, "was confiscated and sold."[57] This "property" included Prime, who was taken by Bainbridge's family first to Monmouth County and later to British-held Long Island. In 1778 Prime escaped and returned to rebel-held New Jersey, where he served in the revolutionary army as a wagon driver. Evidently, as it has been suggested, Prime felt that he had a greater chance of securing his freedom with the rebels.[58]

But, at the conclusion of the war, Prime was reenslaved by a public claimant, John Vanhorn of Rocky Hill. Then, in 1785, Prime, with the apparent assistance of white allies, submitted a petition to the New Jersey General Assembly requesting his freedom. Clearly inspired by rights-of-man rhetoric, the document forcefully argued that "there was something very inconsistent in [whites'] contending for Liberty under an appeal to Heaven, and at the same time selling for Amount to the Publick, the Bodies and Service of human Beings into perpetual bondage." The petition pressed for Prime's liberation by the "Legislature, entitled to that Liberty to defend, secure and perpetuate [for] which the Fields of America have been dyed in the Blood of her Citizens."[59] The petition was granted in 1786.[60] In all likelihood the writing of the petition was mostly the work of local white abolitionists. Yet, should this suggest that Prime's thoughts are absent from the document? The fact that he took the initiative to escape from Long

Island during a time of great social chaos in the New York area, and made it all the way back to his old neighborhood in Princeton, shows that Prime was highly intelligent and most likely played a role in how the petition was written.[61] It is also important to consider that some bondpeople were quite capable of expressing themselves through the written word.[62]

The Revolution also politicized slaves like Yombo who clearly lacked the rudiments of education. In his 1834 deposition for a war pension, Samuel Sutphen, who signed his testimony with an "X," signifying his inability to read or write, stated that "fighting for the white man's freedom" while in bondage warranted him financial support from the government.[63] Whites' exclusive demand for freedom did not fall on unlettered deaf black ears, but was in fact adopted by illiterate slaves seeking to ameliorate their sufferings.

The court docket of Judge Jacob Van Noorstrand, whose circuit covered a large portion of the Somerset County area, is also suggestive of slaves' political astuteness; it mentions several cases of slave subterfuge, truancy, and insolence from 1765 to 1784. Slaves (mostly males) brought before him were convicted of, and condemned to receive a whipping for, such crimes as "Theft of a horse to ride in the night"; "being from home of their masters after nine at night and above 5 miles from home"; "stealing of fowls"; "insult and presumption to assault a white man"; "running out after 9 at night"; "being from master's house 3 nights after 9 o'clock, and taking 2 horses & riding them abroad"; "assault and insult"; "theft & insolence"; and "insolency, assault & battery & breaking Sabbath."[64] This telling synopsis of black agency indicates that truancy's appeal increased among slaves during the wartime chaos. If there was ever a good time for rural Northern slaves, including the physically handicapped, to challenge their oppression through this form of resistance, then the Revolution provided it.

The politicization of slaves in New Jersey (and elsewhere) during the Revolution was most clearly expressed, however, in the number who attempted to escape permanently, often seeking refuge behind "enemy" lines. "The British parade through Bergen, Essex, Somerset, and Middlesex counties," writes Graham Hodges, "resulted in the flight of over fifty slaves in December 1776 alone."[65] Significantly, many fugitives belonged to men serving in the Patriot military, who were hindered in their ability to keep a close watch over their slaves. In 1775 a Somerset County Patriot lamented that "the story of the Negroes may be depended upon, so far at least to them arming or attempting to form themselves. Our militia are gone off in such numbers that we hardly [have] Men in Arms left in those Parts which are least affected to the cause."[66] Thus it was probably inevitable that, in 1775, the slave Tom fled Jacob Holcomb, a resident of Amwell and Lieutenant in the Third Regiment, in Hunterdon County.[67] General John Taylor of Tewksbury, whose slave Ben (as noted earlier) deserted him in 1776, was "an active militia officer in the war, closing his service as colonel of a regiment of state troops."[68] In 1779 Tone and Charles, the slaves of Somerset private Cornelius Van Horn of Readington (Somerset), absconded together with the intention of heading to Staten Island.[69] Hillsborough Township's Peter Dumont served as a private in the First Battalion, in Somerset, when his "Negro man named Toney" escaped in 1780, "endeavoring to go over to the enemy."[70]

Like their compatriot Prime, slaves who fled from officers and privates in the revolutionary army realized fully the contradiction in their owners' contention for liberty sanctioned by God, and simultaneous ownership of the bodies and time of other human beings. "I have often heard them say," wrote William Moraley, that "they did not think God made them Slaves, any more than other Men, and wondered that Christians, especially *Englishmen*, should use them so barbarously."[71] Runaways of men who fought on the Patriot side illuminate the risks whites often incurred for their ownership of, and tyranny over, black people.

Surely, then, it is of no small consequence that Jacob Kline's two sons, John and Jacob, were enrolled in the New Jersey militia during the Revolution.[72] The implication here is that, like Samuel Sutphen, Yombo also heard talk about the "white man's freedom," which would have done little to quell his discontent. Indeed, what is the likelihood that the bondman was in no way affected by either revolutionary discourse or the black insurgency in his midst while enslaved under the elderly Jacob Kline (in 1776 Kline was age sixty-two, whereas Yombo was around age thirty-six)?[73] Interestingly, Aaron Malick wrote a letter to a cousin in 1788 in which he explained that everyone in his brother-in-law's family was well, except for Kline himself. Malick posited, "Old age crowds upon him, which makes him weakly and almost childish."[74] Though it is uncertain exactly when Kline reached this degree of infirmity, we may still assume that he was in no position to maintain tight control over Yombo, particularly when many discontented bondmen—through revolutionary rhetoric, temporary and permanent flight, and insolent behavior—aggressively sought to exercise their own notions of freedom. Indeed, was not Yombo prone to steal and have "outbreaks" long before his arrival on the Old Farm? Did he all of a sudden turn "treacherous" there? Was the admiration he had for his father a sudden occurrence? Perhaps because he was so intractable, Kline offered to sell Yombo, a highly skilled worker, to Aaron Malick, who was "sorely pressed for help."[75]

For William Sutphen, however, "the most favorable" reason why the sale occurred was because "Yombo was a superior currier of leather."[76] Neither he nor Andrew Mellick, who adopts this line of reasoning in his book, were willing to consider the possibility that the aging Jacob Kline could no longer endure such a willful and detestable bondman who had lived through the

Revolution and had experienced its empowering effects. Neither man would consider (or admit) that, like the two New Jersey bondwomen who were advertised for sale in 1780—"one an old one, the other about twenty-eight or thirty years of age"—Yombo was "sold for no fault, but for want of a strict master."[77] Such an admission was to invite further scrutiny regarding the "odious" relationship between Yombo and his allegedly paternalistic owners.

The Dangers of Flight

Yombo's bow-legs and clubfoot would not have been the only things that deterred him from attempting to escape indefinitely. Indeed, it was simply dangerous for blacks to exercise mobility in eighteenth-century New Jersey. William Moraley, for instance, commented that it was useless for bondpeople "to attempt an Escape, tho' they often endeavour it."[78] The New Jersey slave law of 1716 required citizens to whip not only slaves from neighboring colonies who entered the province without the written consent of their owners, but also resident slaves found five miles from their owners' homes without a written pass.[79] As has been shown with respect to Peter Demarest's slave Tom, truants and fugitives could potentially receive more brutal punishment back at the farm. Slaveholders, said Moraley, tended to exercise especial cruelty when punishing captured slaves, even to the point of killing them. Yet they "suffer no Punishment" in doing so, because there was "no Law" against the murdering of slaves.[80] Also anxious about the mobility of free blacks, New Jersey whites passed an act in 1786 stipulating that no manumitted black person could leave his or her county without a signed certificate from two justices of the peace of that county or township.[81] Silvia Dubois remembered "that in those days the negroes were all slaves, and they were sent nowhere, nor allowed to go anywhere without a pass." The former bondwoman spoke from personal experience. Dubois explained that, shortly after her emancipation, she journeyed from Flagtown, Somerset County, to New Brunswick, where her mother still lived in bondage. Along the way, she encountered a hostile white man who inquired, "Whose nigger are you?" Incredulous, she replied, "I'm no man's nigger—I belong to God—I belong to no man." Her antagonist then inquired about her destination, to which she responded, "That's none of your business. I'm free. I go where I please." Upon the realization that he could not overpower this physically imposing woman, "he moseyed off" but told Dubois that he would have her "arrested as soon as he could find a magistrate."[82] Dubois boasted that "he didn't arrest me—not a bit." But, for all her bravado, she fully understood that "anybody had [the] authority to arrest vagrant negroes. They got paid for arresting them and charges for their keeping till their master redeemed them."[83]

Fugitive slaves were often captured and incarcerated in eighteenth-century central New Jersey. In 1779, for example, "a certain Negro Boy named James, who says he belongs to Theophilus Hunt at Morrissania, in [New] York State," was "taken up and brought to the gaol at New-Brunswick."[84] That same year, Godfrey Rhineheart of New Germantown advertised his capture of "a young Negro man, who says his name is Peter." According to Rhineheart, Peter "speaks and understands very little English, and appears to have been but a short time in America," reasons which evidently raised Rhineheart's suspicion of Peter's status as a runaway. Rhineheart took the captive to the "Trenton goal" in Hunterdon County.[85] Likewise, in 1780, Toney, who, as mentioned earlier, escaped from Peter Dumont of Hillsborough, was apprehended and then "hand cuff'd" near Piscataway Town, Middlesex County, but later made his escape from Tunison's Tavern (Somerville).[86] Slave flight in central New Jersey, notwithstanding the wealth of topographical resources, was an extremely risky venture. Despite the social dislocation in the region precipitated by the Revolution, whites were forever mindful of apprehending illegally roving slaves. Indeed, the revolutionary conflict may have heightened their sense of civic duty in this matter, thereby making truancy all the more important to malcontent bondpeople who desired actual freedom.

As a potential runaway, Yombo was further disadvantaged by his illiteracy; that is, he could neither forge a pass nor did he possess the verbal agility required to deceive whites. Without these two critical attributes, it was nearly impossible for a runaway to pass as a free black in New Jersey, or in much of mainland North America. Herein lies the reason for the capture of many fugitives like Peter and James noted above. Unlike their young Morris County compatriot Robbin (alias Leave) who escaped in 1780, they were unable to "frame a smooth story from rough materials."[87] They were not adept at "fast talking" the white man. Fugitives such as Robbin and the aforementioned slave Bood of Hunterdon County—described in 1763 as a "Smooth Tongued Fellow"—exuded a certain confidence that leant greater legitimacy to their mobility.[88] With a written pass in hand, a symbol of white approval, escapees who spoke relatively decent English could potentially deceive even the most suspicious whites.

Of course, we invite criticism in assuming that Yombo actually considered these factors with regard to whether or not he should escape slavery, if he had considered the matter at all. But is it not equally problematic for us to view him as having been completely unaware of his limitations, physical, social, and cultural-linguistic? To do so is to perpetuate Andrew Mellick's depiction of Yombo as a childlike bondman who was ruled by his emotions rather than his intellect.

Profile of Meanness

Unable to escape indefinitely, would Yombo have failed to develop strategies that enabled him to contest, albeit cautiously, whites' unceasing demands and intrusions? Can we rule out his realization that his "disagreeable" or mean disposition could possibly help him achieve this end? Yombo's unpleasantness was not an aberration; there is evidence that other male captives acted similarly. In 1752, for example, the anonymous bondman who murdered his owner, Jacob Van Neste of Branchburg Township, Somerset County, for taking some of his tobacco was described as a "black wretch" who was "large and athletic, and for a long time had been considered dangerous."[89] Arguably, this perception was in part his own doing; that is, he exploited or accentuated his imposing physicality to keep whites at a distance. To put it yet another way, his mean attitude enhanced the potency of his large, dangerous frame.[90] Former Hunterdon County slave Harry Compton was not only "very stout, and very strong," but "had a vicious tendency" that apparently caused the locals, blacks and whites alike, to approach him with a measure of caution. According to Compton's proud granddaughter, Silvia Dubois, "he could put any man upon the ground, white or black."[91] Shortly after Matthew Woodward of Basking Ridge purchased the slave Nathan Woodward from Simon Wyckoff of Readington (Hunterdon), young Nathan gave Woodward "a severe drubbing," making the owner "timid in giving Nate orders." Unable to control the mean boy, Woodward soon sold him to another Basking Ridge resident for "a yoke of oxen."[92]

The historiography of slavery in the New York area suggests that the "dangerous" character of Yombo's three compatriots reflected the particular conditions of thralldom in the region (namely, small holdings and the high rate of turnover among holders), which placed immense physical demands upon bondpeople, and had a negative impact on slave family formation.[93] Further, their hostile dispositions, real or imagined, formed the basis of their day-to-day survival. By invoking fear in whites, they were able to seize some control over their own time and space. To be sure, whites did not take these challenges to their supremacy lightly. It seems doubtful that Jacob Van Neste would have violated his large bondman's supply of tobacco, had he been able to dominate him completely. Van Neste must have realized, as William Moraley did, that tobacco smoking was one of an enslaved male's few means of pleasure and relaxation. "On *Sundays* in the Evening," Moraley noticed, "they converse with their Wives, and drink Rum, or Bumbo, and smoak Tobacco, and the next Morning return to their Master's Labour."[94] The obvious importance of tobacco smoking to enslaved males drove Van Neste to dip into his captive's most prized possession as a means of asserting his authority over him, and he paid for this transgression with his life.

Though Yombo had a "stout" physique, his clubfoot and bow-legs detracted from his overall physical potency.[95] His lamed body appears not to have engendered the same fear in whites as did that of Jacob Van Neste's slave, Harry Compton, or, for that matter, young Nathan Woodward, who apparently had no physical disabilities. To compensate for his bodily shortcomings that increased whites' ability to brutalize and manipulate him, Yombo likely sought alternative methods, such as theft, to enhance his meanness. As was characteristic of bondpeople, Yombo's petty larceny under Aaron Malick doubtlessly had moral foundations. Specifically, it was based on the grounds that the leather goods that Malick claimed for himself were in fact produced by Yombo's time and labor; the bondman was thereby entitled to them as well. For Yombo, theft simultaneously was a means of exacting justice and enhancing his day-to-day survival. Looting served as the basis of his "moral economy."[96] Malick, of course, greatly disproved of this act of resistance and, according to Andrew Mellick, he would give Yombo "a round lecture on the sin of stealing that was delivered with terrible earnest."[97] As a non-Christian whose time and labor had profited whites for years, however, Yombo would have interpreted his stealing much differently. To his mind, he had as much moral authority as Malick and thus he continued to steal. There are also important implications here with regard to gender. As Christopher Booker has pointed out, theft served as a vehicle through which enslaved males could release their frustrations and supplement their (desired) role as providers.[98] Considering the limited ways in which Yombo could exercise his manhood, we can imagine that theft functioned as an outlet for his aggression, while also enabling him to supplement his (and his wife's) meager material existence.

It appears, moreover, that Yombo's thefts evolved into a strategy that put his owners on the defensive, heightening their concern about what he would possibly do next. The fact that Aaron Malick would always check under the seat of the carriage chair for stolen goods before Yombo drove off to visit his wife in Elizabethtown suggests how Yombo's looting evolved into a major preoccupation for Malick. Besides mitigating white authority, Yombo's thievery lent credence to the perception among whites that he was a mean and incorrigible slave whom they needed to watch closely. Advertisements for runaway slaves provide an excellent means of contextualization, illustrating how slave theft was often part of a multifaceted strategy of resistance. Hager, for example, had "stole[n] some goods, and was under a warrant for stealing when she absented herself" from her Morris County owner in 1773.[99] Robert Malcom of Burlington County reported that his anonymous slave who ran off in 1782 had "an iron collar about his neck." This instrument had been used, Malcom explained, because the runaway and another bondman had planned to rob Malcom and then attempt to escape to New York. Malcom characterized his bondman as "a great thief, liar, and drunkard."[100] The Hunterdon County owner of the fugitive bondwoman Catherine was equally acerbic in his 1838 advertisement, describing her as "a noted liar" who "will steal everything she can lay her hands on; and to say the least, this is the fair side of her character."[101] In his view, Catherine's propensity for lying and stealing were symptomatic of her overall impudent nature. Similarly, Yombo's stealing was not a static phenomenon. Rather, it meshed with his other acts of rebelliousness, helping to create a dynamic profile of resistance that underscored his mean disposition.

His "coal black" skin color, as described by Andrew Mellick, was probably another marker of his meanness.[102] By the eighteenth century, Europeans increasingly equated human "blackness" with a lack or absence of civilization.[103] Accordingly, Noah Marsh speculated that his "smooth" talking bondman Robbin was "secreted by some evil minded persons, whose hearts are as black as the fugitive's face."[104] Marsh conceived of Robbin's black face as synonymous with evil and, by extension, that it was the reason why he was both "lazy" and "artful." We are told, moreover, that when a small white boy living near Frenchtown, Hunterdon County, saw a black man for the very first time, he ran home and excitedly told his mother how he "had seen the devil himself down in the meadow by the goose's nest."[105] But despite the many negative connotations surrounding blackness in white thought, Yombo willingly embraced his. He saw his blackness or Africanness as a badge of honor which, in turn, made him appear all the more an outsider in eighteenth-century rural central New Jersey. Alternatively, his conspicuous blackness—accentuated by his theft, donning of earrings, constant tobacco chewing, and refusal or inability to speak intelligible English—further projected the image of a devious, calculating, and mean slave whom whites could not fully trust.[106] Yombo's skin color, like his stealing, made whites suspicious and uncomfortable—a realized form of power for him.

Then again, another plausible explanation for his appearance requires serious consideration. As Shane White and Graham White have shown, enslaved people often saw their appearances, the ways in which they dressed and styled their hair, as matters of great importance, often linked to their African heritage.[107] This was certainly also the case regarding Yombo's hoop earrings. Writing about black natives of Sierra Leone in the late eighteenth century, Thomas Winterbottom, a prominent Scottish doctor, observed that "ear-rings are very generally worn by the natives in much the same way as in Europe, but in some parts . . . it is the fashion to bore a number of holes in the outer circle of the ear, each of which is large enough to contain six or eight small rings."[108] Significantly, an account of Aaron Malick's slaves found in his record book mentions that Yombo "went bare headed"; a similar comment from *The Story of an Old Farm* reveals that "he rarely wore a hat," again suggesting that his head was either shaved or closely cropped.[109] These styles were common among enslaved males and were among aesthetic standards long associated with the Mende (Yombo's purported ethnic group).[110] William Smith, an Englishman who traveled throughout the Guinea Coast in 1726–27, was astonished that both males and females at Whydah "go with their Heads shorn [shaved], and uncover'd, though the Sun is so scorching hot."[111] So, in addition to accentuating his opposition to bondage, Yombo's appearance, even more importantly, bespeaks his African humanity. In light of how the institution of slavery degraded blacks, this attitude in itself can be interpreted as an act of resistance that gained the attention of whites.

William Dunlap, in his recollections of childhood in revolutionary Perth Amboy, wrote of his family's slaves: "My father's kitchen had several families of them of all ages, and all were born in the family of my mother except one, who was called a new negro, and had his face tattooed—his language was scarcely intelligible though he had been long in the country, and was an old man."[112] On the one hand, Dunlap was particularly intrigued by the exotic profile of the "new negro" that distinguished him from those captives who were born and reared on American soil. Then, too, Dunlap's comment bespeaks his incredulity regarding the old bondman's enduring cultural defiance, his strong sense of self that repudiated the cultural hegemony of white society, which Dunlap (a gifted artist and pioneer of the American theater) basically promoted. Yombo's determination to hold on to his cultural roots evoked similar emotions from whites, which he obviously relished.

Yombo's apparent refusal to embrace Christianity similarly enhanced his mean persona. Slaveholders generally welcomed their captives' attendance at white church services, which usually were characterized by racial clientage or paternalism.[113] In her memoir about her childhood in the Princeton area, Margaret Nevius Van Dyke Malcolm reveals how her family attempted to inculcate their slaves with religion. She explains that every morning in her grandparents' home "a goodly string of Negroes" would enter the hall room and stand at the foot of the stairway to hear the prayer given by the family patriarch, Mathew Van Dyke. Moreover, the slaves attended the religious home of the Van Dyke family, Kingston Presbyterian Church, where they faithfully, and supposedly with utter compliance, sat in the gallery "reserved for the Negroes." With a tinge of nostalgia, Malcolm proudly wrote, "Ours [slaves] were all communicants, a godly set."[114] But, given her nostalgia, we cannot take her account totally at face value. She fails to consider the possibility that the black communicants were currying favor with whites, that their faithful attendance at white church services was partly a strategy of survival. In 1784 Sip of Somerset County was charged in court "with insolency, assault & battery & breaking the Sabbath." He was acquitted after he "fell down on his knees before Mrs. Catrina Vroom, widow, and pronounced not to do these things again."[115] His promise to observe the "Sabbath" again was perhaps the most effective way he could show repentance and regain his owner's confidence. Quamino Brokaw (the subject of chapter 4) explicitly stated that he went to church to show that he was "a good boy."[116]

Yombo would have none of this. He had no desire to demonstrate compliance to whites through Christianity (a means by which owners attempted to "civilize" and control slaves) or otherwise.[117] Still, the power of whites required some degree of deference on his part; his survival required that he make adjustments, even in terms of his personality. Even though Yombo had to capitulate to white hegemony, he greatly depended on his African culture, the basis of his identity and self-respect, to mitigate the harsh realities of slavery. He capitulated and perhaps even changed in ways that were recognizably African and therefore empowering.[118]

Yombo's mean persona invested him with the power to convert physical space within the Malick household into his own, namely, "the seat by the fireplace in the outer kitchen."[119] "As a rule, the niggers," posited Silvia Dubois, "had no other light, and no other fire than [the kitchen fire]— they had to stay in the kitchen—this was their part of the house, and here they had good times, too. The white folks were in another part of the house."[120] And, as William Dunlap remembered it, his father's kitchen, in addition to serving "as the place where I found playmates (being an only child), and the place where I found amusement suited to, and forming my taste, in the mirth and games of the negroes," was a kind of meeting place for "the variety of visitors of the black race."[121] Despite commenting about the kitchen from very different vantage points, both Dubois and Dunlap demonstrate how enslaved blacks, through their "mirth," "games," and sense of community, had created their own separate worlds in this part of white people's homes. For Yombo, the kitchen served a slightly different and empowering function: it was a site where he could further promote his oppositional stance. He used his conspicuous physicality and "evil" disposition to accentuate his throne, as it were, by the outer kitchen fire. This represented Yombo's personal space, which surely no one—black or white—dared to enter without his permission.

Conclusion

For all the credit he deserves for introducing us to Yombo, Andrew Mellick portrayed him in *The Story of an Old Farm* as nothing more than a juvenile-acting "darkey." Yombo's anger is alluded to but never discussed explicitly, probably because this would have undermined Mellick's claim that his ancestors practiced paternalism. Small wonder, then, that Mellick depicted Yombo not as a truly dynamic presence on Aaron Malick's farmstead, but rather as a periodically irrational slave who lacked awareness with regard to his physical surroundings, the political climate during the Revolution, or how whites attempted to monopolize his time. In fact, Yombo serves as an element of amusement in *The Story of an Old Farm.* His presence adds "color" to Mellick's long and often convoluted narrative of local "white" history. The purposes of this chapter have been to recover, from Mellick's descriptions, the defiant persona Yombo had constructed for himself, and to restore the memory of him as a rational, even powerful agent in a racially hostile society.

In doing so, however, this discussion, like Andrew Mellick's, basically presents Yombo in narrow terms, as a man lacking real personal depth, largely because we have no real understanding of Yombo's behavior out-side of the Old Farm, away from white scrutiny. We are unable precisely to determine, for example, what kind of relationship he had with his wife. That Yombo would make the trek from Bedminster to Elizabethtown to see her suggests that theirs was a marriage of love, grounded in mutual caring and understanding. Indeed, "abroad marriages" were not easy on enslaved women and men. They involved not knowing the daily welfare of one's mate, who could be brutalized or sold without the other partner's ever learning about it. In short, abroad marriages added to the immense burdens of bondpeople. And yet, Yombo and his wife attempted to stay together, testimony not only of their love and devotion to each other, but also of Yombo's other personality as a warm and concerned husband. He probably, then, was not completely a rebel as portrayed here and in *The Story of an Old Farm.* He was an individual of multiple dimensions.

And yet, Yombo was a malcontent bondman, an issue that deserves scholarly inquiry. Again, it is probable that Yombo's obstinacy was a mani-festation of his parent's alleged suicide (an issue that Andrew Mellick appears to have conveniently ignored); his African heritage, which rein-forced his sense of self-worth; his inability to see his wife more often; and his disdain for the way in which whites seized control over his body and time. Certainly, time was not an abstraction for bondpeople, but a very real element in their lives. For the enslaved, having time of their own was per-haps as vital to their day-to-day survival as stealing and praying. Time that they seized themselves and that was allotted by holders allowed Yombo and enslaved persons in general to retain a sense of their humanity. As a result, captives contested the appropriation of their time vigorously, and often used truancy as a means of disrupting continuity on the farmstead.

Time was gendered as well. Black men, more so than black women, were perceived by whites as potential threats. So it behooved enslaved males to try to reappropriate some measure of their own time, as this enabled them to maintain an even greater degree of social-psychic distance from white scrutiny. By manipulating the negative images whites had of them, Yombo and his menacing male counterparts were possibly able to achieve this end. In a way, it was more advantageous for bondmen that whites feared rather than loved them. Still, we cannot dismiss the possibility that Yombo's meanness had negative consequences. After all, it was a behavior that, like the cool pose or tough-guy image of contemporary black men—carefully crafted performances that convey pride, strength, and self-control, and that obscure anger and disappointment in the presence of others—was essentially forced upon him by a lack of effective survival tactics. And, like black males today who embrace the cool pose, Yombo may have suffered because of it. "The masking central to cool pose," it has been argued, "also trains the black male in the art of self-deception"; thus, "he may lose the ability to know his own feelings, to feel them keenly, or to express them to others when it is safe to do so."[122] Yombo incurred a similar risk in surviving through meanness.

Finally, Yombo, perhaps like many other bondmen throughout the African diaspora, was a product of his circumstances under thralldom. His anger, defiance, and meanness were all manifestations of the oppressive and "odious" nature of eighteenth-century New Jersey slavery. Rather than allowing whites to dominate him without retribution, Yombo used their own fears about his body, color, and culture to terrorize them and thereby enhance his chances of survival. As whites had done to him, Yombo added an element of anxiety to their daily existence. Thus it comes as no surprise that the local whites never forget about "Old Yombo." Even in death, he won their full attention.

Chapter 4

Threat of a (Christian) Bondman

While Yombo's combative temperament speaks dramatically to the heroism of enslaved males, more bondmen perhaps chose Quamino's method of diffusing white people's endless scrutiny of their allegedly dangerous physical (sexual) presence. At first glance, the *Memoir of Quamino Buccau* appears to be a rather uninspiring account of Quamino's life in slavery and freedom. Yet, upon closer examination, the *Memoir*, which author William Allinson composed as a romantic racialist tract, powerfully elucidates the tenuous existence of enslaved males in the eighteenth-century rural North, and how their religiosity helped to promote their day-to-day survival. Specifically, Quamino's exploitation of and receptivity to Christianity demonstrates how the religiosity of bondmen could help them fashion identities that were agreeable to the white population, while also serving as a vital means of strength, support, and resistance for the enslaved themselves.

Liberated in September 1806, Quamino lived most of his life in bondage in the rural Somerset County area, which, by 1790, had emerged as a major center of slaves in the Middle Colonies. The 1790 federal census reported 1,810 slaves in Somerset, 22 percent of the 8,196 total slaves in East Jersey. Somerset had the second largest enslaved population in the region as well as in the state.[1] In the 1770s, Quamino also experienced bondage as a rented or hired slave in the Hudson River Valley of New York—that is, in Poughkeepsie Township, Dutchess County. Although, by 1771, there were 19,883 "Blacks" in New York (which constituted the largest enslaved population north of Maryland), more than one-third of this black population (12,383 total people) was located in the Hudson River Valley, with Dutchess accounting for 1,360 people, or 10.9 percent of it. This figure nearly approximates the county's 1790 enslaved population of 1,856, indicating that the majority of blacks in 1771 were held in bondage.[2] In short, Quamino labored and, more importantly, survived as a bondman in areas where slavery was highly valued, and where bondpeople were regarded as subhuman and thus dangerous.

What role did religion play in Quamino's life in a region where whites intensely feared and brutally treated enslaved blacks? Around age eighteen and seemingly cognizant of what his maturing (male) body signaled to whites in the rural and socially turbulent revolutionary North—circumstances that inspired numerous captives to liberate themselves—Quamino viewed Christianity as a means of presenting himself to his Patriot owners as an agreeable or "good" slave. Like any person oppressed because of race, class, or gender, he learned how to read the expectations of his superordinates while remaining inscrutable. That is to say, Christianity allowed Quamino to engage in the politics of self-presentation. Yet, in the aftermath of a life-changing conversion experience, Christianity assumed a more meaningful, and thereby more empowering, role in his life. As a result, his Christian faith worried his once protective owners, who believed that it was potentially subversive. Thus, notwithstanding William Allinson's romantic racialist propaganda in the *Memoir*, it is evident that Quamino's religiosity was not only dynamic but also threatening to the established order.

Perils of Childhood

According to Allinson, Quamino's life in bondage originated under a man known only as "Buccau," a surname which does not appear in any eighteenth-century sources for the "vicinity of [New] Brunswick," and is apparently a corruption stemming from Quamino's illiteracy.[3] An analysis of several key points in the *Memoir* has led to the conclusion that this "Buccau" was probably Isaac Brokaw, a Dutch land- and slaveholder of the Eastern Precinct (Franklin Township).[4] Hence, this chapter will refer to Isaac Brokaw and his sons as Quamino's original owners. In 1771 the elder Brokaw hired out nine-year-old Quamino "for a term of years to a person of the name of Schenk."[5] Prior to this fateful business transaction, Quamino's life was rather ideal when compared to that of many other enslaved Northern youth. While enslaved blacks in the New York hinterland typically lived with only one or a few other compatriots, and frequently were bought and sold among white relatives, Quamino had a relatively stable family life consisting of two parents, four elder siblings (a brother and three sisters), as well as "friends" (fictive kin?) in the New Brunswick area. Moreover, he represented Isaac Brokaw's "only young cub," or favored slave.[6] Then, suddenly, the youth was stripped of these human relationships, and thereby deprived of the emotional attention and support system so critical to the psychic needs of children.[7] The severance of human relationships is a common theme in antebellum (Southern) slave narratives written by Frederick Douglass, Harriet Jacobs, Henry Bibb, William Wells Brown, and other former blacks in bondage. Slave (or, more accurately, ex-slave) narratives vary in terms of geographical location and time period, yet they typically underscore how slavery and the slave trade severely undercut the childhood of blacks.[8] Quamino's narrative (like the narratives of Silvia Dubois and Sojourner Truth, former Mid-Atlantic captives) indicates that this harsh reality was not only endemic to black Southern children (the subject of several notable historical studies), but also characterized the lives of enslaved youth on the other side of the Mason-Dixon line, who have typically been elided in slavery discourse.[9]

As shown in the tragic life of Phillis, who was enslaved in Hunterdon County, transplanted slaves became susceptible to gross mistreatment. During the early 1800s, Phillis's owner, Henry Post, sold an entire corn crop to save his irresponsible brother from the consequences of a "drunken frolic," which in turn had placed Post's household in a state of financial distress. To alleviate the crisis, Post hired out Phillis, an "efficient lady's maid, seamstress, and nurse," to a man who probably resided in Cranbury Township, Middlesex County, under the expressed agreement that he return Phillis to Post in one year. As the end of the year approached, Phillis's mistress, Martha or Mattie (Anderson), began to worry about the slave who had been given to her as a present from her father. After he borrowed enough money from his neighbors to buy Phillis back, Martha's husband went in pursuit of the slave and eventually found her in Monmouth County. The physically delicate woman was crippled upon his arrival. In addition to working an entire season as a field hand, she has been subjected to brutal whippings. The deadly combination of hard physical labor and barbarous treatment rendered her body permanently crooked. Unable to lie in a bed, Phillis spent the remainder of her life confined to a cradle specially made for her.[10] Such was the horror that possibly awaited a slave who became someone else's property in a different area or neighborhood (though, admittedly, this could have also led to an improvement in conditions and treatment).

Initially, Schenk (presumably John or Paul) employed Quamino "as a house servant," most likely in Somerset County, which perhaps alleviated the devastation of the youth's separation from his previous existence. Then, around 1773, Schenk took the youth with him when he relocated to Poughkeepsie. Young Quamino was forced to survive without family and friends in this part of the distant New York frontier, which, as William Allinson puts it, "contrasted strongly with its present aspect." He quoted Quamino as saying, "There was . . . so much wild varmints there"; "not a week elapsed," Allinson clarifies, "without his seeing wild bears swimming across the noble Hudson."[11] The purpose of this commentary was not to inform the reader about how Poughkeepsie had changed over time, but to underscore Quamino's sense of vulnerability in a new and threatening land, where, in addition to "wild varmints," he may have also encountered a dangerous human element in "blood thirsty [Indian] savages and Frenchmen."[12]

Silvia Dubois, a former central New Jersey slave in the 1790s, allows us to peer into Quamino's emotional state in his new surroundings. As a teenager, Silvia was forced to relocate with her owners to rural Susquehanna, Pennsylvania; she left behind her mother and siblings, from whom she was initially separated as a child. She recalled feeling "a little glum" one day, having no desire to clean her owners' barroom as the mistress had ordered. Thereupon, the mistress scolded Silvia, who then "sauced her." The mistress responded to this act of impudence by striking Silvia with her hand. But Silvia still refused to submit, and actually struck back the mistress with even greater force. Silvia explained, "The first whack, I struck her a hell of a blow with my fist. I didn't knock her entirely through the panels of the door, but her landing against the door made a terrible smash, and I hurt her so badly that all [the white people in the bar] were frightened out of their wits." Realizing that "it wouldn't do to stay there," Silvia fled to Chenango, New York, where she says she "went to work." This potentially disastrous situation could not have turned out any better for Silvia. Faced with the fact that his wife and slave could no longer coexist, Minna Dubois freed Silvia shortly afterward.[13]

Along with demonstrating the intense hostility that existed between some enslaved Northern women and their mistresses, Silvia Dubois's reminiscences force us to consider seriously how transplanted blacks were susceptible to feeling depressed.[14] Though Silvia was a strong-minded individual, she still experienced moments of loneliness and sadness which apparently stemmed from her loss of contact with family and friends. Given the relative stability that characterized Quamino's old family life, not to mention his emotional attachment to Isaac Brokaw, it is plausible that he too had a difficult time staving off bouts of feeling "glum" while in Poughkeepsie. As in Silvia's case, these low feelings could potentially have affected his ability to excel at his work, the only sphere of his young life in which he could exercise some control. His reputation as a dutiful servant was perhaps seriously challenged in his new and threatening environment.

Quamino's sense of vulnerability was further exacerbated by the fact that the youth, who no doubt represented Schenk's only slave or one of a few, did not have access to the type of psychological support that a so-called slave community could provide.[15] Thus, like any young person living closely with his elders, he would have viewed Schenk as a sort of father figure, whom he tried to please at all costs.[16] Interestingly enough, after he had been liberated, Quamino created a social world in which he interacted primarily with prominent white clergymen and reformers like William Allinson.[17] As a free man, Quamino sought the acceptance and approval of white males in positions of authority, a pattern of behavior that arguably was rooted in his childhood in bondage.

Hence, it comes as no surprise when William Allinson mentions that Schenk and others attempted to purchase Quamino from Isaac Brokaw. We may interpret this as evidence that the youth had proven himself as a compliant and reliable servant. Even so, "he was compelled [by Schenk] to witness every public execution, with the idea that a salutary lesson would thus be impressed." One "peculiarly distressing" execution involved an enslaved male, "about twenty years of age," who had set fire to his owner's "barn and outbuildings," destroying a considerable amount of grain and livestock. Allinson vividly describes the man's brutal execution:

> He was fastened to a stake, and when the pile [of wood] was fired, the dense crowd excluded the air, so that the flames kindled but slowly, and the dreadful screams of the victim were heard at a distance of three miles. His master, who had been fond of him, wept aloud, and called to the Sheriff to put him out of his misery. This officer then drew his sword; but the master, still crying like a child, exclaimed, "Oh, don't run him through!" The Sheriff then caused the crowd to separate, so as to cause a current of air; and when the flame burst out fiercely he called to the sufferer to "swallow the blaze"; which he did, and immediately he sunk dead.[18]

Considering both the rarity of slave arson in Poughkeepsie and the time frame in which Quamino was enslaved there (roughly 1773–80), the executed bondman in question appears to have belonged to Poughkeepsie resident Jacob Van Benchaten. In 1775 he was burned alive for setting fire to Van Benchaten's house and barn.[19] Enslaved people who committed arson against their owners usually did so in retaliation "for some private offense or injustice."[20] Presumably, Van Benchaten violated his bondman's own sense of justice, thereby turning the otherwise amiable servant ("as nice a coloured man . . . as you wish to look at," stated Quamino) into a vindictive rebel.[21]

This and other public executions must have had a devastating impact on Quamino's mind. For public executions were not just community death rituals; they were also exercises in mental torture from which no enslaved person would have escaped unscarred, psychologically. Consider, for example, the 1752 burning of the bondman who had murdered his owner, Jacob Van Neste of Branchburg Township, for using his tobacco. His execution was attended by slaves from the surrounding area who, according to local legend, were so traumatized by what they had witnessed "that they did not eat any meat for a long time afterwards."[22] To reiterate the impregnable force of white hegemony, as well as the power of the law, Sheriff Abraham Van Doren apparently conducted the execution from his horse, "riding with drawn sword between the spectators and [the] fire."[23] This burning, along with all public executions, was intended to make the black spectators internalize the horrible consequences of challenging their subordinate position, and remind them of their lack of humanity, devoid of personal notions of justice. To put it another way, the purpose of these terrifying spectacles was to induce the so-called slave mentality, defined as the lack or absence of self-worth, self-confidence, personal autonomy, and independent thought.[24]

Slavery, writes Orlando Patterson, was principally "a relation in domination," and the use of violence was essential "in creating and maintaining that domination."[25] In the minds of slaveholders, forcing their human chattel to observe public executions was a part of the business or politics of slavery. Thus, not even a reputedly "good" slave like Quamino was exempt from these exercises in racial dominance. Indeed, the older and stronger he became, the more of a physical threat he represented to white public safety, increasing the probability that he would begin asserting himself like the Dutchess County slaves Cuff and Trace. By the time of his escape in 1753, Cuff, around thirty years old and physically "well-set," had earned the reputation as a "very flippant" and "plausible smooth Tongue[d] Fellow."[26] In 1763 Trace, who ran away at age twenty-five, was deemed a "spry well-built Fellow" who also "looks very brazen" and "talks flippent [sic]."[27] As a slaveholder, Schenk could not risk the possibility of Quamino's running away, let alone acting "flippant" or "brazen" and developing a "smooth" or deceptive tongue. Public executions reinforced his power and authority over Quamino, reminding the youth of the necessity of demonstrating full compliance at all times.

The cautious manner that the bondman Dick Melick assumed in the presence of whites has strong implications for interpreting Quamino's behavior as he developed physically. Dick and his family were sold to Andrew Mellick's Bedminster Township ancestors in 1798. Known as a good black whose family reflected his positive "virtues," Dick was "quiet," "courteous," and "dignified in appearance" upon meeting the Malicks for the first time. Although he described New Jersey slavery as a benevolent institution, Mellick conceded that "heavy-set" Dick, who was also "of a good dark color," may have consciously diffused the presence of his physicality when interacting with whites.[28] It would have behooved Quamino to tread with similar caution around Schenk, who obviously became increasingly alarmed if not intimidated by the presence of his young male captive's body.

In addition, Quamino had to endure the fact that "the unsettled state of the country during the Revolutionary war, prevented communication with his old master" and thus his family.[29] There were forts and troops positioned along the Hudson River, raids by the British forces, incidents of espionage, and sequestrations. This ominous state of affairs was dramatically captured by Poughkeepsie resident Elizabeth Tappen. In a letter written to her husband Peter in July 1776, she says, "Almost every Tory in the County was hunted up by the Yankie's & Brought to County Committee . . . then we had news of the ships moving up the river, Troops flocking in here like swarms of Bees, People that live at the river moving everything away."[30]

Many discontented slaves exploited these turbulent conditions by running away. Dutchess County newspapers, for example, contain advertisements for sixty fugitives who absconded between 1777 and 1783.[31] A number of Hudson Valley fugitives aspired to reach the British, who, by the end of 1776, had established a long offensive line extending from Tappan, in the lower Hudson Valley, to Monmouth County.[32] As a case in point, in 1779 Pomp of Poughkeepsie was suspected of escaping to the British.[33] His female compatriot Bridget, who for many years was enslaved under the Van Cortlandt family of Westchester County, held similar aspirations; she had planned to lead five other enslaved women across British lines to freedom. Their escape, however, was foiled by a female member of the Van Cortlandt family.[34] The prevalence of such surreptitious activity among blacks was not conducive to the maintenance of slave discipline. In Albany, therefore, a strict curfew was enforced and "troublesome blacks were deported to New England as a preventative measure."[35] There can be little doubt that Quamino's required attendance at the execution of the "nice" bondman for committing arson (apparently in 1775) was related partly to the social disorder that slaves exploited to liberate themselves.

During these unstable times, Quamino had "relinquished the hope of again seeing his former friends." Around 1780, however, his fate suddenly changed, when Schenk was visited by "a stranger" who had been sent to retrieve Quamino for the Brokaw family.[36] Subsequent to their conversation, Schenk asked Quamino, who was about eighteen years old, "whether he would like to see his father and mother, his master and mistress, his young masters and mistresses, &c." To the youth's affirmative reply, Schenk responded with apparent disappointment, "Well, your master has sent for you, and this man has come to take you." Upon learning that he was going back home, Quamino's emotions got the best of him. "Overcome with this too sudden announcement," states William Allinson, "he burst into a violent and uncontrollable fit of crying, and for hours cried aloud as though he had been beaten—unable to answer questions, or to stay his emotions at the kindest efforts to pacify him." To Allinson's inquiry "whether it was joy that affected him," Quamino retorted, "It seems so, sir—I don't know, and I didn't know then—it struck me to the heart."[37]

Clearly, Allinson places emphasis upon Quamino's uncontrollable sobbing to demonstrate further his extreme vulnerability. At the same time, however, we cannot ignore how his lack of emotional control in this instance also signifies his identification (by Allinson) with the figure of the childlike romantic racialist Negro. Still, this should not diminish our appreciation of his emotional suffering, which was perhaps so profound that it was practically beyond his own comprehension. Nell Irvin Painter, who challenges historians to deal with the enslaved as psychological people, reminds us that, according to psychologists, emotional deprivation, sexual abuse, and physical and mental torture can lead to "soul murder" among children, which is typically characterized by depression, low self-esteem, and anger.[38] In light of this assessment, can we ignore how the many hardships that Quamino endured—the loss of family and friends, the witnessing of public executions, the deterioration of racial relations during the Revolutionary War, and the daily pressure of fulfilling the expectations of a slave—had probably compromised his psychic health and hence his ability to fashion his own identity?

The lives of Sojourner Truth (born Isabella) and Silvia Dubois allow for greater comprehension of this issue: not only were both women held in rural Northern bondage (collectively from the 1790s through the 1820s), but as children they were separated from their families.[39] In her excellent biography of Truth, Nell Irvin Painter explains that it was not until long after she had been liberated that Truth realized the absurdity of her "extreme anxiety" to please her owner, John Dumont.[40] But, like Dubois, Truth was abused as a child and, as a result, found ways to explain and excuse the beatings she received from Dumont, whom she looked upon as a god. Painter notes, "Even as an adult, she reckoned that he was in a position of authority over her, and when she did wrong, it was fitting that she paid the price."[41] Similarly, Silvia Dubois described Minna Dubois as "a good man and good master" who "never whipped me unless he was sure that I deserved it."[42] She went so far as to compare her former owner with George Washington and other great white men of his age: he was tall, handsome, brave, commanding, graceful, and widely respected. Thus, when asked by her amanuensis if disorderly New Jersey blacks were deserving of the whippings they received by whites during local community events, she hesitantly replied, "Yes, sometimes—most always, I expect. They had to lick 'em; there was no other way; they had to make 'em mind."[43] Despite decades of living in freedom, and largely on her own terms, Dubois was unable to reconcile fully with white people's racial brutality, reasoning that since she and other blacks had invited abuse, whites were justified in their violence.[44] Troublesome blacks, she reluctantly conceded, warranted the brutal treatment they received from such important men as Minna Dubois.

Silvia Dubois and Sojourner Truth reaffirm that slavery's continued assault upon the bodies and minds of blacks could result in circumscribed identities. Their experiences strengthen the assumption that the hardships of Quamino's childhood, and in particular the terrifying executions that he never forgot, also had a profoundly negative impact on his young, impressionable mind, influencing him, likewise, to identify strongly with his abuser. As gender plays an important role in the construction of identity, it is only logical, moreover, that these childhood hardships greatly affected his ability to fashion a particular model of masculinity for himself. Indeed, the construction of gender conventions among the enslaved was done under extreme duress, under persons who viewed them only minimally as women and men, and principally as exploitable chattel. For enslaved women, this duress included the specter of sexual exploitation, especially rape, whereas for enslaved men it involved the alleged threat of their (potent) sexuality to white womanhood, and the particular danger they posed to the safety of whites in general.[45] Schenk's insistence that Quamino attend public executions was related to these kinds of fears about black males—fears that must have had a tremendous influence on how Quamino would perceive himself as a man in the future.

Christianity and the Politics of (Male) Survival

Upon his return to New Jersey, Quamino's "young associates were so grown beyond his knowledge, that he felt like a stranger in his childish haunts," avers William Allinson.[46] Significantly, what Allinson fails to mention is that Quamino, likewise, would have returned home not as a "young cub," but as a physically developed young man whom his owners may not have fully recognized. After all, he had made only "several" visits to New Jersey during his seven or so years of exile in Poughkeepsie. "When nearing the age of manhood," Quamino made an important decision that evidently was influenced by this reality. Allinson explains that his protagonist became "steady in his attendance upon religious meetings, walking several miles through all kinds of weather," and he adds: "His own account of the motive for going was, that he 'liked to have the name of being a good boy.'"[47] Since enslaved blacks typically attended the churches of their owners, Allinson may possibly be referring here to Isaac Brokaw's church home, the Reformed Dutch Church of the Raritan (Somerville).[48] Quamino's rationalization that attending religious meetings enhanced his reputation as a "good boy" among whites bespeaks his awareness of his vulnerability as a black man in a white-dominated society. No longer able to perpetuate his nonthreatening status as a "young cub," given his grown body, he attempted to reclaim this benign image through compliant behavior buttressed by Christian passivity. We must realize that not every enslaved male was capable of, or interested in, Yombo's strategy of direct, oppositional resistance. Enslaved males (and females) were complex individuals who survived and resisted in ways that made the most sense to them—even in ways that, by today's standards, might seem cowardly or unmanly.

Still, we cannot assume that Quamino's attendance at religious meetings reflected no desire on his part to identify with his owners, namely, with the patriarch Isaac Brokaw. Again, he spent most of his life trying to gain the approval of white men, powerful evidence of slavery's lingering impact on his conduct. But, at the same time, Quamino was a slave in a black man's body, a fact that made his day-to-day existence undeniably precarious. As in Dick Melick's case, it was in Quamino's best interest to develop strategies that reinforced his obsequiousness and, by extension, reassured his owners of their safety. His attendance at religious meetings, which was probably inspired by his experiences in racially turbulent Poughkeepsie, emerged as one of these strategies at a time when race relations in New Jersey were growing worse, partly as a result of the Patriots' conflict with Great Britain.

It is unlikely that the Brokaw family would have been unconcerned about the hostile environment that the Revolution created and that slaves used to their own advantage. The Brokaws' military participation on the Patriot side is suggestive of men who felt the need to crush those forces, white and black, that threatened their "freedom." Three of Isaac Brokaw's sons—Caspares, Isaac, and Abraham—saw varied but extended military service as fighters and guardsmen in New Jersey as well as Staten Island. These ardent defenders of the Patriot cause, and other Brokaw family members, would not have tolerated any aberrant behavior from blacks. This point is exemplified in the person of Abraham Brokaw, who became a minister after the Revolution and was later ordained in the Dutch Reformed Church. Prior to his ordination, however, he served four (monthly) tours of duty in Elizabethtown in 1779, "watching the enemy night and day."[49] The "enemy" included "the Negro slaves in Elizabethtown," who, that same year, had plotted "to rise and murder their masters." All the blacks suspected "to be involved in the plot were locked up, while the others were kept under close surveillance."[50] Abraham Brokaw's intense scrutiny of oppositional forces apparently did not end with his military service. As William Allinson explains, Quamino's "young master," presumably Abraham Brokaw, "who, although a professed minister of the gospel, gave no attention to the religious culture of his slaves—his policy being, (to use Quamino's word,) to keep them 'igarent,' that they might be more serviceable."[51]

It was in this environment that Quamino turned to religious meetings as a means of enhancing his survival. But, as suggested by his young owner's refusal to provide his slaves with religious instruction, for fear that it might inculcate them with knowledge and thereby power, this strategy entailed an element of risk. As shown in the runaway slave advertisements placed by James Leonard (of Middlesex County) and John Bryan (of Somerset County), some owners actually questioned the sincerity of their slaves' religiosity. In 1740 Leonard reported that his runaway, Simon, "Pretend[s] to be a great Doctor and very religious and says he is a Churchman."[52] Similarly, Bryan repudiated his bondman Gilbert's religiosity by explaining, in 1786, that he "can read very well, pretends to be religious, and sometimes undertakes to preach."[53] We will never know for certain if Simon and Gilbert were sincere in their religious faith. Yet we can safely conclude that Leonard and Bryan had equated the bondmen's displays of religiosity with a subversive craftiness that threatened their authority. The bondmen were thus deemed religious pretenders, as malcontents who seditiously exploited the word of God. Quamino's religious devotion risked similar scrutiny from his owners, especially the suspicious minister.

Conversely, the renowned piety of Cuffy Barnet (d. 1844) demonstrates how it was possible for Quamino and other enslaved males to acquire a modicum of respect and thereby protection through their adoption of Christianity. During Sunday services at Lamington Church in Bedminster, Cuffy, a bondman, always sat at the farthest end of the segregated gallery pew, located above the pulpit. Every black churchgoer was aware of his seat and never failed to yield it to him.[54] Cuffy, moreover, often attended the funerals of black communicants and, when no ordained (white) minister was present, provided the requisite prayer. But, even more revealing, he was empowered as a kind of lay preacher, supplementing the sermons of the minister with suggestions and pragmatic remarks to his fellow blacks. And he achieved this high status within the church despite his rather conspicuous and intimidating physicality. Charles Bartles, a prominent lawyer in nearby Flemington Township, vividly recalled a chance encounter with Cuffy when the bondman was driving a team of oxen. Bartles "said that it was not the deep, coarse voice, nor the heavy, rugged hands, nor the brawny back of this pious man which so attracted his attention, but a pair of monstrous feet that kept pace with the bovine pair."[55] Although Bartles, and doubtless other whites, viewed him as a kind of racial monstrosity, Cuffy was regarded as a devout and well-behaved slave who became a role model to his black peers. His religiosity made him appear less threatening to whites—that is, more like a human and less like a beast.

We cannot, therefore, dismiss the possibility that Cuffy, or Dick Melick for that matter, utilized religion as a buffer of sorts against oppression. Given the few means of defense at their disposal, they could not afford to ignore how religion might help them to mitigate their physical presence. This does not mean, however, that the bondmen were insincere Christians; certainly, the important role that Cuffy played in the spiritual lives of his black coreligionists, making sure, for example, that they were prayed for at their funerals, is indicative of someone who took religion seriously. Yet the reality of his and Dick's existence as large black men in a racially hostile society does raise the issue of how their religiosity possibly served multiple functions: as a source of enlightenment, salvation, self-worth, service, and, less discernible, protection. Similar to Quamino, Cuffy and Dick were in no position to disregard the negative image of the black man in the white mind, and the ways in which Christianity could assist them in wearing the mask of subservience.

Coming to God

Religion acquired greater personal meaning in Quamino's life following his conversion experience around 1780. William Allinson writes:

One Sabbath evening, returning home from meeting, he had impressions of a striking character; his imagination being evidently much acted upon. As he trod the familiar way, a new road appeared to branch off to the right hand, leading up to the mountain. Intent on pursuing it, he hastened to look into it, and saw distinctly "a dry, smooth path," leading upward as far as he could see; but, as he was about to enter it, (to quote the old man's own words,) "I heard a noise like a half-a-dozen horses, coming after me, rattling as hard as they could lay their legs to the ground." He turned his head, and the illusion was broken. The old man's tears trickled, as he said, "and there, sir, I lost it. I thought," said he, "that it was a token for something or other."[56]

The incident left Quamino in a state of distress. Before going to work early the next morning, he got on his knees and began to pray. The "Saviour" (Christ) then presumably spoke to him, saying, "Let not your heart be troubled. Ye believe in god, believe also in me." Thereafter, explained Quamino, "everything was glorious around me—everything seemed engaged praising God!" By "yielding his whole heart" to God and acquiring the "unspeakable Gift" of God's glory, perhaps for the first time in his life, Quamino was instilled with an inviolable sense of conviction.[57] At the very least, his self-esteem, courage, and hopes were bolstered. Indeed, the passage that begins "let not your heart be troubled" comes from the book of John (14:1), and is followed by a verse that states, "In my Father's house are many mansions" (14:2), a phrase that we can interpret as a promise of equality and inclusion. The passage is later repeated with the injunction not to "be afraid" (14:27). As we have seen, Quamino had much to fear in his young life. But, with God on his side, he did not have to "be afraid" any longer.[58]

The religious conversion experience of William Boen (1735–1824), who lived in slavery and freedom near Mount Holly, Burlington County, warrants our consideration. During the French and Indian War, William's owner sent him into the woods to cut down trees. William felt terrified of the Native Americans who came lurking about his neighborhood, and whom the local whites accused of killing and scalping people. Thus he was afraid to work alone in the woods. While in his terrorized state, William thought to himself "whether I was fit to die."[59] Shortly afterward, when he felt condemnation, the deeply troubled bondman stood quiet and still in the woods as "a flaming sword passed through me." This experience showed him how to prepare for death: he had to serve God faithfully. William, in fact, now believed that he "had two masters." God, whom he considered his "new Master," wanted him to leave one of the trees standing on the hillside, which went against the orders of his "old master." Though distressed by how his "old master" might react to this act of defiance, he left the tree unmolested. The bondman had placed his religious duty above obedience to his white owner. But, as it turned out, his owner never seriously questioned him about the tree, and eventually he cut it down himself. Still, William viewed this as a significant incident: it showed him that "my new Master will make [a] way for me, and take care of me, if I love him, and mind him, and am attentive to this my guide, and rule of my life."[60] William, as Quamino would eventually do, put all his troubles in God's hands. God would somehow make a way for the two oppressed slaves, if only they put God first in their lives.

It would appear that, like the religious conversion experiences of ante-bellum Southern slaves documented by Clifton Johnson in *God Struck Me Dead*, those of Quamino and William were galvanized by their oppression. The more than forty slave conversion experiences presented in Johnson's book "conform to the normal pattern for all such experiences": they begin "with a sense of sin and nonrealization and terminate with one of cleanliness, certainty, and reintegration, the very three things every Negro was denied in life." As Johnson points out, "the antebellum slave was not converted to God. He converted himself to God. In the Christian God he found a fixed point, and he needed a fixed point, for both within and outside of himself he could see only vacillation and endless shifting."[61] Quamino and William's lives in bondage were similarly characterized by a dreadful state of uncertainty and instability. This condition led them to a crossroads in their lives where they, too, sought God to help put them on a stable path. The bondmen had reached the point in their suffering where they needed, and were ready, to come to God.

Another important point to consider is that Quamino's spirituality was syncretic, encompassing both European and African elements. Instead of receiving God within a (white) church or religious community, where his humanity was most likely denied, he had his revelation in the open air amid trees, rocks, and waterways—symbols of divinity in African culture.[62] His first name, which is discussed in chapter one, also points to an African dimension to his Christian faith. Apparently given to him by his parents, Quamino's name bespeaks his African heritage, the mention of which is conspicuously absent in the *Memoir*, and which may well have encouraged his attraction to Christianity.

African and European cosmologies had much in common, including that humans were once immortal, that the use of magic could kill, and that the spirit lived on after death. It was relatively easy for enslaved Africans and their descendents to identify with the essential elements of Western Christianity and to adopt them as their own without completely abandoning some of their old beliefs—a premise that has strong implications for Quamino's own conception of Christianity.[63] And yet, we have no reason to believe that William Allinson had any appreciation for religious paradigms espoused by members of a degraded race that, in his opinion, needed Christian white men like himself to advocate on its behalf.

Indeed, had Allinson acknowledged the probable cultural nuances of Quamino's religiosity, it would have problematized his very safe portrayal of Quamino as an exemplar of Christian humility and devotion.

In addition, Allinson makes no mention that Quamino's conversion experience occurred within the context of the Methodist evangelical movement in revolutionary North America. Of no small consequence, upon receiving his freedom in 1806, Quamino (and wife Sarah) joined the Methodist Episcopal Church in Burlington County.[64] This begs the question: Why and when did Quamino become attracted to Methodism? Significantly, prior to the end of the Revolution, the Methodist Church, which was founded by English abolitionists, had vociferously denounced the institution of slavery, advocated universal salvation and individual religious experience, sponsored illiterate black preachers, and provided African Americans with a deeply emotional religious experience.[65] The Dutch Reformed Church, by contrast, did not begin accepting black communicants until shortly after the war.[66] In 1773 itinerant Methodist minister Benjamin Abbott made note of the interracial love feast that he held at the Basking Ridge home of William Alexander or Lord Stirling. "The power of the Lord," he enthused, "came down in a wonderful manner among the black people, some cried aloud and others fell to the floor, some praising God, some crying for mercy." Afterward, Abbott and "brother S[tirling] went among them, where he continued upwards of an hour, exhorting them to fly to Jesus the ark of safety."[67] Former Basking Ridge slave Nathan Woodward (d. 1901) emerged as a prominent figure at Methodist revivals in the area. According to a newspaper report on his life, "He would take part in the praying and exhorting. He was also a good singer and would stir an audience by the touching way he sang the old revival hymns."[68] Although racism increased in the Methodist Church following the Revolution, the church's relative liberalism and acceptance of religious self-expression inspired many African Americans, perhaps including Quamino while he was yet in bondage.[69] Even so, his Brokaw owners would not have approved of his associating with the Methodists, whose egalitarianism challenged the validity of the Brokaws' ownership of blacks. But even if Quamino's attraction to Methodism was rooted in his enslavement, William Allinson had little incentive to reveal this fact. Clearly, Quamino appeared less threatening to white America in 1850 as a poor, humble, and free black man who embraced Methodism than as an oppressed slave empowered because of it.

In sum, contrary to how William Allinson presents it, Quamino's religious conversion experience was most likely a complex phenomenon precipitated by a culmination of psychic, cultural, and social forces that, in the end, allowed him to see himself as much more than a slave. He had been transformed into one of God's children. And he would soon prove what his young owner feared most about slaves' exposure to Christianity.

Perils and Limitations of Religious Power

As William Allinson describes it, the day that life turned "glorious" for Quamino as a result of his finding God brought about a change in "the youth [which] was conspicuous to all who knew him. He was diligent in attention to all his duties, but he had no inclination to talk with anyone."[70] Quamino's young owner, who believed that religion was not conducive to making slaves "serviceable," took a particular interest in the bondman's changed demeanor. One day Brokaw followed Quamino into the family barn and listened carefully as the illiterate slave prayed "with great fervency." The minister did not like what he heard, and a conflict between owner and slave ensued: "On his return to the house, [Brokaw] questioned [Quamino] sharply, saying repeatedly, that to be talking thus when he was alone, he must be talking to the Evil Spirit." Still incensed by the accusation, Quamino told Allinson, "I knowed better than that. I wasn't after the Evil Spirit. I didn't want to have anything to do wid him." In the aftermath of the conflict, Allinson maintains, "Quamino understood the nature of that peace which is independent of external circumstances, being given 'not as the world giveth' [John 14:27]."[71] Allinson cites this biblical passage to emphasize how, following the dispute, Quamino had fully entered the next phase in his life, where there was no reason for him to fear external circumstances, including hostile slaveholders, in the earthly world. In his new life, peace, derived from salvation, came from serving his "true master"—God.

The struggle between Quamino and the Brokaws over his religiosity did not end with the dispute between slave and "young master." William Allinson remarks that "on the first day of the week he would get the carriage ready, and when his master had started, he would walk several miles across the fields to meeting, and back; but, as he was certain to be faulted, and sometimes even 'cuffed,' if not at home in time to take the horses, on the arrival of the family, he always left the congregation before the completion of the service."[72] Accordingly, as John Blassingame has argued, "the more pious slaves persisted in attending religious services contrary to the order of their masters and in spite of floggings. In this test of wills the slave asserted that his master could inflict pain on his body, but he could not harm his soul. . . . Clearly, religion was more powerful than the master, engendering more love and fear in the slave than he could."[73] The Brokaws placed few if any restraints on Quamino's desire to attend church meetings prior to his conversion experience, when his intention was to demonstrate his compliance. Owing, however, to their apparent awareness that his religious empowerment and devotion threatened their authority over him, the family, or at least certain of its male members, believed it was necessary to check his religious autonomy.

This conflict hints at the emergence of Quamino's nascent masculine identity. We can discern how, after he became endowed with the power and protection of God's grace, his sense of manhood was rooted not only in surviving with dignity from day to day (which, in and of itself, was a heroic act for American bondmen), but also partly in religious devotion and situational open resistance.[74] The development of his masculine sense of self would have put him increasingly at odds with his owners, especially when his personal life was at stake.

Around 1789 "a person" from Baltimore, Maryland, offered Isaac Brokaw a large sum of money to purchase Quamino. Brokaw, who had earlier declined offers from Schenk and others to buy Quamino as a youth, asked the adult bondman "if he was willing to be sold." Quamino "replied in the negative," yet "the subject was left overnight for consideration."[75] This was the first time, as far as we know, that Quamino had openly or assertively opposed "his old master," something that he surely did not relish but was forced to do. His removal to Maryland would have separated him not only from Sarah, whom he married around 1788 and refers to in the *Memoir* as "my woman," but also from immediate family members and friends.[76] In addition to his religious empowerment and devotion, Quamino's masculine identity was undoubtedly based upon his tenuous family relations, notably with respect to Sarah.

Daniel Black, in *Dismantling Black Manhood*, argues that the brutal experience of bondage made it nearly impossible for enslaved males to exercise manhood as fathers, husbands, and warriors, the concept of manhood in precolonial West Africa that bondmen in America attempted, strenuously, to emulate. White hegemonic forces, Black insists, persistently undercut the ability of enslaved males to act as fathers, husbands, and protectors, who nevertheless coveted these unstable roles.[77] Edward Baptist examines the masculine identity of enslaved males from a different vantage point. In his illuminating essay on slavery in the antebellum plantation frontier, Baptist describes how adopting the role of caretaker enabled black men to assert themselves within the slave community, and provided them with the opportunity to establish relationships that critically assisted their own survival.[78] Like his male compatriots who took the precarious roles of father, husband, protector, and caretaker seriously, Quamino could not consider himself a man by failing to stand his ground on behalf of his loved ones, particularly his "woman," Sarah. In regards to Sarah's death in 1842, William Allinson wrote, she "was considered by those who knew her best, to be a woman of piety and worth, and not inferior to her husband—to whom, indeed, she was a helper in spiritual as well as temporal things."[79] Similar to the enslaved males delineated by Baptist, Quamino's sense of manhood was not only a social construction, but it was also a *relational* social construction in which Sarah played the most important role. In the end, he was left with no other choice but to defy Isaac Brokaw's proposal to sell him south, an act which irreparably altered their already fragile relationship.

A number of historians have cogently demonstrated how religion, the belief that God was on their side, played a critical role in fostering a rebellious consciousness among enslaved people.[80] Conventional wisdom indicates that Quamino's defiance of Isaac Brokaw's proposal to sell him was abetted by the support and strength he drew from his Christian faith. In historical terms, his Christian-inspired stance, as it were, breached the etiquette characteristic of all power relations—that is, the code of silence and consent—and carried "the force of a symbolic declaration of war."[81] On a personal level, his stance conveyed to Brokaw that there was a limit to his masked subservience, a limit to how far he would serve the patriarch's economic interests at the expense of his own well-being; it communicated to all his owners, in fact, that he was not merely a saleable object and would thus stand his ground when his humanity or sense of justice was violated. For a slave, especially one who had been intensely inculcated with the notion of black capitulation to white power, such an admission, public or private, would have been a significant psychological victory. But did this admission come without any costs? Did it not confirm the suspicion that certain Brokaw family members felt regarding the danger inherent in exposing slaves to Christianity? Did it not enhance Quamino's physical potency and in turn undermine the Brokaw men's masculine sensibilities? In short, did not this psychological victory imperil Quamino's life?

Perhaps even more important than his Christian-inspired, heightened sense of determination and self-worth, Quamino had allies in the Brokaw family. The patriarch's wife resolutely opposed the idea of sending him to Baltimore, declaring, "None of my slaves shall go there—that's Ginney [i.e., Guinea]." To her mind, even the upper South represented a distant and alien territory. It was the Brokaws' "eldest son," however, who, upon "discovering Quamino's unwillingness to be sold," successfully persuaded his father not to go through with the impending sale.[82]

Following Isaac Brokaw's death around 1789, "it was provided, that Quamino, his brother, and three sisters, should have the privilege of choosing an owner among their late master's children; or, if they preferred it, of seeking another purchaser." Not surprisingly, Quamino "chose the eldest son" (presumably Caspares Brokaw) as his new legal owner, in appreciation for his having saved him from possible removal to the distant South.[83] The bond between them was eventually shattered, however, when, several years later, "the faithful servant received from his master an unreasonable and severe blow, when he was conscious that he had done no wrong—which so wounded his feelings, that he immediately announced his determination to work for him no longer." The incensed owner "reminded him of the choice he had made," but changed his position after learning for the first time why Quamino had chosen him as his owner. Brokaw granted the bondman permission to look for a new owner, and around 1792 sold him to a neighbor named "Smock."[84]

The conflict between Quamino and Brokaw indicates that, although enslaved blacks were not legally protected by the law, they were still afforded some customary rights or privileges that they could use against their owners. Bondpeople fulfilled their obligations to their owners in return for recognition of certain rights, including reasonable standards of discipline.[85] Still, the practice of slave quitting (the means by which Silvia Dubois's mother, Dorcas Compton, was also able to replace her abusive owner) represented a direct affront to the authority of slaveholders; it struck at the very heart of white male patriarchy.[86] In other words, slave quitting involved an element of risk, endangering the life of the man or woman who dared to employ this tactic. A slave who decided to quit his or her owner needed an inviolable sense of moral conviction as much as local custom. For Quamino, this was provided through his strong religious faith; it empowered his decision to leave a man who had come to his rescue during a critical moment in his life.

The piety of Cuffy Barnet again serves as a critical means of contextualization. Cuffy was enslaved under Dr. Oliver Barnet, who practiced as a physician in New Germantown (Oldwick). Barnet was a deist: he advocated reason and logic over revelation or tradition as the basis for believing in God. His lack of religious devotion did not meet the approval of his bondman, who "audibly groaned over his master's frequent lapses from a correct life," and "fervently prayed, both in public and private, for his early conversion."[87] Even though Barnet owned Cuffy, the bondman did not necessarily view the physician as possessing a superior sense of morality and spirituality. This point is further demonstrated in a conversation that allegedly occurred between them. Barnet is said to have stated, "Cuffy, I intend to be buried on my own land, and have reserved a place for you close beside me. When I rise, you may also rise with me. Wait upon me in the other world the same as in this." And Cuffy retorted, "I am much obliged, but rather guess not. The Devil might come along some dark night and take the darkey for the Doctor."[88] This exchange (if it is in fact credible) speaks directly to Cuffy's Christian rectitude. Through the humble and deferential guise of Sambo, Cuffy declared that he did not need Barnet to help him get to heaven. This would be achieved through the merit of his own righteousness.

A similar righteous indignation made it impossible for Quamino to stop attending religious meetings and to endure Caspares Brokaw's abuse. As a child of God, he was empowered, if not required, to defend his humanity. With regard to William Boen's God-inspired refusal to cut down all the trees as his owner had ordered, his amanuensis wrote, "It was sufficient to test his faith and love; and though a simple circumstance, it was probably of great use to him ever after, as by it he was taught to be faithful in little things, and thus become ruler over more."[89] It appears that, like Boen, Quamino also had a moral imperative to defy his "old master," and thereby reaffirm the authority of his "new Master."

Why did Caspares Brokaw strike Quamino in the first place? Certainly, this act of violence was not elicited by any recalcitrant or indolent behavior on the part of Quamino. There are at least three plausible reasons to consider. First, as indicated earlier, slaveholders used naked force to maintain hegemony. Though Brokaw had previously acted as an ally of Quamino's, he was first and foremost his owner. The "unreasonable and severe blow" Brokaw dealt the "faithful servant" represented the brutal politics of slavery. The physical altercation between Bergen County resident Peter Kipp and his bondman Jack, in 1753, suggests that this was not an isolated occurrence. Kipp testified that, while he and Jack were heading to one of his fields, "on the road he gave the said negro a blow which the said negro resisted and fought with his master, striking him several blows." Afterward, Jack appropriated an ax, with which he "threatened to kill his said master and his son, and then destroy himself." Thereupon, Kipp "ran away" but later "returned with assistance."[90] Kipp's testimony at the trial does not mention that Jack had done anything wrong prior to responding violently to his owner's attack (for which the bondman was eventually burned to death). This leads us to believe that Kipp felt he could discipline his slave— his property—through the use of physical force whenever he decided such correction was necessary. A local New Jersey historian who has analyzed the incident concurs: though Kipp was "the first assailant . . . as a master," he deemed himself empowered to chastise the slave."[91] As Kipp saw it, he had the right, as a slaveowner, to strike Jack as a way of reinforcing his dominance over the slave—thinking that closely parallels Brokaw's striking of Quamino. And yet, secondly, Brokaw's attack was probably as much personal as it was political; it also reflected Brokaw's anger at the way in which Quamino's religiosity had undermined his authority. That is, Quamino's faith had threatened Brokaw's masculinity, which, invariably, was dependent upon the denial of that of the loyal captive.[92]

Third, Brokaw's attack bespeaks an owner who was intimidated by his slave. Though it has been discussed in previous chapters, the murder of Jacob Van Neste is again worth mentioning. Van Neste was wealthy, successful, and highly respected within his community, but he was unable to exercise complete control over his large and intimidating bondman. Thus Van Neste decided to help himself to the slave's tobacco, an act that he must have known would infuriate (and emasculate) the slave who had no choice but to endure the indignity. Van Neste succumbed to the temptations of his power and prestige, which had been compromised by his inability to conquer the black male menace effectively. Brokaw evidently felt likewise about Quamino, who now possessed not only physical but also spiritual power.

That said, not every white man who encountered Quamino was threatened or intimidated by his religiosity. In William Boen's case, in fact, he and his owner got along "very well" after "his change" or conversion experience; their relationship was so good, in fact, that William was later given his freedom.[93] Quamino's survival partly depended upon forming alliances with white males who perceived his faith as a positive asset, if not as an affirmation of white supremacy. In fact, it was white males who helped him to preserve his marriage to Sarah, "a slave on a neighbouring place." Shortly after they were married, she was "sold to a distance of five miles, and for some years they met only once a week." As a result, their fragile marriage and family life faced even greater uncertainty:

> One Sabbath morning he [Quamino] went to see her, and found that she and her infant had been sold, leaving her little son, a boy nearly four years old. She now had a hard mistress; but, through the efforts of her husband, she was purchased by a neighbour, and, at length, on the removal of the purchaser, Quamino induced his second master, Smock, (to whom he was sold when about thirty years old,) to buy her.[94]

Neither the anonymous "neighbour" nor Smock would have come to Quamino's aid had they perceived his religiosity as having a negative influence on him. Their willingness to do so suggests that, by living a virtuous (Christian) life, by continuing to project the image of himself as a good boy, Quamino was able to establish a rapport with a number of whites whose help he could solicit in times of crisis.

Quamino was in no position to solicit favors from whites as a religiously empowered slave imbued with a sense of his own self-worth. To put it differently, he was more likely to approach whites with utter deference grounded in religious humility. After Smock had sold him and Sarah to Dr. John Griffith of Essex County around 1798, Quamino, at the advisement of some friends, asked Griffith, "If I should outlive master, would master please to give me free?" Although his tone was meek and humble, the otherwise amiable physician, "losing his self-possession in angry excitement, vented much passionate language" toward "tender-spirited Quamino [who] burst into tears."[95] Griffith's acrimonious response to Quamino's request for freedom (made around the passing of New Jersey's gradual abolition law of 1804) indicates that the doctor was offended by what he perceived was a bold act on the part of his slave, whom he later admitted "would make out [well] if you were free."[96] As suggested here, though Quamino was endowed with God's grace, he had to tread cautiously and with humble deference around white males, including his allies. (Indeed, when John Griffith's son, William Griffith, later asked Quamino, "Would you like to be free?" Quamino hesitantly replied, "*I don't know, Sir.*")[97]

The death of John Griffith in 1805 further illustrates how Quamino's Christian identity was subjected to the dictates of race. As William Allinson writes,

> Quamino was sent to get advertisements printed, and to post and circulate them about the country; and, although he and his wife were included in the list of chattels, and he fully expected to be sold with the rest of the estate, he faithfully executed the commission. He carefully collected all the items of his master's property, in preparation for the sale, "with good will doing service, as to the Lord." The vendue having commenced, he and his wife became objects of much attention to the multitude gathered on the occasion, and Quamino was repeatedly asked whether they were to be sold.[98]

Once again, Quamino was put in a situation where he had to subordinate his status as a child of God to that of a humble slave whose fate was controlled by other men. Yet God had remained with him during his time of crisis. Writing about noted black abolitionist Frederick Douglass, Vincent Harding remarks, he "was not deeply involved in organized religion, neither while in slavery nor as a free man, but he did imbibe intensely of the nineteenth-century understanding of Providence, of the rational, loving, guiding hand of the Divine." "This religious conviction," he adds, "was of great importance, for it brought to his thought and life what might be called a radical hope, a strange and mysterious faith which . . . had a profoundly strengthening effect, allowing Douglass to maintain himself in the midst of discouraging realities."[99] Quamino had also trusted profoundly in the Divine, or God, seeking its love and guidance during his own moments of despair. And, like Douglass, Quamino derived strength from his religious convictions, which allowed him to push forward, as evidenced by his ability to do "good will" as in the name of the Lord. But, for him to have projected such strength may have invited the wrath of certain whites, which he could not risk when his marriage was hanging in the balance. When asked during the auction about where he and Sarah "were to be sold," Quamino appears to have remained mute. The bondman's silence and ensuing "relief" upon learning that he and Sarah now belonged to William Griffith, "who had manifested kindness and sympathy during the seven years" they toiled under William's father, convey humble deference and not an outward (bold) hope in the power of God.[100]

The notion that there was a time and place for carrying oneself as God's child under slavery appears even more evident during Quamino and Sarah's 1806 manumission interview in Burlington County. William Griffith, a prominent Burlington abolitionist, had promised Quamino that he would have them manumitted. But first the couple had to prove to the manumission committee that they were in good health and would not become burdens on society. With so much at stake, a strategy was needed. On reaching Griffith's office (the site of the interview), Quamino says, "I made my bow to the [white] gentlemen." When asked how he felt, the bondman responded, "I feel very well, I tank you, Sir: I feel very well in my limbs."[101] His deferential bow and response signify more than slavish conformity; they also comprised a deft performance of black manhood and survival. An important aspect of black manhood is the "capacity to think, talk, and act quickly," all of which were required of Quamino as he fielded the many questions asked him.[102] His performance met with success: the committee concluded that he and Sarah "would be able to do well for themselves." In this and other such performances, Quamino was living up to his responsibility as a family man. Correspondingly, Quamino explained to William Allinson that he and Sarah stood before the committee "as if we were just married."[103] Quamino saw their interview as a marriage ceremony in which he played the role of groom, of a responsible adult who was the head and protector of his family—a man who would be more able to exercise or fulfill these roles.

Even so, Quamino's masculine posture in this instance was necessarily divorced from the power he received from God's grace. The dictates of survival required that he temporarily subordinate God, reminding us of how enslaved males were unable to present themselves as men fully on their own terms. Life as a free man did not necessarily change matters. Upon his and Sarah's liberation, William Griffith "promised to show Quamino that he would teach him how to get along"; and, in fact, Quamino and Sarah "were then hired to him for ten dollars per month."[104] Could Quamino realistically assume a manly posture buttressed by God's grace when he depended on the mercy and guidance of white males in a world where free blacks were characterized as lazy, slovenly, and inferior?

Conclusion

Despite his efforts, William Allinson is unable to prevent us from conceiving of Quamino in terms contrary to the nonthreatening romantic racialist Negro. Three incidents in particular—(1) Quamino's initial decision to attend religious meetings, (2) his refusal to go to Maryland, and (3) his decision to quit Caspares Brokaw for assaulting him—reveal that Quamino was capable of acting deceptively as well as with rage. Could it have been possible for Quamino to feel no anger or even hatred for men who cursed him, abused him, and fragmented his family—men who treated him as if he were chattel? How was this possible when his faith confirmed his inclusion within the human family? Allinson may have been cognizant of Quamino's rage, because, after all, he indirectly brings these issues to our attention. Yet, had Allinson acknowledged Quamino's rage in the *Memoir* (and how it was fueled by his reception of God's glory), he would have been unable effectively to depict Quamino as a victim of racial oppression who, as a result of his Christian passivity, represented no threat to white society.

Beneath this image was a man who may well have been somewhat skeptical of white people. When William Griffith told Quamino that he would liberate him, Quamino decided not to share this news with Sarah. As he told William Allinson, "I never told my woman—no, Sir, I kept it still."[105] Although Griffith had shown much "kindness and sympathy" to Quamino, the bondman still did not completely trust him at his word. One can understand his position when considering how previous white male allies had eventually betrayed his confidence. Thus, while Quamino's decision to withhold Griffith's momentous decree from Sarah reflects how he embraced the role of family protector (that is, he wanted to spare Sarah from possible heartbreak), it also suggests how Quamino was necessarily distrustful of whites.

Indeed, the politics of the *Memoir* belie the reality of Quamino's precarious existence as a black male slave in American society. Despite his demonstration of compliance, his owners demonstrated varying degrees of hostility toward him. These episodes expose the contrived physical rendition of Quamino as nonthreatening (as discussed in chapter 1). They suggest that Quamino may have in fact possessed real physical presence—enough for Schenk to terrorize him through murderous public spectacles, and enough for Brokaw to attack him without real provocation. In his physical prime, Quamino was the black man whom Schenk feared would possibly rise up against the institution of slavery, and whom Brokaw feared had found a new master in God. In a way, the *Memoir* illuminates white men's anxiety over the presence of enslaved males in the eighteenth century. Alternatively, it speaks to why Quamino and other black males would turn to Christianity to mitigate their physical potency and enhance their reputations as good boys. It points to how Christianity emerged as a dynamic weapon in their lives, and had multiple social, psychic, political, and spiritual dimensions.

Notwithstanding the psychological trauma that he experienced in slavery and literally took to his deathbed, Quamino was a shrewd survivor of racial oppression who had, in a sense, learned how to psychologize white people. Although rendered an "impossible witness" to his own life story through William Allinson's manipulative romantic racialism, Quamino nevertheless exemplifies the nature of the black threat in early American society—a black person who was necessarily and strategically deceptive.[106]

Chapter 5

Work, Family, and Day-to-Day Survival on an Old Farm

Much like Quamino, Dick Melick survived the hardships of eighteenth-century rural Northern slavery by navigating cautiously around whites, while at the same time embracing the perilous responsibilities of father, husband, and protector under bondage. In a manner similar to, yet different, from Quamino, Dick shows that not all bondmen embraced Yombo's strategy of overt resistance. Still, in his own way, as the consummate family man, Dick was a strong and resilient bondman. This was no small feat when considering that he was as "dark" as Yombo (whose skin color was "coal black"), and probably had a larger physique than either Yombo or Quamino.[1] Whites would have thus been as aware of Dick's physical presence (and the potential threat that it represented) as they were of the "black" bodies of his two compatriots. But, despite this and numerous other hardships, Dick coveted his role as a dedicated family man.

Andrew Mellick provides a rather imaginative account of Dick and his family's arrival at Aaron Malick's Bedminster Township farmstead "in the spring of 1798":

> In fancy we see these colored people as they reach their new home, and stand a little abashed and nervous while receiving welcome from their new mistresses. Dick is of a good dark color, heavy-set and dignified in appearance, courteous and quiet in demeanor, while Nance does the talking and laughing for the family through thick lips which partially cover a full set of white teeth. She is lighter in color than her husband, and very short—not to say fat. You know where her waist is because you see her apron strings, but with that feminine badge removed, to locate her zone would be like establishing the equator—a matter of calculation rather than visual certainty. Her breadth affords a good cover for her three frightened children, who peer shyly from behind her ample skirts at the new "white folks," at the same time taking curious note of Daniel's flock who form a background to their mother and grandmother. . . . A few pleasant words, emphasized with cookies, soon calm their agitation, and it is not long before parents and youngsters are at their ease and taking kindly to their new surroundings.[2]

Needless to say, this passage reflects how Mellick's book was representative of late nineteenth-century hegemonic literature that racialized or essentialized dark peoples.[3] Conversely, Mellick's negative, reductionist depiction of Dick and Nance speaks to how the vicissitudes of bondage shaped the gender dynamics of their marriage, requiring Nance to assume certain roles of family leadership that invariably undermined Dick's patriarchal status. "Every one said," Mellick maintains, "that Dick was a 'most likely nigger'; every one was right, for he was an exemplary, pious black of sterling parts, and his family but reflected the virtues of the sire."[4] Dick, as this comment suggests, projected the image of a responsible, Christian, and dominant family man. Yet the truth of the matter was that he was unable to exercise manhood fully on his own terms, a reality that may have had a great impact on his wife and children. That is, we must seriously consider that Nance's burdens as an enslaved woman were related partly to the particular hardships of her husband, who represented a greater physical threat to white society and could exercise his manhood only in limited ways.

In addition to their gender-related hardships, Dick and Nance's daily lives, as we shall see, were often devoid of adult interaction with other blacks and consumed with hard, dangerous work. Still, to borrow the words of Shane White, they "were not passive ciphers, helplessly swept along by currents of repression and discrimination and controlled solely by whites."[5] They refused to allow slavery to strip them of their humanity, of how they perceived themselves as a respectable man and woman.

The couple's first known owner was General John Taylor of Tewksbury Township, who "offered Dick and his family to Aaron [Malick]" after "he had become financially embarrassed, and finding it necessary to sell some of his slaves."[6] In this respect, they were more fortunate than many other enslaved blacks, for many New Jersey slaveowners had little compunction about severing blacks' family ties.[7] It is difficult to approximate how long Dick and his family were enslaved under Taylor. Even so, it seems reasonable to assume that they spent some years in Tewksbury prior to their arrival in Bedminster.

When the family arrived at Aaron Malick's farm and tannery in 1798, Dick was about forty-nine years old and Nance around age thirty-seven.[8] Nance may have had some European ancestry, since Andrew Mellick described her as having a lighter skin color than her husband, whose African roots were slightly more discernible. Dick was also known by the name "Ballod," which approximates the name "Balla," found among the Hausa, Mende, Bangi, Bobangi, Poto, and Ngombe peoples of Africa.[9] Thus, it is possible that, like Yombo, Dick was a native-born African.

While enslaved under Aaron Malick, Nance was responsible for the domestic chores as well as nursing the old owner and his wife, Charlotte, while Dick—who served as a kind of body servant for Aaron—eventually came to manage the farm on his own. The enslaved couple had five children: Diana (also called Deon), born August 9, 1791; Sam, born September

1794; Dick, born December 22, 1796; Joe, born March 4, 1800; and Ann, born March 4, 1806. The family remained intact until Aaron's death in 1809, at which point the four older children were sold to four separate owners; they were to serve as indentured servants for terms ranging from seven years, for eighteen-year-old Diana, to nineteen years, for nine-year-old Joe. Nance, Dick (the father), and baby Ann remained on the farm.[10] Andrew Mellick does not mention it, but manumission records for Somerset County indicate that Nance was manumitted by John Davenport of Bedminster, in 1821.[11] Dick, conversely, does not appear in the manumission records, which suggests that he died prior to Nance's manumission. Neither does baby Ann, whose fate is unknown. We do know, however, that young Dick was freed by Bedminster resident Jacob Kline in 1824; that Diana apparently gave birth to a daughter named Nancy in 1805, and was freed by Margaret Biggs of Readington Township, Hunterdon County, in 1812; and that Sam was freed by "John McCown, a Pluckamin [Somerset] farmer."[12] Sam supposedly "made his home at Dr. Van de Veers [probably Dr. Henry Van De Veer of Hillsborough Township] and married one of the doctors [sic] colored girls, raised several children, and there died." Apparently, moreover, "Sam had a failing, he liked rum," a vice that he certainly did not learn from his image-conscious parents.[13] As a freedman, however, Sam was able to create a relatively stable, long-term family life for himself, something that his father had strenuously attempted but was unable to accomplish.

Gender and Rural Isolation

The contributions of Shane White and Graham Hodges are indispensable to our understanding of Dick and Nance, who were enslaved within the orbit of New York City but, at the same time, lived a rural existence, like their compatriots in Monmouth County. White and Hodges have demonstrated that slavery in both places was a harsh institution, in some respects worse than Southern bondage. The small size of slaveholdings (on average about two or three slaves per family), the frequent dispersal of slaves among white relatives, and the high turnover of slaveholders, was detrimental to black family formation.[14] Similarly, as Gary Nash and Jean Soderlund have demonstrated for Pennsylvania, the Northern bonded family was, at best, a fragile creation.[15] The modest holdings and cruel parceling of enslaved persons also impeded the development of black culture by forcing (to varying degrees) assimilation or adoption of European culture. This type of ethnic isolation was especially difficult to overcome in the hinterland, where enslaved Northern blacks were most prevalent. White writes that, on a day-to-day basis, rural slaves "came into contact with a much smaller number of compatriots than did their urban counterparts, which inevitably limited development of the networks that were so extensive and important for city slaves."[16] As pointed out by Hodges, "the most common condition for Monmouth's slaves was to live and work in ethnic isolation."[17]

The 1790 census, though incomplete, helps us to contextualize Dick and Nance's social existence under the ownership of General John Taylor in Tewksbury. It reported only 326 total blacks (268 enslaved and 58 free) for the townships of Lebanon, Readington, and Tewksbury combined. Apparently this tabulation was reasonably accurate: the more comprehensive 1810 census gives a total of 365 blacks for the three Hunterdon County townships. In Tewksbury that year, there were 126 blacks (66 enslaved and 60 free) out of a total population of 1,308. Blacks represented just 9.6 percent of Tewksbury's population; there were only four black persons (women, men, and children) per square mile.[18] This situation does not bespeak a very active social life for free and enslaved blacks in Tewksbury.

One of the many tragedies of American slavery (particularly endemic to the rural North) was the frequent movement of captives from one isolated area to another. The lack of black comradeship Dick and Nance experienced in Tewksbury may have only slightly improved in neighboring Bedminster Township. The 1790 census indicates that there were just 173 blacks (169 enslaved and 4 free) out of a total population of 1,197 in Dick and Nance's future home. Only 14.4 percent of Bedminster's population was black; there were just 5.3 blacks per square mile. Bedminster's reported black population in 1790 had not changed much by 1810: the enslaved population was 161, and no free blacks were recorded, an indication, perhaps, of a hostile environment for persons of African descent.[19]

The isolation experienced by enslaved persons in Tewksbury and Bedminster was not representative of all New Jersey blacks, however. By 1790 East Jersey was a major center of slaves in the North and, according to Peter Wacker, there existed especially dense areas of blacks in "eastern Bergen County, central Somerset with some adjoining townships in Hunterdon and Middlesex, and northern Monmouth County."[20] Enslaved women and men in these rural areas at the end of the eighteenth century had more opportunities than in previous years to establish networks among themselves as well as more stable relationships with black people in general. But these were still difficult tasks.

By comparison, captives in West Jersey (where slavery was a relatively minor institution) generally lived lonelier lives. As evidence, in 1790, Sussex County, roughly 890 square miles, had a total of 504 blacks (439 enslaved and 65 free), or 0.5 blacks per square mile. Burlington County was around 870 square miles; however, its total black population that year was a paltry 825 (227 enslaved and 598 free). Here, too, was less than one black person per square mile. The lack of significant black population density also characterized the smaller West Jersey counties in 1790. Cape May

County, for example, about 250 square miles, had a total black population of 155 (141 enslaved and 14 free); that is, less than one black person per square mile. This was also the case with regard to Cumberland County: around 520 square miles, with 258 total blacks (120 enslaved and 138 free).[21] The 1810 census reported that the black population in Sussex had increased to 747 (32.5 percent of the population); in Burlington to 1,039 (20.6 percent); in Cape May to 192 (19.3 percent); and in Cumberland to 589 (56.2 percent).[22] These percentages, in terms of the number of black persons per square mile, do not reflect significant changes in the black population in these four counties.

Clearly, the evidence here supports Shane White and Graham Hodges's views of slave isolation. As was typical of rural Northern bondpeople during the late eighteenth and early nineteenth centuries, Dick and Nance lived without the daily support of an extended black community, which was crucial to the survival of enslaved blacks in the South and urban North. Indeed, since they lived on the periphery of both Hunterdon and Somerset Counties' denser black populaces, the couple may have been even more isolated than many of their rural and urban Northern counterparts.

What does this analysis mean in terms of gender? For Nance, it indicates that she did not have access to the type of dynamic female slave camaraderie that, Deborah Gray White argues, characterized slave life on Southern plantations. According to White, if slave women "seemed exceptionally strong it was partly because they often functioned in groups and derived strength from numbers."[23] This was not the experience of most women enslaved in New York's hinterland, though there were exceptions. Writing about her privileged childhood in rural Middlesex County, Margaret Nevius Van Dyke Malcolm recalls that, after her grandfather's female slaves had completed their work "each day in the Winter, they went to their spinning wheels, kept in the kitchen."[24] As Deborah Gray White has written, "female slave domestic work sealed the bonds of womanhood forged in the fields and other work places."[25] Given the scarcity of black women in Bedminster, Nance probably had to depend on both Charlotte Malick and her daughter-in-law, Margaret Melick, for some semblance of friendship, and perhaps for family security too.[26]

Although Nance was unable to partake in bonding experiences with other black women on the Old Farm, she did not succumb to her circumstances. Specifically, she and Dick were able to forge some semblance of an alternative culture of survival that helped to soothe the pain of their enslavement in the rural Bedminster area: they not only attended social events, but also organized annually an elaborate dinner for their friends during the Christmas holiday.[27] Thus, despite overwhelming circumstances, they managed to create a meaningful social life for themselves that was perhaps as meaningful as that of many enslaved urban blacks. Still, we must acknowledge that living in rural isolation was a harsh aspect of their daily lives that was impossible for them, or any other enslaved person, to overcome completely. This was especially true in the case of Nance, who was relegated to domestic service and always at the beck and call of her owners. While it is conceivable that working and living in Aaron Malick's home gave Nance certain material privileges, it is equally plausible that her life in this house resembled that of a jailed prisoner under close surveillance.[28]

By contrast, Dick's position as general farmer not only provided him with a greater degree of mobility, but also likely put him into contact with a wider circle of people. Still, it would be incorrect to assume that rural isolation did not greatly affect his life. Significantly, drinking alcohol, gambling with dice, and fiddling and dancing were common activities among bondmen in eighteenth-century New York City. This vibrant underground black culture, which typically manifested in black-owned taverns and dance houses, was critical to enabling bondmen to exercise their manhood in the company of other black males. Bondmen did not define themselves as "men" through interactions with women only; they also did so with other men within their own masculine spaces.[29] The type of social environments that facilitated the masculinization of urban black males did not, however, exist in either Tewksbury or Bedminster, or in much of the early Somerset County area, for that matter.

Hunting provided a possible alternate setting for forging or performing manhood. According to Nicolas Proctor, hunting was a critical masculine proving ground for antebellum Southern whites and, to a lesser degree, enslaved blacks. For white males, the hunt enabled them to demonstrate their prowess, self-control, and mastery. Frequently accompanied by their slaves into the field, owners used hunting outings to confirm white supremacy.[30] The enslaved, however, viewed the hunt much differently, namely, as "an opportunity to ameliorate their condition." For enslaved blacks, the hunt, or the game they acquired from the hunt, "provided them with a supplementary food source, an item for trade, and a measure of autonomy." But, rather than keep their kills to themselves, enslaved hunters would share them with their friends and family. In doing so, enslaved hunters "strengthened the power and cohesion of the slave community as a whole."[31] Further, by sharing their game, enslaved hunters assumed the coveted masculine role of provider and, in the process, challenged the emasculating nature of white (slave) society. That is to say, enslaved hunters denied the totality of their owners' power and confirmed their own masculine prestige to their family and friends.[32] At the same time, hunting was a male bonding experience. Kenneth Greenberg, for example, has interpreted the woods of the hunt as a space where black and white men "played together, away from the world of women," but never "in such a way that threatened bondage."[33]

In her recollections, Margaret Malcolm wrote how "in the Winter, all the gentlemen in the country [including the men in her family] would take a long, covered, four-horse wagon or team, and fill [it] with provisions, and three or four Negroes, and tents, [and they would] start for a gaming expedition in the Pines, generally lasting three or four weeks, a regular shooting frolic, returning with deer, rabbits, quail, everything in the game line including cranberries, enough to last a year, a barrel of them." It appears that hunting expeditions also empowered the "Negroes" mentioned here, allowing them to interact with one another, if not to demonstrate their masculine prowess. If "Grandpa, Father, Uncle Isaac and Negroes started in high glee" during these festive occasions, as Malcolm maintains, then the hunt would have meant as much to the black participants as it did to the men in Malcolm's family.[34] This point is worth mentioning because such masculine interactions were beyond the reach of Dick and most other enslaved males in and around Somerset County. In a sense, slavery in the rural North impeded the masculine development of black males to an even greater degree than did Southern bondage. Small wonder, then, that Dick relished his role as a dedicated family man. He turned to, perhaps even depended on, his family for masculine empowerment.

The gendered lives of slaves in the Somerset County area were not stunted solely by rural isolation. Another contributing factor was that black people were not a monolithic group who thought and behaved in exactly the same ways, and who saw themselves as having a common destiny. Consequently, conflicts and tensions—no doubt exacerbated by their oppression—naturally existed among persons in bondage.[35] To illustrate, Tone, the slave of Somerset resident Matthew Ten Eyck, was tried in court in 1771, "for stealing bacon & tobacco" from another of Ten Eyck's bondmen, Simon.[36] Tensions among blacks in the Somerset area could also turn fatally violent, as when, in 1767, James Caster's bondman Harry "came to Rynier Van Neste's house and told him that he had killed Jupiter," a fellow slave who belonged to Jeromes Van Neste. Harry confessed to striking "Jupiter on [the] head with a stand, the foot of which was a square block weighing 5–6 pounds."[37] Moreover, in 1802 a slave named Brown belonging to Philip Case of Hunterdon County killed a fellow slave, with whom he had argued earlier in the day, over "some slight provocation" as they went into the kitchen later that evening. Brown struck his victim on the head with a trammel that he seized from the fireplace. He subsequently was hanged for his crime.[38] Blacks also held low opinions of each other. Silvia Dubois, who has on several occasions graced the pages of this study, had nothing but contempt for "a cowardly nigger."[39]

To this point, Dick and Yombo were probably not the best of friends on the Old Farm. They had different family obligations (unlike Dick, Yombo lived apart from his slave wife), strategies for dealing with whites (Dick acted deferentially, whereas Yombo was openly defiant), as well as separate work spaces on the Malick plantation (Dick was general farmer and Yombo a tanner). Evidently, the two men interacted mainly in the outer kitchen and, even there, Yombo occupied an area by the fireplace that functioned as his personal space.[40] Indeed, would a churchgoing family man like Dick (whom whites considered a "most likely nigger") have closely associated himself with a malcontent, non-Christian like Yombo (who was prone to thievery and "outbreaks")? By the same token, can we assume that Yombo had much if any respect for the way Dick lived his life as a docile and humble Christian? Although rural isolation and the common oppression they shared as enslaved males might have encouraged Dick and Yombo to develop a cordial relationship, these factors did not necessarily compel them to view one another as natural allies who instinctively sought out the other's company. Divergent personalities, value systems, and family obligations were not easily overcome even on farms and plantations where only a few blacks lived—factors that could impede the ability of slaves to construct models of masculinity and femininity for themselves.

Modes of Survival

How did Dick and Nance survive their isolation and precarious family life? Andrew Mellick would argue that their complacent behavior was largely a consequence of the "kindly" treatment afforded slaves in Somerset County.[41] It cannot be denied, however, that Northern bondage—that is, the small holdings, close living conditions between black and white, and the almost complete absence of gang labor—provided slaves with some leverage when dealing with their owners. We may assume that, out of necessity, allies for Northern bondwomen came in the form of white women, with whom they had intimate and regular contact in the household. For example, Mellick writes that Nance was Charlotte Malick's "devoted attendant, cook, and skilful housekeeper," and was later "equally faithful" to Margaret Melick.[42] The memoir of Margaret Malcolm provides another, more interesting example: upon the death of her Middlesex County mistress, Lydia Van Dyke, in 1840, the bondwoman Peggy Van Dyke, in addition to receiving her freedom, inherited all of Lydia's "parlor furniture . . . $700.00 to build a 'shack' and some silver, to recompense her for her faithful service."[43] Presumably, Lydia and Peggy had developed a close friendship in the "small roomed house" they occupied together on the Van Dyke plantation. Some bondwomen went to great lengths to demonstrate their faithfulness to their mistresses. In 1769, for example, an anonymous bondwoman of Burlington County attempted to rescue her mistress, who had been shot and brutally beaten by her jealous husband.[44] (Domestic violence knew no racial boundaries either.) Nance may have had strong feelings for her mistresses, because, according to Mellick, her display of grief at Charlotte's death on March 13, 1802, "was as deep and sincere as that of any other member of the household."[45] His comment suggests that Nance grieved solely out of love for Charlotte; he fails to consider that her sorrow was probably more a consequence of losing her semblance of family protection. As we shall see, Charlotte was fond of Nance's family, strong evidence not only of the bond that existed between the two women, but also of the matron's role as the enslaved family's principal protector.

But even if Nance was able to have meaningful relationships with her mistresses, there is no reason to believe that these relationships would have been based on racial equality. As Elizabeth Fox-Genovese has pointed out, although "gender ascribed white and black women to a common sphere within the household," they were separated by "race and class."[46] Andrew Mellick explains that Charlotte Malick, a descendent of a Quaker family that disproved of the institution of slavery, initially was against her husband's decision to buy Nance's family. Subsequently, her "affections soon went out to these worthy bondspeople, causing her prejudice against slavery to wane daily."[47] Charlotte's racial paternalism suggests that she became cognizant of who was the slave and who was the mistress in her house. Nance was certainly also aware.

Dick's relationship with Aaron Malick and his son, Daniel Melick (who lived on the farm with his family and was his father's business partner), was certainly also strained by the realities of race and class as well as gender.[48] As a sexually virile and thickly built black man, Dick could potentially subvert his owners' dominance over women, children, and slaves. Indeed, he constituted an even greater threat to them than Yombo, whose club foot and bow-legs mitigated his physical potency. The existence of such tensions would have undermined the possibility of racial egalitarianism between Dick and his adult male owners, despite Andrew Mellick's claim that "for a number of years much happiness in their mutual relations came to bond and free; their lives moved on with but little friction," save, of course, "an occasional outbreak from Yombo."[49] As Quamino's bondage (discussed in the previous chapter) demonstrates, it behooved enslaved males to tread with caution even around white males who had proved themselves to be critical allies. If anything, Dick, Aaron, and Daniel realized that the prosperity of the Old Farm (and the preservation of Dick's family) depended largely upon their getting along, if only in a superficial manner.

Outside the white household there were other more important avenues for social contact for enslaved blacks, especially at church. Dick and Nance were devout Christians who regularly attended church on Sundays. Like many captives, they probably attended their owners' church: Zion Lutheran Church in New Germantown (Oldwick), where Aaron Malick usually worshipped.[50] The enslaved couple had to sit in the "gallery" along with the other black churchgoers, among whom were some of the same blacks they entertained during the Christmas holiday.[51] Despite its racist implications, the gallery may have actually helped to facilitate a sense of camaraderie among African Americans, as well as soothed their painful week-long bout with isolation.[52] At any rate, there can be little doubt that white church services provided Nance, Dick, and their compatriots with some needed release from the strictures of bondage. But it was probably the happenings outside of church that meant the most to them and other blacks in the rural North: Sunday church services for slaves were occasions for visiting, sharing news, and picnicking with other blacks. It was also a time for potential courting; not surprisingly, enslaved men and women took pains to look their very best for the services.[53]

In a sense, Sunday was like a one-day holiday for the enslaved. William Moraley, an indentured servant in colonial New Jersey, commented that, on Sunday, the slaves' only free day during the week (except in the event of a slave's wedding day), "they banish . . . all Thoughts of the Wretchedness of their Condition."[54] Sundays may have allowed slaves like Dick and Nance—that is, servants living in sparsely settled backcountry areas—to get from other blacks what they could not get from their owners: unconditional emotional support and social equality. But they would first actually have to congregate, which was no small task in the densely forested, hilly, rocky, often pathless, and expansive backcountry.[55] The social activities of Silvia Dubois suggest that some blacks managed to do so. Dubois recalled going to church regularly and walking "a good way to [camp] meeting—to Pennington, to Princeton, to Hopewell, and to Harlingen," adding that, "I'd walk ten miles to a camp meeting—further, too." Not surprisingly, she was indifferent about returning to her owners: "I guess no nigger was ever so glad to get home," she remarked.[56] In a similar tone, Moraley noted that, at the end of each Sunday, slaves would "return to their Slavery," that is, back to the realm of their owners' property.[57]

The holiday season was particularly significant for Dick and Nance. To demonstrate his ancestors' benevolence, Andrew Mellick underscores the fact that, every year between Christmas and New Year's Day, the slaves on the Old Farm would give a party to which only the "older colored people of respectability were invited." Blacks belonging to the Gaston, Kline, Linn, Van Doren, Van der Veer, and other local white families, he quips, used "large and heavy words" and addressed one another "as Mr., Mrs., or Miss." The entire feast was "under Nance's supervision, and in quality and quantity was credible alike to her as a cook and to her old master as showing the liberality and kind feelings he extended to his slaves." (Mellick explains that, as testimony of Aaron Malick's affection for Nance and Dick, he chose not to refer to them as slaves during this special occasion, saying instead, "*No, Sah, Sarvunts if you please.*")[58] From this we can deduce both that Nance earned high praise and attention at the Christmas parties, and that she drew strength from her day of celebrity around her family and friends. At any rate, she was a major contributor to and organizer of the "colored society" that existed in the area.

The Christmas parties were equally empowering for Dick. As Andrew Mellick posits, "at the supper, after a lengthy grace fervently uttered by the one [slave] supposed to be the most gifted, even staid Dick Melick, who took upon himself the service of the table, displayed airs quite foreign to his generally modest deportment."[59] Arguably, Dick viewed the holiday dinners as rare occasions where he could safely assert himself both verbally and physically in the presence of whites. Similar to those patriarchs who traditionally carve and dole out the family turkey on Thanksgiving Day, Dick's "service of the table" signified a public exercise in manly authority, reaffirming his family status in the presence of those blacks and whites in attendance. "As a social construct," Nicolas Proctor emphasizes, "gender meant little unless verified by appreciable observers."[60] In the end, the Christmas parties were as much Dick's time to assume center stage as it was Nance's—if not more so.

The couple's spirits were also lifted by the fact that, during this holiday week, they could visit other blacks and wear their best attire.[61] Wearing good clothing allowed the enslaved to distinguish the owner's time from their own. Decent, clean, and expressive attire (whites generally perceived the latter as comic and distasteful) bolstered slaves' self-esteem and reinforced their self-awareness—in other words, demonstrated their personal pride. Equally significant is that such attire symbolized black peoples' rejection of their oppressors' values.[62]

For Dick, wearing his best clothes also reinforced his status as a dignified family man, as Andrew Mellick's description of Dick and his family's departure for the militia celebration known as General Training reveals. First, "Nance and the children were placed on chairs in [the] front" of the wagon. Then "Dick, in his Sunday clothes and displaying a most conspicuous nosegay, would . . . seat himself on the foreboard, seize the reins, and with the stalk of a long whip against his shoulder and the lash hanging behind him, would set off with his happy family."[63] In part, this scene reinforces Aaron Malick's paternalism, for the "happy family" would not have been able to attend this much-anticipated affair without either Aaron's consent or the use of his horse and carriage. Moreover, the elements that Mellick describes—the separate seating arrangements, Dick's accentuated "Sunday clothes," and his mastery of the beasts—form a composite of Dick as undisputed family boss. His good attire, and the manly respectability it conveyed, reinforced the bondman's (tenuous) patriarchal rule. It goes without saying that he must have relished those moments, particularly during the week-long holiday season, when his manhood was on full display.

One might assume that, given Dick and Nance's isolation in rural Bed-minster, they would have made it a point not to cut off any interaction with other blacks. And yet, at their annual dinners they limited invitations to the respectable. Perhaps they did not feel that living in bondage meant having to settle for whatever company happened to exist in their neigh-borhood. After all, they were Christian, respectable, and mature persons, and people generally want to keep company with persons who they believe are more like themselves. Should enslaved people have been any different? Certainly, respectability was not just a European-American concept. Olau-dah Equiano, for example, who allegedly was kidnapped from West Africa as a child and sold into slavery, wrote of the barbaric and uncouth behavior of Europeans as compared to the civility of native Africans.[64] Older blacks like Dick, Nance, and Yombo may have retained more of African culture than did the younger generation.

In reality, though, enslaved blacks in the eighteenth-century rural North, both young and old, had limited access to authentic African cul-ture. Thus it is understandable that the enslaved here would succumb, albeit differently, to what Ira Berlin has called "the larger forces of Euro-American life."[65] In no uncertain terms, bondpeople's conformity to the dominant European-American culture "confirmed rather than challenged the existing order." But, at the same time, white traditions, such as dinner parties at Christmastime, allowed the captives "to express themselves more fully than the narrow boundaries of slavery ordinarily allowed."[66] In retro-spect, Nance and Dick's exploitation of these social outlets allowed them to enliven not only their own existence, but also that of their children, com-patriots, and owners.

But was Dick and Nance's use of white culture totally apolitical? Andrew Mellick wrote the following about their Christmas parties: "Although whis-key, cider, and metheglin [a kind of mead] were always furnished the lowly guests, a too-free indulgence would not have been countenanced by the hosts, nor was it ever known, the whole party always conducting themselves most decorously and politely, endeavoring as far as possible to be 'jes like white folks.'"[67] On the face of it, or as Mellick would have us believe, the slaves' modest consumption of alcohol reflects only their desire to emu-late whites. Yet, when considered in the context of whites' general concern over slave drinking, this modest alcohol consumption takes on a different meaning, one that speaks to Dick and Nance's attempt to protect their good Christian names, their only real means of defense against the horrors of Northern slavery.

Although the consumption of liquors or spirits was a vital part of everyday life in eighteenth-century New Jersey and throughout the American colonies, whites were never completely at ease with slaves' access to alcohol. This sentiment is reflected in a 1797 New Jersey law that made it illegal for tavern-keepers and inn-holders to sell "vinous, spirituous, or strong liquors" to servants and slaves without their owners' consent.[68] From the perspective of whites, slaves' consumption of alcohol was a double-edged sword, of sorts. On the one hand, permitting slaves to drink alcohol was a means through which owners could demonstrate their benevolence. For example, during mealtimes, Garritee (or Charity) Quick of Somerset County would stand in the kitchen doorway holding a flask of apple whiskey, from which the family slaves, beginning with the oldest, would take a drink and then depart, with hat in hand, thanking her in either Dutch or English.[69] On the other hand, alcohol could seriously affect black behavior. For one, liquor caused some slaves, such as Tom and Betty Ryder of Somerset, to take their own lives by accident. In 1794 the "very much intoxicated" Tom fell off a steep bank and died, and in 1803 Ryder, "intoxicated with liquor," drowned as she attempted to cross a brook.[70] Liquor also induced slaves to escape. A serial runaway, Jack of Middlesex County, had again escaped in 1774, a habit that was fueled "by drinking too much, and other misdemeanors."[71] Similarly, George of Hunterdon County, who allegedly was "much addicted to liquor," escaped in 1783 "in a drunken fit, leaving his best cloathes behind him."[72]

But, most disconcerting to whites, liquor emboldened blacks against their owners. As we have already seen in chapter 2, the Somerville slave conspiracy of 1734 was undermined by an intoxicated bondman who boldly told a white male passerby that, in due time, he would learn that the bondman was his equal as a man. Liquor likewise inspired the fugitives Linden (of Somerset County) and Peter (of Salem County) to challenge white authority. As Linden's owner put it in 1767, "He is addicted to strong liquor and when drunk troublesome"; several years later, in 1776, Peter's owner stated that the captive was "fond of strong liquor, and when drunk very saucy, and talks a great deal of his abilities as a farmer."[73] Another revealing incident of alcohol-related black resistance involved the bondman Sam, who belonged to highly vilified New Jersey Tory Bernardus La Grange. In 1775 Sam pled drunkenness as the cause of his assault and insult of John Beekman. Sam must have been under the influence, for he attacked Beekman—a white man—in his own home.[74]

Given these incidents, it is not surprising that, when William Veghte of Somerset County expressed interest in buying Enoch Johnson's slave, he inquired if the slave was faithful in his duties and "free of the vice of drunkenness." After Johnson assured Veghte of this, Veghte paid him $375 for the slave. Around 1820, however, Veghte sued Johnson for deceit. According to Veghte, the bondman possessed a number of faults, not the least of which was his addiction "to the habit of Drinking."[75]

In light of all the controversy surrounding New Jersey bondpeople's drinking of alcohol, one can discern why Dick and Nance made sure that they and their black guests did not overindulge in strong drink during their Christmas parties. The 1834 memoir of William Boen, a poor, illiterate, and devout former Burlington County slave, emphasizes that he had "obtained the friendship, esteem, and respect of all classes of his fellow-men" in part because of the alcohol-free lifestyle he adopted while in bondage.[76] Had Boen ever been known to indulge in any kind of alcohol consumption, he would have jeopardized all the respect and good will accorded him. Similarly, any significant amount of alcohol consumption by Dick and Nance and their friends would have sullied the couple's image as virtuous, trustworthy blacks.[77] Thus the modest drinking of alcohol during their Christmas parties was not simply an emulation of white behavior; it is also an indication of their acute sense of survival. More than just celebratory occasions, the Christmas parties served as public confirmations of racial subservience that promoted the couple's good reputation among scrutinizing whites.

Another event that black New Jerseyans eagerly anticipated was General Training. This one-day interracial affair, which occurred in mid June, was supposed to celebrate the day when all the troops of the county were drilled; as Andrew Mellick points out, however, General Training was considered a grand holiday, frequently marked by heavy drinking of rum and fighting.[78] Similarly, another scholar of New Jersey history writes, "Training days, in all communities, were parodies on warlike preparations, but in isolated areas . . . they exceeded all orgies known to modern civilization." Scores of people dressed in their Sunday best, he adds, would march "to the inspiring music of drum, fife, and bugle."[79] African Americans were admiring spectators. General Training allowed the lowly and oppressed (black and white alike) to earn some money. Specifically, "booths were set up for the sale of cakes, pies, beer, and rum," and when the militia had completed its drills and ceremonies, activities such as gambling and horse-racing were arranged for the entertainment of the people.[80] Certainly, from the viewpoint of many of those persons who gambled and became intoxicated, General Training symbolized more than a celebration of New Jersey's armed forces: particularly with respect to isolated bondpeople on small farms, this and other festivals, as pointed out by Shane White, "helped to break up the work year" and "provided a rare and valued opportunity" for them to get together with other blacks.[81]

Dick and Nance always attended General Training while enslaved in Bedminster. The couple and their children would leave for the Pluckamin grounds (southern Bedminster) by wagon at early morning and return at nightfall. Both Nance's ginger cakes (bolivars) and Dick's root beer were sold at the event. While many of their compatriots were set on getting drunk and having a good time, the business-minded couple was set on making their own money, evidently for the purpose of establishing some semblance of economic independence. To be sure, after running out of cake and drink, they took some time to enjoy the festivities. Andrew Mellick mentions that Dick's "spirits [were] lightened by the pleasures he had experienced," a comment that speaks to Dick's burdensome existence as both an overworked farmer and large black man in a white-dominated society.[82] Yet Mellick says nothing about how Nance felt. Silvia Dubois recalled that General Training was the most important holiday for her and African Americans in general.[83] At the very least, General Training was both a welcome and calculated respite from Nance's many chores in Aaron Malick's household.

Gender and Slave Labor

In addition to her often meager social existence, Nance was required to work hard. Indeed, her enslavement demonstrates both the inequities and hardships of work performed by New Jersey bondwomen. Andrew Mellick explains that, while she was "duly installed in the outer kitchen at the east end of the house," Dick soon "had nearly the entire control of the farm, which he managed with great prudence and intelligence; being always faithful to the interest of his master, he was rewarded with a leniency and trust that few white people in the same situation would have enjoyed."[84] Like many New Jersey bondmen, Dick was spared the isolation and restriction of the household and the mistress's surveillance. Jobs as sailors, stage drivers, boatmen, stablemen, and farm managers generally were not seen as appropriate for women.[85]

Yet kitchen or household service did not necessarily mean unrelieved drudgery for enslaved women; in fact, it could manifest as a real source of power. David Demarest recalled that the slave Sarah had a tremendous amount of authority in his grandfather's Bergen County household. "She alone knew what we were to have for our meals. She prepared the meats, gathered and prepared and cooked the vegetables. . . . Nobody trespassed on the domain of Sarah. Even grandfather bowed in submission."[86] Notwithstanding this power, Sarah was still a slave.

Because of male bias and the absence of a real plantation economy in New Jersey, enslaved men most likely had better opportunities than women for dealing effectively with the stress and frustrations of living in bondage. Despite David Demarest's comments about Sarah's household authority, there was little opportunity for the majority of domestic servants (usually women) to develop autonomy, with their mistresses looking over their shoulders, and with no support from fellow blacks. Enslaved males, who labored primarily as farmhands, at least had the comfort of the openness of the land, which put a degree of social-psychic distance between themselves and whites.

Nance had little choice but to exist as a beast of domestic burden. Initially the care of Aaron and Charlotte Malick and general oversight of the household were daughter-in-law Margaret Melick's responsibility. For Margaret and her husband Daniel, Nance's arrival in 1798 must have been a stroke of good fortune. What was apparently perceived as too great a physical burden for Margaret, a mother of four children at the time, did not apply to Nance, who was also the mother of several children, and who probably was mostly responsible for everyone's health and nutrition, for clean and pressed clothing, and for the overall dignity of the household, that is, all of the essentials of a well-to-do rural lifestyle. Presumably, Nance's daughter Diana, as well as the younger boys, would eventually assist their mother with her chores.[87] But the overall success of this domestic work, which may have included spinning wool and flax, knitting, and making butter and cheese, rested mainly upon Nance's shoulders.[88]

Little is known of both the working conditions of Northern households and their ill effects upon enslaved women. The Malick house, like many other larger homes during the eighteenth century, had two kitchens: the "outer kitchen," which Andrew Mellick comments was Nance's principal station, and the "farm kitchen, or living-room." Mellick refers to the farm kitchen as the mistresses' "kingdom." It had a deep fireplace for all the cooking, and was the center of home activity; that is, it was where "the meals were eaten, friends were entertained, and the spinning done."[89]

By contrast, the outer kitchen was smaller in size and had a door that led to a garden, suggesting that Nance's domestic duties extended to this area. Moreover, it had a massive "Dutch oven" for baking. Andrew Mellick romanticizes the family oven as the source of proud foods.[90] Evidently he never did much baking. There can be little doubt that the oven produced a sweltering and stifling heat that caused fatigue. These problems must have worsened during the long winter months, when the doors were closed. In addition, the handling of heavy firewood was required to keep the capacious oven heated to just the right temperature for proper baking. Certainly, Margaret Melick was more than glad to relinquish the outer kitchen to Nance, who spent a large portion of her life baking, both for whites and for her own family (but more for the whites). It is also plausible that the fumes from these fiery ovens, at some point, affected the enslaved woman's health. As pointed out by Susan Klepp, confinement "for long periods in a drafty, smoky room did no good to people prone to respiratory infections."[91]

The fireplace in the farm kitchen was probably also hazardous to Nance's health. Although the farm kitchen may have been the mistresses' personal domain, Nance would have done much, if not most, of the work in it—including the handling of "warming-pans, flat-irons, skillets, tea-pots, and other [potentially dangerous] necessities"—because Charlotte Malick was getting old (she died at the age of sixty-seven), and Margaret Melick, who died in 1807, had borne a total of ten children prior to Daniel Melick's second marriage in 1808.[92] (Nance most likely dedicated most of her time to the Melick children.) Theophile Cazenove, a Frenchman who visited New Jersey in the 1790s, observed that not all rural white women were afforded a servant like Nance. "The wives have the care of the house, and besides they have a number of children, 5, 6, 7, 8. So they have more work than they can do, with no help, except one or two old and dispirited colored women."[93] In light of rural white women's burdensome existence, it is doubtful that the mistresses on the Old Farm would have failed to put Nance, a conscientious servant and dedicated mother and wife, to work in the dangerous and exhausting farm kitchen.

Andrew Mellick reveals that the procedure for washing clothes also entailed an element of danger. First, "a roaring fire was built alongside the wash-house—on the bank of the brook [located on the Old Farm]—over which was suspended an iron pot in which the clothes were boiled." After the dirt had finally loosened, "the coarse clothing was put in the pounding barrel and well thumped with a wooden pounder until the dirt was sup-posed to be eliminated."[94] This back-breaking, time-consuming, filthy, and risky job, which was done seasonally, was one that many mistresses prob-ably attempted to avoid, if they could. Indeed, laundry work was gener-ally associated with black women in the North.[95] African American women, both slave and free (since there were few job opportunities available to freewomen), had little choice but to submit to laundry work and general domestic work. They had to endure on a daily basis the deadly fumes, cuts, lacerations, burns, bruises, and strained muscles that accompanied house-hold labor in white people's homes. Arguably, the numerous potentially lethal duties within the household required an even greater sense of alert-ness than agricultural labor.

Life on the Edge

Andrew Mellick gives no indication that Nance and Dick ever rebelled against all this dirty and dangerous work. And they may not have. Why? The most obvious reason would be that they were afraid of having their family broken up.[96] Another probable explanation was the very real threat of Northern white violence. It has been alleged that, as a group, Northern whites acted significantly less brutally toward blacks after the colonial era. Arthur Zilversmit, for example, argues that, "by the time of the Revolution, most northerners had ceased to regard the Negroes as the treacherous, uncivilized creatures they had once seemed to be, and they slowly modified their treatment of the subject of race."[97] Yet it is clear that numerous heinous acts of violence were committed against slaves well after the Revolution. In 1792, for example, "Samuel Hunt of Maidenhead, a man of 70, had brutally whipped to death, his young negro slave woman."[98] The whipping was so brutal that it prompted an investigation by Hunt's wife, who was aided by a male relative. The coroner for the case observed that "a more painful death than she must have suffered can scarcely be possible."[99] In another incident, in 1799, Amy Reckless of Salem County told the Pennsylvania Abolition Society that her mistress had "knocked two of her front teeth out with [a] brush handle and on other occasions pulled handfulls of hair from her head."[100] Silvia Dubois bluntly referred to her former mistress as "the very devil himself," explaining that "she'd level me with anything she could get hold of—club, stick of wood, tongs, fire-shovel, knife, hatchet, and anything that was handiest—and then she was so damned quick about it too."[101] Yet it was the mistress's husband, Minna Dubois, whom Silvia recalled as treating both her and especially her mother, Dorcas Compton, rather cruelly. Silvia and Dorcas were, simultaneously, casualties in the racial assault waged against black people, and the victims of the harsh nature of backcountry life. Silvia long remembered the brutal backcountry: "Them old masters, when they got mad, had no mercy on a nigger—cut 'em all up into strings, just leave the life, that's all. I've seen 'em do it, many a time."[102]

Interestingly, Silvia noted that only disorderly blacks were treated harshly during General Training and other "big days" in Flemington, the seat of justice of Hunterdon County. After the constables had captured unruly slaves, she says, "they'd tie 'em right up without judge or jury, and pull off the shirt, and put [the whip] right on the bare hide. My God, how they licked 'em—cut the hide all in gashes. . . . That's the way they used to fix the old slaves—give 'em a holiday to have a little sport, and then if they had any fun, lick 'em till they'd have a sore back till the next holiday come."[103] It was open season on blacks even during a licentious affair like General Training. Hence, General Training may not have been a completely pleasurable affair for Dick and Nance.

Like many owners, Aaron Malick was intolerant of blacks' intemperance, as evidenced by his verbal condemnations of Yombo's disruptions. Of course, one cannot compare Aaron's tirades to either Minna Dubois's, his wife's, or the constable's sadistic behavior. Yet one would also have difficulty arguing that Aaron's outbursts had absolutely no effect on his slaves. They may well have served as a painful reminder to Dick and Nance of the real brutality that existed outside of Aaron's homestead.

Andrew Mellick makes a provocative remark that further hints at the couple's sense of vulnerability on the Old Farm. "In the winter of 1792–93," he explains, "Daniel Melick went on a trading voyage in Georgia," where he attended two slave trials. Mellick provides no details about the first trial, but he indicates that the second trial concerned "two negro women for 'poisoning their mistress.'" The women "were found guilty, and sentenced to have their right ears cut off and to be branded on the forehead with the letter P."[104] Though Mellick frequently speculates about his ancestors in his book, he says nothing about why Daniel may have attended these trials, or mentioned them in his journal, which apparently is now extant. Of course, it is possible that Daniel went out of sheer curiosity; that is, he was interested in observing how the court system in the South dealt with the sensitive issue of slave criminality. Yet another, and arguably more plausible explanation, is that his attendance at the second trial was an affirmation of white solidarity, demonstrating his allegiance to the institution of slavery. If so, then his attitude may not have been much different from that of the anonymous individual who attended the Somerville slave conspiracy trials of 1734, who, we will recall from chapter 2, not only described the rebels as dangerous monsters, but also believed that strict laws governing the behavior of slaves were absolutely necessary.

At first glance, it might appear that Daniel's interest in the Georgia slave trials related in some way to Yombo's disagreeableness. But equally disturbing to Daniel would have been the slave conspiracy that occurred on the Bedminster property of Richard McDonald in 1788. That year, three slaves, known as young Sam, elder Sam, and Dine, were convicted of "setting fire to a barn property of Mr. McDonald." After McDonald whipped young Sam for stealing and then selling a gun of his, the angry youth told elder Sam and Dine about the punishment. The two adults "urged him to seek revenge by burning the barn and [said] they would assist him," following through on their promise one September night.[105] Because of his age and confession, young Sam appears to have received a pardon for his role in the conspiracy.[106] Conversely, Dine and elder Sam were hanged together at Gallows Hill near Somerville.[107]

Undoubtedly, the McDonald slave conspiracy, which local whites continued to discuss well into the late nineteenth century, served as a sobering reminder of how the black populace in the postrevolutionary era was not fully trustworthy. Whites were surely stunned to learn (from young Sam's confession) that, about ten years earlier, Dine had "set fire to her master's barn which was entirely consumed[,] and since that time was guilty of poisoning her mistress but was never discovered until now."[108] Given how enslaved blacks ceaselessly resisted oppression, and in ways not always detectable to whites, it is no wonder that General John Taylor's offer to sell Dick's family to Aaron Malick "was given much serious reflection and provoked warm and earnest discussions in the living-room of the old house." Although Daniel (as Andrew Mellick suspects) "urged the purchase,"[109] would he have failed to consider the possible dangers of owning blacks, even those with impeccable reputations? While Daniel and his parents no doubt debated the morality of owning slaves (as they did prior to purchasing Yombo), the issue of slave resistance—in both the North and South—was difficult to ignore.[110] Such a conversation would have had grave implications for Dick and Nance, and would have required them to tread cautiously around their owners, who were already daily confronted with Yombo's obstinacy.

White people's perception of slaves as mere property further illuminates Dick and Nance's vulnerable condition. At the Federal Convention in 1787, William Paterson, governor of New Jersey, stated unequivocally that he could "regard negro slaves in no light but property. They are not free agents, have no personal liberty, no faculty of acquiring property, but on the contrary are themselves property, and like other property entirely at the will of the Master."[111] As evidenced by the unscrupulous exportation of New Jersey slaves to plantations in Louisiana in 1818, Paterson did not stand alone in his pitiless position.[112]

Although there were probably variations in the treatment of slaves, the fact of the matter was that slaves were disposable chattel, and so were Dick and Nance and their children. Interestingly enough, Aaron Malick's will referred to them as "Inventory," along with "'old' & 'new' bark house [and] hides & skins."[113] More revealing is the enslaved family's emotional response to Aaron's death in 1809. As Andrew Mellick solemnly explains, "Then Dick and his family knew what trouble was. Not only did they honestly grieve at the lost of a good master, but they knew they must be sold and possibly separated."[114] The weeks between Aaron's death and their auction "wore heavily on, though only too fast when the thought of separation and the loss of a happy home confronted the poor slaves."[115] Whether Aaron was a "good master" or his slaves lived in a "happy home" is a matter of perspective. In no uncertain terms, however, the events involving the bonded family's break-up are indicative of slaves' precarious living, of parents who had earlier explained to their innocent children the brutal realities of bondage, of the lack of control that enslaved people had over the most basic of human relationships.

As a mother, Nance was probably particularly devastated by the pending break-up. "Slave mothers," Wilma King tells us, "lived and prospered only to the extent that their children did. They shared each others triumphs and defeats. Their lives were so firmly interlocked that they did not behave as individuals with singular purposes."[116] The loss of their children was more than many enslaved mothers could possibly bear. While at Perth Amboy in 1797, William Dunlap, who was a member of the New York Manumission Society, made note of an enslaved woman who was separated from her child: "The Mother by her cries has made the town re-echo & has continued her exclamations for two hours incessantly & still continued them."[117]

Still, it is important not to underestimate the grief black men experienced over the fragmentation of their families. Though it is certain that Dick's anguish over his family's inevitable separation largely reflected his own parental instincts, another factor undeniably came into play as well: his inability, as the head of his family, to protect it. Despite his efforts and sacrifices (which likely included his public acceptance of his "slave" name, a reinforcement of his compliance), Dick was essentially powerless to defend against losing what he obviously believed belonged to him. If nothing else had ever troubled his masculine conscience, the thought of having his precious "flock" parceled out like mere inanimate objects would have tortured it beyond repair.[118]

Slave-Owner Negotiations

At the same time that the Northern slave regime oppressed blacks both physically and psychologically, there were cracks in its armor that worked to the advantage of the enslaved. Rather than providing for the total emancipation of slaves, the New Jersey legislature instead enacted several comparatively beneficial laws for slaves (and owners) during the postrevolutionary era. One of the measures of the law of 1788, for example, required owners to have their slaves taught how to read before the age of twenty-one, with a penalty of £5 for noncompliance.[119] This may well explain, in part, why Aaron Malick paid for two months of Dick's son Joe's schooling.[120] Arthur Zilversmit has argued that the law of 1788 "made the relationship of master and slave more like that of master and apprentice": as apprentices, who were given "the same procedural rights in courts of law as white men," black New Jerseyans could further strengthen the bargaining power they already had as invaluable skilled workers.[121]

Andrew Mellick was probably correct in assuming that the sale of Joe and three of his siblings as indentured servants was the result of an earlier compromise made between Aaron Malick and the children's parents. On the one hand, Aaron's estate could ill afford the expense of four manumissions,[122] given that New Jersey slaveowners were required by law to give security for manumitted slaves, a strong deterrent against immediate emancipation.[123] On the other hand, Dick and Nance, both of whom were invaluable and faithful servants, would naturally want their children freed. The problem, however, was that the freed children would have been forced to live in abject poverty. It would seem, then, that the situation called for a resolution between the two parties—indentured servitude.

The negotiating may not have ended here. The law of 1788 also prohibited the export of slaves without their consent or that of their guardian.[124] According to the law, Dick and Nance had some say regarding their children's new addresses, which were in New Germantown and Elizabethtown, respectively, and relatively close to their parents. Of course, because the parents were slaves, whites would have had the ultimate say. Even so, was it simply a coincidence that the four children were purchased by men whom Dick and Nance had already known?[125] As further evidence of their bargaining power, and good name, Diana was promised that she could visit "the old folks at Christmas each year."[126]

The enslaved couple did not possess nearly the same bargaining power regarding Ann's future. The New Jersey gradual abolition law of 1804 (as outlined in the introduction) curtailed the rights of slaves and strengthened that of owners. But perhaps the most damning evidence of the decline in Dick and Nance's negotiating power are manumission records for Somerset County, which do not report a single Ann who was freed between 1805 and 1844.[127] This evidence suggests that Ann, who was born in 1806, was either dead or in some form of bondage when Nance was freed in 1821.

The condition of Ann's siblings was also less than perfect. Life as an indentured servant could be rather perilous. William Moraley wrote, "The Condition of bought Servants is very hard. . . . Upon Complaint made to a Magistrate against the Master for Nonperformance, the Master is generally heard before the Servant, and it is ten to one if he does not get his Licks for his Pains, as I have experienced upon the like Occasion, to my Cost."[128] His commentary apparently also holds true for the late eighteenth century, when a number of white indentured servants had run away evidently because of maltreatment or dissatisfaction, or both.[129] In short, indentured servitude did not guarantee an easier, more comfortable life for Dick and Nance's children. Besides their subjugation to possible abuse, these youths also belonged to a supposedly inferior race. For the majority of blacks—enslaved, indentured, and free alike—there was no escaping either of these hardships, a reality that must have caused the parents more pain than we will ever know.

How were Dick and Nance's children treated by their new owners? How did they respond to the family's forced separation? *The Story of an Old Farm* provides no insight regarding these inquiries. But found in one of Andrew Mellick's correspondence books is a telling reference made with regard to Sam, the second oldest child, who was purchased by the Reverend John McDowell of Elizabethtown. William McDowell, a relative of Reverend McDowell, wrote to Mellick in 1889 that Sam had "lived with the doctor, until he became so saucy that he was sold to John McCown."[130] William McDowell makes no mention why Sam, a seemingly well-behaved child on the Old Farm, turned unruly under Reverend McDowell, who was unable to control him.[131] Yet the reason behind his acting out seems obvious: the family's separation angered him. Nell Irvin Painter points out that one of the defining characteristics of soul-murdered children is the tendency to respond to their trauma by engaging in hostile behavior.[132] Apparently, Sam did not adapt well to his new environment and expressed his anger through "saucy" (mean) behavior, perhaps fueled by his fondness for rum. While no clues exist regarding the emotional state of his other siblings, they certainly experienced varying degrees of emotional trauma as well. The fact that Diana was given the promise of seeing Dick and Nance every Christmas testifies to her and the other children's emotional attachment to the "old folks," and the limited opportunities they had to indulge their affections.

Gender Relations

There are two possible reasons why Nance may have played a major, if not the lead, role in discussing the children's future, as well as other family business, with Aaron Malick. First, it was probably more risky for bondmen than women to act assertively in the company of whites, especially white males, whose authority they most threatened.[133] Needless to say, many New Jersey bondmen suffered indignities for confronting white men; Mingo, for instance, was whipped for going public about his owner's rape of his wife.[134] We must question, then, the commonly held belief among whites that Dick "'was a most likely nigger.'" Generally speaking, antebellum whites viewed African Americans as either foot-shuffling Sambos or potentially murderous Nat Turners. Winthrop Jordan writes that, "in all societies men tend to extrapolate from social status to actual inherent character, to impute to individuals characteristics suited to their social roles."[135] John Blassingame has stressed that, because of the high "distortion in people's perception, observation, and interpretation of the behavior of other individuals," scholars should be careful of relying "solely upon their reports," and he adds: "Prior experiences, situational factors, cultural frames of reference, and selective inattention all influence perception of individual behavior."[136] Racist attitudes make for even more distortion of Andrew Mellick's (and others') account of Dick and Nance. In sum, those whites who claimed to have known Dick's true character were probably misinformed. His quiet demeanor may well have been a mask he wore around whites for the purpose of protecting both himself and his family from any potential danger.

And, second, Nance may have possessed stronger emotional and social ties with the children. As noted, Andrew Mellick suggests that, on meeting Aaron Malick's family for the first time in 1798, Nance and Dick's three small children hid behind their mother. Although Mellick's account of this episode seems devoid of any real evidence (he says that we can imagine the slaves as they arrive at their new home), at the same time, he openly acknowledges the anxiety that undoubtedly arose between new owners and (especially) their newly acquired slaves, an observation that would seem to indicate that his story was not based on total fiction but contains a germ of observed truth. In other words, in their day-to-day lives, the children probably did gravitate more toward Nance for protection and nurturing, thus causing her to have a stronger inclination to deal with Aaron Malick in matters regarding the family.

This analysis does not suggest that Dick was rendered mute regarding family issues. As mentioned earlier, one of his and Nance's sons was also named Dick. Herbert Gutman has convincingly argued that incidences of children named after enslaved fathers strongly dispute the frequent and negative assertions that enslaved men were inattentive, absent fathers.[137] Slave naming practices are strong evidence that enslaved fathers played an active role in decisions affecting the family. Moreover, they indicate that many family decisions under slavery were the product of the private agreements between black men and women.

But at the same time that we may refer to Dick and Nance's marriage as a partnership, a closer look at their activities at General Training indicates that their relationship was not based on total gender equality. Dick's root beer was sold for two cents a glass, whereas Nance's ginger cakes were priced at a penny each. The fact that they set these prices themselves would logically suggest that Dick was considered the family breadwinner, and that Nance's financial contributions were secondary. Though this difference in price may have been attributed to a higher cost in making a barrel of root beer, what happened after General Training says something entirely different. Dick would take all the money ("his pockets full-weighted with big copper pennies"), implying that he was in charge of the family purse-strings. The bondman now had "pocket-money for all his needs for months to come, and some to drop in the black bag each Sunday morning at church when the deacon passed it in the gallery, which Dick always did with a most reverential bow."[138] Donations to the church were one of the few ways in which black men under slavery could demonstrate their manhood in the presence of whites without serious repercussions. Again, black men's mere potential to act dangerously threatened whites. Displays of manly dignity from up in the segregated gallery did not engender such heightened sensitivity. Given the rareness and importance of such masculine exhibitions, we can surmise that they were often done at the expense of black women. Even though Nance worked as hard as Dick in what was perhaps a more dangerous (domestic) setting, she evidently was still at the mercy of her proud husband's masculine dictates.

It would come as no surprise if the dynamics of their marriage were influenced by gender relations in Africa. Socioeconomic practices in Africa were brought across the Atlantic and reinforced by slavery. The double duty of being mother and laborer (outside of the house) was nothing new to enslaved African women. To be sure, it is easy to conceive of African women's substantial economic responsibilities and autonomy as real power. But, as Claire Robertson reminds us, "in Africa even daily subsistence decisions—when to plant, what to plant, how much grain or other staple to dole out—

were often controlled by men, although the division into 'women's' crops and 'men's' crops sometimes mitigated that control"; at any rate, "patriarchal rather than matriarchal authority was the dominant norm." In light of this, says Robertson, "we have had to discard romantic notions of egalitarian precolonial Africa, even while recognizing that colonialism created or vastly exacerbated existing economic inequalities in African societies."[139] Although in terms of economic power black men and women were equal under American slavery, older African American men like Dick still may have embraced patriarchal ideology. If so, then Nance was oppressed on all fronts—that is, by race, by class, and by gender. She persevered nonetheless.

Conclusion

Dick and Nance tell us a great deal about how blacks may have experienced married life under rural Northern slavery during the late eighteenth and early nineteenth century. We can see clearly that the couple survived a range of rather difficult experiences: the brutal social climate of their time; the monotony and hazards of domestic and agricultural labor; periodic isolation from other blacks; chronic family instability; and, most painful of all, the eventual sale of at least four of their five children. These hardships called for them to exert mental and physical strength and self-reliance. They did, but for seemingly particular reasons. That is, they had partners who were probably always a part of their adult lives, owners who were demanding but probably never cruelly abusive, and five children who needed their strength and love. These amenities, however, did not come without a price; in fact, they required enormous sacrifice on their part.

Perhaps most admirable about the enslaved couple is how they survived—by appearing docile while working together to protect their family. Certainly it was difficult for them to have to smile and grin in the faces of whites. For, despite their willingness both to work hard and to demean themselves, their family could be, and eventually was, ripped apart in an instant. This must have been a bitter reality, especially when the disaster of separation finally occurred.

Dick and Nance's enslavement together demonstrates much more than their grace and family dedication at all costs, however. It also conveys black community consciousness. On the surface, the holiday dinners and General Training festivities appear simply as mechanisms of white control. When examined more closely, however, it is clear that these and other social events fostered enslaved blacks' self-esteem and self-worth. Enslaved people were not merely imitating whites during these festive occasions. They were also expressing their own humanity or heritage and demonstrating skills they had cultivated, which, in turn, made slavery more bearable, but certainly not acceptable.

Equally illuminating, Dick and Nance's marriage reveals that, despite the precarious nature of such unions under slavery, there were African American couples who strove to live their lives as normal people—who loved, who at times shared, who worked together in the name of prosperity, and who tried to raise and protect their children the best they could. The black couple's survival of the vicissitudes of slave family life, for more than a decade, was no doubt attributable not only to constant communication on both their parts, but also to their willingness to compromise and comfort one another. As a black man, Dick was under extreme pressure to maintain both his dignity and his manhood. We can only guess that Nance was cognizant of this fact and did what she could to ease her husband's burdens, even at her own personal expense.

In a way, Dick was a kind of ultra patriarch who seems to have seized nearly every opportunity to demonstrate or exercise his manhood. This role, however, perhaps represents not so much who Dick was as a person, but who he was forced to become under slavery—a man whose family and destiny were controlled by the will of other men. For all his size, strength, and virility, he was essentially reduced to the status of a child under General John Taylor and Aaron Malick. And yet, he endured and gave of himself to Nance and the children in ways that rendered him all the more vulnerable as a black man in bondage. If a real man is one who sacrifices for his family at all costs, then Dick certainly personified this particular notion of manhood. For Nance, then, it was probably fairly easy for her to sacrifice some, if not much, of her own pride and autonomy for Dick. This is not to say that Nance was a weak woman who bowed in submission to her husband; to the contrary, she was as strong and resolute as Dick. But she also fully understood how slavery assaulted her husband's dignity on a daily basis, how it had reduced him and his family to objects that whites could buy and sell with impunity.

By the same token, Dick surely realized how much Nance had sacrificed for their family and championed his identity as a father and husband. Dick was not a man all by himself; he needed Nance to help him reach some degree of his manly potential. No doubt, then, like both Yombo and Quamino, Dick was a warm, caring, and giving spouse who greatly appreciated how his wife had enhanced his existence, as both a person and a man, in a brutal society that often failed to recognize him as either of those things.

In the final analysis, Dick and Nance, like all enslaved people, did what they believed was necessary to survive with dignity from one day to the next. Consequently, they were able to help sustain not only their individual selves but also their family, their community and, to some extent, their race. They were a remarkable couple indeed.

Epilogue

"Losing It"

I could have concluded this study in any number of ways. And, in fact, I considered several promising lines of thought. Eventually, however, I chose to close my discussion with an incident involving a slave who has fascinated me nearly as long as Yombo, Dick, and Quamino—the bondman York, owned by John Blanchard of Woodbridge. York's behavior in this incident, which was both tragic and comical, underscores the anger, frustration, and alienation of enslaved males in eighteenth-century New Jersey. Indeed, it may serve as a metaphor for black men living in American society throughout the ages. The following account is based on the court testimonials that three white males—Benjamin Bishop, David Bishop, and William Edgar—provided on June 28, 1760, six days after the incident.

The Bishop brothers and Edgar testified under oath that on Sunday, June 22, around five o'clock in the afternoon, York was seen approaching the house of Moses Bishop (Benjamin and David Bishop's brother) with a drawn sword in one hand and a pistol in the other. Along the way, the bondman stumbled and fell into a brook, wetting his pistol. After getting out of the water, he not only began brandishing the sword about, but also struck it violently into the door of Moses Bishop's house, muttering the words "son of a Bitch" several times. Not quite satisfied with this terrorizing display, he struck the sword into several other objects in his path. At some point, York appeared at one of the open windows of Moses's house and struck something inside with the sword as well. This action terrified the women inside the house, and they cried for help to Benjamin Bishop, who was in a field near his brother's house at the time (the whereabouts of Moses are never revealed in the testimonials). Shortly thereafter, a group of white men, consisting of Benjamin Bishop, Richard Kelly, John Moore III, and John Carlisle, gathered at the scene and discussed how to handle the slave. Carlisle suggested that they knock him down with a stake, then take away his weapons. Thereupon, all four men got stakes and called after York, who had gone to the other side of the house. He retreated slightly, turning frequently and wielding the sword as the men approached him. Kelly was the first to attempt to strike him, using a cedar fishing pole he had also acquired during the pursuit. The pole broke and Kelly dropped it; he then threw a stake at York, striking him in the shoulder. Carlisle immediately knocked down York, who had been staggered somewhat by Kelly's blow. The four men then bound his hands together behind his back.

While York lay prostrate on the ground, William Edgar inquired into the matter and suggested that York's assailants untie him. (It is not known whether Edgar was an antislavery sympathizer.) As soon as York was free, he jumped up and grabbed a crab-net, with which he attempted to strike Richard Kelly. Once again, however, John Carlisle seized the bondman and threw him to the ground. As the two scuffled, Kelly kicked York twice, and the four men bound him a second time. A short time later, York's owner, John Blanchard, appeared and untied him. He told his slave, who was lying on his stomach, to get up and go home, then struck him several times with the rope that had been used to tie him. The "surly" bondman got up but did not leave as instructed, an act of impudence that infuriated Blanchard, who dealt him more blows. After walking about two or three yards, York either fell or lay down in the mud. Blanchard fetched him from the mud and again ordered him to go home. After York finally began walking toward Blanchard's house, Edgar advised Blanchard to make sure "the Negro did not get something in his hands, with which he might do mischief."[1]

I have been unable to find any additional information regarding this rather bizarre confrontation. It is not known if York received additional punishment by Blanchard, if he was sent to the whipping post, or if he was eventually sold or even killed. (Still, it is very unlikely that he was not at least severely punished.)[2] And, most importantly, it is not clear why he decided to terrorize the white community that particular day in June 1760. Like many other cases or incidents of slave resistance, we are left to make sense out of fragmented pieces of tantalizing information. Yet, as this study has attempted to demonstrate, the silences in the sources may prove as exciting and rewarding as what is actually said in them.

At first glance, the York incident may seem somewhat amusing: an angry black man comes stumbling and bumbling his way into the neighborhood, wielding his wet gun and sword, frightening the white citizenry as he stabs everything in sight while using profane language, but is eventually captured by anxious white males who subdue him, not once but twice, and release him to his incensed owner, who bids him to go home but eventually has to go and fetch the black man-child, who instead decides to lie in the mud. The first time I read the court testimonials, I nearly fell out from laughter, because they seemed so preposterous to me. And, indeed, I assumed (and still believe) that York was drunk. What else could explain such a bizarre scenario? After all, "many slaves," as John Blassingame has written, "tried to drown their anger in the whiskey bottle, and if not drowned, the anger welling up was translated into many other forms."[3]

But, over time, I sensed that York must have experienced a great deal of alienation and despair. Although I found it difficult to incorporate him into the body of this study in a serious fashion, I also had great difficulty differentiating him from his compatriots who have been discussed in these pages. Periodically over the years, I have shared my thoughts about York with my wife, explaining how I empathized with him and understood why he was so angry. After one of my many York rants, she shrugged her shoulders and calmly stated, "He lost it." In those three words, she basically summarized what I had been thinking about York and enslaved males in the rural North for years.

I interpret the phrase "he lost it" to mean that the circumstances of York's life had pushed him over the edge, causing him to have little or no regard for the consequences of his actions, regardless of how they may have frightened the local whites. But what were the circumstances of his life? As we might expect, the court testimonials are silent on this matter. Or are they? In most cases of law, enslaved black New Jerseyans did not serve as witnesses. They were allowed to testify in court only when their evidence was used against other slaves.[4] Apparently, then, only the three previously mentioned white males had testified on June 28. York's feelings or version of what happened six days earlier were of no interest to the court, a fact that speaks to his sense of alienation in a white-dominated world that viewed him as subhuman, as John Blanchard's property. To be sure, York had one owner but many "masters" in whites who were obligated as "citizens to assert their authority over servants and slaves."[5] It was of no concern to Blanchard, his neighbors, or the court why York had "lost it" that day, only that he did. In retrospect, York's attack was probably related to how he was perceived and treated, not as a person or man, but rather as exploitable chattel. Perhaps nothing in particular had caused him to appear at Moses Bishop's house wielding his sword, other than the fact that he lived every day of his life as a lowly slave. As a slave, he was required to submit always to whites, which called for him to assimilate, change, and suppress his true feelings and desires. This in itself would have been enough to cause him and many other bondmen to lose all sense of composure, thereby rendering them dangerous to their oppressors. (The whiskey bottle functioned as a dangerous kind of truth serum that exposed the ugly feelings and desires harbored by the vast majority of American bondmen.)

It was this very reality about enslaved blacks that neither William Allinson nor Andrew Mellick cared to address. Allinson clearly thought better of presenting to the world the maimed, pessimistic, and angry Quamino whom his abolitionist uncle had visited in 1805. At age forty-two Quamino had decided to put his trust in the other world where he could escape from poverty and oppression—that is, from white male domination. Though well-intentioned perhaps, Allinson diffused the anger of "the injured, outraged slave" (as noted in the "Plea for Liberty") and, consequently, helped to promote the myth that Northern slavery was a relatively benign institution seldom if ever confronted by black rage.

This myth, of course, was further promoted by Andrew Mellick and members of his generation, who saw themselves as more enlightened than the "slave South." Though they, too, had a slave past, it was unlike the South's brutal "peculiar institution" of enslaved black majorities, an ideology buttressed by the notion, widespread in the late nineteenth century, that black people were inferior and required continued benevolence from whites in central New Jersey. Accordingly, Mellick portrays Dick as the good or "likely nigger" on Aaron Malick's plantation, phraseology that was not used in the original account of the Old Farm. Dick serves not only as Yombo's alter ego but as proof, according to Mellick, that slavery on the Old Farm was not wrong or immoral. "Likely," or mild-mannered, Dick made it easier for Mellick to reconcile his family's slaveowning past, which caused him more than a little embarrassment. For the sake of his ancestor's good name, Mellick needed Dick to appear as good and bereft of anger, as a prime example of what was supposedly admirable about slavery in Somerset County. Mellick needed the "likely" bondman Dick in much the same way that antebellum white Southern writers needed the docile Sambo, whose purpose, states John Blassingame, was "to prove the essential goodness of Southern society."[6]

Yet, just as it is doubtful that the openly discontented Yombo never experienced moments of genuine happiness, it is unrealistic to surmise that Dick was devoid of anger and suspicion, particularly during those ominous weeks between Aaron Malick's death and the sale of his estate. As Andrew Mellick describes the situation, "The sale commenced at the barns, when, after the hay, grain and other property had been disposed of, the people were invited to the house to buy the 'niggers.'"[7] Though, for the sake of his family, Dick appeared an agreeable slave during these frightening times, his quiet compliance neither reflected his true feelings nor was an issue that his biographers had an interest in exploring. Dick's family constituted his greatest, if not his only real, source of happiness. How, then, was he always "likely," with his family living in a precarious state that eventually brought them to their degrading auctioning and ensuing fragmentation? As Quamino indicates, even "a nice coloured man" (read: Jacob Van Benchaten's bondman) lived perilously close to "losing it." Indeed, those slaves who demonstrated utter compliance, yet in the end had their families and honor violated, were prime candidates for angry, destructive behavior.

Owing, in no small part, to the politics and racism of Northern white males in the nineteenth century, many Americans today (including my students) can scarcely imagine that there were bonded males on the brink of madness in places such as central New Jersey and upstate New York (where I currently live and teach), that race relations in the North were once so bad, and that there might be some justification for why many black males today remain angry in the age of the country's first black president. If for no other reason, the York incident is important to discuss because it helps us to see rural Northern slavery as it really was—a battlefield where enslaved blacks fought whites for the preservation of their minds and bodies.

For three reasons, I sense that this was not the first time York had directed his fury against the local whites. First is the comment that Moses Bishop said his own "Negro Fellow" made: "There comes York with his Cudgel."[8] The tone here seems almost causal, as if the "Negro Fellow" had seen York act this way before. Second is William Edgar's inquiry into the incident and ensuing request that York's attackers untie him. Whatever they told Edgar had convinced him that the slave's actions did not warrant such treatment, again suggesting a pattern of behavior. And third is John Blanchard's demand that York return home, a comment that bespeaks a frustrated owner who had had yet another confrontation with his unruly bondman. In saying all this, I am not tying to minimize the seriousness of York's offense. After all, white males felt threatened enough to congregate and collectively assail him. I am merely suggesting that York was a potentially dangerous slave whose anger the local whites had learned to tolerate, in much the same way that whites had learned to tolerate Yombo's "disagreeable" disposition.

Yet, as Blanchard's brutality indicates, white tolerance of slave anger did not translate into acceptance, but rather into incessant hostility between owners and slaves, a fact that both William Allinson and Andrew Mellick downplay. To this point, it seems inconceivable that Aaron Malick attempted to control Yombo through blistering verbal condemnations alone; it is doubtful that he never sought to emulate the behavior of those "old masters" who, Silvia Dubois recalled, "had no mercy on a nigger." The relationship between owners and slaves begot violence—violence that Malick and his brother-in-law doubtlessly employed on occasion as well. Very few slaves escaped physical violence, let alone an angry bondman whose defiance called for violent reprisal. As we will recall, diligent and trustworthy Quamino evoked white hostility and violence for merely having his humanity (and anger) affirmed by his religious faith, which, in turn, undercut his owners' masculine authority. Thus, one can appreciate why Dick, who was physically powerful, seldom if ever demonstrated his anger to his owners: it would have been deemed as a declaration of war. Dick was not necessarily cowardly but cautious around white males who could disrupt his family relations at any given moment. Like countless black men throughout the ages, Dick suffered in silence.

Black nationalist leader Malcolm X and comedian Richard Pryor, astute observers of race and racism, keenly understood black rage. Cornell West, in his illuminating interrogation of race in contemporary America, writes, "Malcolm X articulated black rage in a manner unprecedented in American history," adding that, "the substance of what he said highlighted the chronic refusal of most white Americans to acknowledge the sheer absurdity that confronts human beings of African descent in this country—the incessant assaults on black intelligence, beauty, character, and possibility."[9] Part of Malcolm X's appeal to the masses of angry black men (and women) was that he developed a gendered political rhetoric that urged black men to reclaim their manhood, stolen by white slavers and negated by two centuries of racist, segregationist policies.[10] Malcolm X's legacy continues to manifest today, especially among black youth who have, in the words of Michael Eric Dyson, "rightly fixed on Malcolm's rage at racism and economic misery." "Angry words from his speeches," Dyson observes, "have appeared in rap songs, on posters, and on T-shirts."[11]

Though he was not Malcolm X's peer as a spokesman for the oppressed black masses, Richard Pryor, whose comedic style came of age through and with the Black Power movement, nonetheless brilliantly communicated black rage during the 1970s.[12] Pryor grounded his outrageous standup routines in the harsh realities of American racism, revealing "how it perpetuates the ideologies of slavery."[13] In doing so, Pryor, like Malcolm X, spoke for many angry and embittered black people who were unable to speak for themselves. In his 1974 album *That Nigger's Crazy*, recorded live in San Francisco, he addressed African Americans' subjugation to white police brutality and humiliation. As he explains it,

> You get your shit together, you work all week and then you get all dressed. . . . Say a cat makes $120 a week and gets $80 if he lucky. Right, and he go out . . . be drivin' with his old lady out to a club and the police pull over. "Get out of the car! There was a robbery, a nigger look just like you! Alright, take your hands up, take your pants down, spread your cheeks!" Now, what nigger feel like having fun after that? . . . You go home and beat your kids. . . . Gonna take that shit out on somebody."[14]

Glenda Carpio argues that "a nigger" here, for Pryor, "is someone whose life can be taken randomly, whose integrity and self-respect can also be taken—and in extreme ways, as the insinuation of sodomy suggests—despite his efforts to work hard (even at little pay) and to live according to the rules."[15] Pryor uses the "N" word in this scenario to suggest that, much like their enslaved forefathers, marginalized black men in post-civil-rights America routinely had their manhood and dignity publicly assaulted, and had access to few if any constructive outlets to express their anger.

And black rage was (and is) in no way limited to males, the youth, and the working class. For example, bell hooks, a prominent black female intellectual, wrote a powerful essay about a "killing rage," about the anger that surfaced in her after a day full of racist harassment. "With no immediate outlet," she confesses, "my rage turned to overwhelming grief and I began to weep, covering my face with my hands."[16] In another important essay about the importance of moving beyond black rage, hooks posits, "Many African Americans feel uncontrollable rage when we encounter white supremacist aggression. That rage is not pathological. It is an appropriate response to injustice. However, if not processed constructively, it can lead to pathological behavior—but so can any rage, irrespective of the cause that serves as a catalyst."[17]

It is far easier for scholars of the twentieth and twenty-first centuries to acknowledge the need to find constructive ways to vent or express rage that a white supremacist society inspires. Yet we cannot even begin to fathom how difficult it was for enslaved persons to find constructive outlets for the very real rage that they experienced. Unprotected by the law, stripped of integrity and self-respect, besieged by brutality, and rendered completely invisible, many enslaved men and women were consumed by a deeply rooted anger for which there was "no immediate outlet" in the confines of the racially brutal and sparsely populated rural North. No doubt the enslaved gained much-needed solace from religion and African mores: religion clearly served as a critical means through which Quamino could channel his anger and frustration, as did Yombo's fragmented African identity, structured around his father's prestigious and seemingly heroic (manly) image. But was the utilization of such resources always enough to quell the anger of blacks under a system that ruthlessly denied their humanity and systematically assaulted their sense of self?

This was obviously more than the captives belonging to Jacob Van Neste, Robert Hooper, and Obadiah Ayers could possibly bear, causing them to commit violent acts of murder that may have been inspired by their African roots and, in the case of Hooper's bondman, lack of assimilation. In each case, as in York's, one gets the sense of despondent persons who could no longer endure acquiescing to the white power structure, and who had little to look forward to each day in their lives. Perhaps being ordered and censored by white women, and having one's tobacco pinched would not have been perceived as so utterly offensive if these men had possessed, like Dick, a loving and supportive family, as well as "colored" friends who shared their pain. But it seems that these bondmen, or York for that matter, were not afforded such love and friendships in their respective places of enslavement, though it is said that the bondmen belonging to Van Neste and Ayers had black male accomplices. Perhaps these accomplices were friends, but how many friends did such outcasts really have? This question is particularly apt in the case of Ayers's bondman, who had not only exploited but also planned either to kill or to frame his young, "new Negro" accomplice.[18] In any event, his anger clearly had gotten the better of him, resulting in the brutal death of a vulnerable young person pining for home in Africa. His behavior (contemptible though it was) underscores how the enslaved, unlike privileged black academics, were unable to deal with their rage by whipping out a pen and pad to discuss the legacy of American slavery, or to express their hostility in the presence of a white man who was complicit in the racism they were experiencing that day. With few constructive outlets, black rage under slavery could potentially imperil the lives of both the carrier and those blacks in his or her presence. Surely, like frustrated colonized (African) subjects who would commonly draw their "knife at the slightest hostile and aggressive look from another colonized subject," some bondpeople vented their pent-up aggression toward their fellow compatriots, and for the slightest reasons.[19] Recall the slave Brown, who was hanged for murdering a fellow bondman over "some slight provocation"?

Just as the rage of enslaved blacks could bring them (and other blacks) great harm, it could also potentially empower their lives. "Rage can act as a catalyst inspiring courageous action," observes bell hooks.[20] By demanding that bondpeople repress and annihilate their rage to conform and assimilate, owners were advocating that blacks remain complicit in their efforts to exploit and oppress. By refusing to surrender their rage, bondpeople were repudiating white supremacy while at the same reclaiming or reaffirming their emotional subjectivity. In this context, York's tirades and Yombo's "outbreaks" appear as much more than expressions of their pent-up frustrations; alternatively, we can read them as bold declarations of their humanity. For them, we may argue, to be angry was to remain alive under slavery's yoke. To relinquish their anger—the catalyst of their freedom struggle—was to die under the system, which may have actually happened to York. But at least he would not have died while complicit in his own suffering. In short, "losing it" was not necessarily a bad thing.[21]

Therefore, it is quite possible that Yombo's rebelliousness made a positive impression on Dick, albeit they probably viewed each other with suspicion. In his discussion of group survival within Southern slave quarters, in *Roll, Jordan, Roll*, Eugene Genovese distinguishes between "bad niggers" and "ba-ad niggers"—the longer the *a* is prolonged, the greater is the implied homage paid—who appear frequently in Southern plantation literature. Generally speaking, Genovese writes, "the 'ba-ad nigger' gave the white man hell, whereas the 'bad nigger' terrorized other blacks." In truth, however, as he remarks, "most ba-ad niggers were sometimes just bad, and vice-versa."[22] Consequently, slaves tended to view their "bad" men with ambivalence: on the one hand, they had the strength and courage to defy the system, and on the other hand, they brought distress to their compatriots both in terms of their violence (which could be misdirected at them) and because their actions often resulted in more work for everyone. Nihilists who lived on the margins, enslaved bad men were sources of both anxiety and inspiration.[23]

Unlike the actions of these "bad" or "ba-ad" individuals, however, Yombo's defiance appears to have had little, if no, negative bearing on Dick's life: again, Aaron Malick trusted him enough to run his entire farm. So Dick could have had great admiration for the way Yombo relentlessly refused to die under a brutal and callous system that, in the end, did its best to emasculate them both. If Yombo did indeed bring some discomfiture to Dick's life—serving, for example, as a solemn reminder of the reality of racial antagonism in and around central New Jersey—Dick could also take some comfort in how Yombo gave the white man even more hell. To be sure, Dick and Yombo were as similar as they were different. In Yombo, Dick could have seen his own anger (and vice versa). Indeed, as they stood together inside Malick's house during the auctioning sale, and perhaps in the tradition of the cool pose, they were both "niggers."

In light of the ambivalence that enslaved Southern blacks demonstrated toward the bad men in their communities, we cannot say with absolute certainty that the "Negro Fellow" who had announced York's angry entry into the neighborhood was currying favor with whites. Though this was possibly part of his motivation, in giving fair notice to whites, he could have also been trying, indirectly, to save York's life. White society had rendered the "Negro Fellow" invisible (and thus unimportant) in much the same way as it did his sword-wielding compatriot. That is to say, like Yombo and Dick, he and York perhaps had more in common than they did not.

Admittedly, like the *Memoir of Quamino Buccau* and *The Story of an Old Farm*, this analysis (and study) is a product of its time. "History is always produced in a specific historic context," comments Michel-Rolph Trouillot; "historical actors are also narrators, and vice versa."[24] *Manhood Enslaved* has been written at a time when scholars no longer view the enslaved as Sambos, but as gendered persons with real agency. Needless to say, it is inconceivable to me that Yombo, Dick, Quamino, and York were the *actual* persons described in white-authored (hegemonic) sources. As a black American man who is rather conscious of his masculine sensibilities and has experienced his fair share of racism and unremitting anger, I am compelled to view them as complex persons who struggled constantly with their identities and emotions. In a sense, then, I am no less objective than my white male counterparts of the eighteenth and nineteenth centuries. Idealistically, the "truth" about these intriguing bondmen and their compatriots is located somewhere between what I and whites have said about them.

Then again, Silvia Dubois did not necessarily ask for scholars to write the "truth" about black folk. She merely wanted them to be taken into "account," to be considered seriously as historical actors. This study, its subjectivity aside, earnestly attempted to do this for her and her central New Jersey compatriots.

Notes

Introduction

1. *Second Census of the United States: 1800* (New York: Norman Ross, 1990), 1.

2. C. W. Larison, *Silvia Dubois, A Biografy of the Slav Who Whipt Her Mistres and Gand Her Fredom,* ed. and trans. Jared C. Lobdell (1883; repr., New York: Oxford University Press, 1988), 51; see also 5–12, 20, for discussion of the years of Silvia's birth and death.

3. For an engaging overview of slavery in New Jersey, see Giles R. Wright, *Afro-Americans in New Jersey: A Short History* (Trenton: New Jersey Historical Commission, 1988), 18–27.

4. For foundational studies, see John W. Blassingame, *The Slave Community: Plantation Life in the Antebellum South,* rev. ed. (New York: Oxford University Press, 1979); Deborah Gray White, *Ar'n't I a Woman? Female Slaves in the Plantation South* (New York: Norton, 1985); and Elizabeth Fox-Genovese, *Within the Plantation Household: Black and White Women of the Old South* (Chapel Hill: University of North Carolina Press, 1988). See also Jacqueline Jones, *Labor of Love, Labor of Sorrow: Black Women, Work, and the Family from Slavery to the Present* (New York: Norton, 1985), chap. 1. For important recent studies, see, for example, Jennifer L. Morgan, *Laboring Women: Reproduction and Gender in New World Slavery* (Philadelphia: University of Pennsylvania Press, 2004); Emily West, *Chains of Love: Slave Couples in Antebellum South Carolina* (Urbana: University of Illinois Press, 2004); Rebecca J. Fraser, *Courtship and Love among the Enslaved in North Carolina* (Jackson: University of Mississippi Press, 2007); and Edward E. Baptist, "The Absent Subject: African American Masculinity and Forced Migration to the Antebellum Plantation Frontier," in *Southern Manhood: Perspectives on Masculinity in the Old South,* ed. Craig Thompson Friend and Lorri Glover (Athens: University of Georgia Press, 2004), 136–73.

5. On antebellum white opposition to educating slaves, see especially Carter Godwin Woodson, *The Education of the Negro Prior to 1861* (1919; repr., New York: Arno, 1968), chap. 7. The modest literacy of Northern slaves and the movement to have them educated is discussed in Arthur Zilversmit, *The First Emancipation: The Abolition of Slavery in the North* (Chicago: University of Chicago Press, 1967), 24–28, 159, 188–89. For explorations of these themes on the state level in New Jersey, see Marion Thompson Wright, *The Education of Negroes in New Jersey* (New York: Columbia University Teachers College, 1941), 20–21, 23–25, 34, 56, 63, 71–76, and Graham Russell Hodges, *Slavery and Freedom in the Rural North: African Americans in Monmouth County, New Jersey, 1665–1865* (Madison, WI: Madison House, 1997), 60, 61, 70, 71, 116, 156.

6. On the forces inhibiting and promoting the education of free blacks, see Woodson, *Education of the Negro,* 159–69; Marion Thompson Wright, *Education of*

Negroes in New Jersey, esp. 34–35, 49–50; John Hope Franklin, *The Free Negro in North Carolina, 1790–1860* (1943; repr., New York: Norton, 1971), 165–74; Leon F. Litwack, *North of Slavery: The Negro in the Free States, 1790–1860* (Chicago: University of Chicago Press, 1961), chap. 1; Benjamin Quarles, *Black Abolitionists* (New York: Oxford University Press, 1969), 106–15; Ira Berlin, *Slaves Without Masters: The Free Negro in the Antebellum South* (New York: Pantheon, 1974), 76–78, 285–86; James Oliver Horton and Lois E. Horton, *Black Bostonians: Family Life and Community Struggle in the Antebellum North* (New York: Holmes and Meier, 1979), 70–76; Leonard P. Curry, *The Free Black in Urban America, 1800–1850: The Shadow of the Dream* (Chicago: University of Chicago Press, 1981), 150, 161–67; Gary B. Nash, *Forging Freedom: The Formation of Philadelphia's Black Community, 1720–1840* (Cambridge, MA: Harvard University Press, 1988), 22, 208–29, 269–70; Patrick Rael, *Black Identity and Protest in the Antebellum North* (Chapel Hill: University of North Carolina Press, 2002), 175–80, 182–83, 296; and Leslie M. Harris, *In the Shadow of Slavery: African Americans in New York City, 1626–1863* (Chicago: University of Chicago Press, 2003), 64–65, 137–39, 142.

7. On the problems and utility of black testimonials about Southern slavery—a contentious issue among scholars—see, for example, John W. Blassingame, "Using the Testimony of Ex-Slaves: Approaches and Problems," *Journal of Southern History* 41 (1975): 473–92; David Thomas Bailey, "A Divided Prism: Two Sources of Black Testimony on Slavery," *Journal of Southern History* 46 (1980): 381–404; Norman R. Yetman, "Ex-Slave Interviews and the Historiography of Slavery," *American Quarterly* 36 (1984): 181–210; and William L. Andrews, *To Tell a Free Story: The First Century of Afro-American Autobiography, 1760–1865* (Urbana: University of Illinois Press, 1986), esp. 2–4, 6, 9–10, 16–17.

8. See the bibliographies in Stanley Feldstein, *Once a Slave: The Slaves' View of Slavery* (New York: Morrow, 1971), 305–14, and Andrews, *To Tell a Free Story*, 333–47.

9. Officially, New Jersey in the eighteenth century was divided into two provinces, East Jersey and West Jersey. By 1790 the former (where slavery became more entrenched) comprised Bergen, Essex, Middlesex, Monmouth, and Somerset counties; and the latter Burlington, Cape May, Cumberland, Gloucester, Hunterdon, Morris, Salem, and Sussex counties. (See note 36.) In more recent times, New Jersey has been conceptualized as North, South, and Central Jersey, though not everyone accepts these regional designations.

10. William J. Allinson, *Memoir of Quamino Buccau, A Pious Methodist* (Philadelphia: Longstreth, 1851); Andrew D. Mellick Jr., *The Story of an Old Farm; or, Life in New Jersey in the Eighteenth Century* (Somerville, NJ: Unionist Gazette, 1889). Book copies of the *Memoir of Quamino Buccau* appear to be extremely rare. I examined a book copy at the Schomburg Center for Research in Black Culture, Manuscripts, Archives, and Rare Books Division, NY. However, I initially found the *Memoir* on microfilm in Special Collections, Alexander Library, Rutgers University, New Brunswick, NJ. See also the following website designed by the University of North Carolina at Chapel Hill Libraries: http://docsouth.unc.edu/ neh/ allinson/allinson.html. On elite texts, see, for example, James C. Scott, *Weapons of the Weak: Everyday Forms of Peasant Resistance* (New Haven, CT: Yale University Press, 1985), 28–37.

11. William Allinson indicates that Quamino was born near Brunswick, New Jersey, in February 1762 and died in Burlington County, New Jersey, in November

1850. These dates appear reasonably accurate. The 1850 census also places Qua-mino's birth in 1762, noting that he was eighty-eight years old at the time of the census. Moreover, according to Burlington County death records for the period 1848–67, Quamino died on October 30, 1850, at the age of eighty-seven; hence, he was born in 1763. See Allinson, *Memoir*, 28–29; US Census of the City of Burlington (NJ), 1850 (microfilm), Library of Michigan, Lansing; and New Jersey Vital Statistics, Vol. C. (1848–78): Burlington County Deaths (1848–67), p. 399, New Jersey Department of State, Division of Archives and Records Management, Archives Section, Trenton (hereafter New Jersey State Archives).

12. George M. Fredrickson, *The Black Image in the White Mind: The Debate on Afro-American Character and Destiny, 1817–1914* (New York: Harper and Row, 1971), chap. 4, esp. pp. 108–9. For a divergent interpretation of romantic racialism, see Joanne Pope Melish, *Disowning Slavery: Gradual Emancipation and "Race" in New England, 1780–1860* (Ithaca, NY: Cornell University Press, 1998), 184n33. See also Mia Bay, "Remembering Racism: Rereading the Black Image in the White Mind," *Reviews in American History* 27 (1999): 651–52.

13. Kenneth E. Marshall, "'Ain't No Account': Issues of Manhood and Resistance among Eighteenth-Century Slaves in Nineteenth-Century Literature Pertaining to Central New Jersey" (PhD diss., Michigan State University, 2003), 22, 23.

14. This point on local dogma is discussed further in chapter 1.

15. According to Mellick, *Story of an Old Farm*, 611, Yombo was seventy years old upon the death of his Bedminster, Somerset County, owner, Aaron Malick, in 1809. Hence, Yombo was born around 1739. Yombo is said to have died "several years" after his 1809 departure from Bedminster (612). A reasonable assumption is that he deceased around 1819, that is, ten years after his relocation to Elizabethtown in Essex County. Dick was about forty-nine years old when he and his enslaved family arrived at Malick's farmstead in 1798, which places his birth around 1749. See Aaron Malick Record Book, 1809–18, MG 898, box 1, folder 1, New Jersey Historical Society, Newark. Manumission records for Somerset County indicate that Dick's wife, Nance, was manumitted in 1821. Dick, however, does not appear in the manumission records, which leads us to assume that he died prior to this date. See note 53.

16. See H. C. Brearley, "Ba-ad Nigger," *South Atlantic Quarterly* 38 (1939): 75–81; Clarence Major, ed., *Juba to Jive: A Dictionary of African-American Slang* (1970; repr., New York: Penguin, 1994), 17, 244; Eugene D. Genovese, *Roll, Jordan, Roll: The World the Slaves Made* (New York: Pantheon, 1974), 436, 625–30; and Lawrence W. Levine, *Black Culture and Black Consciousness: Afro-American Folk Thought from Slavery to Freedom* (New York: Oxford University Press, 1977), 407–20.

17. For a provocative discussion on slave dissimulation, see Robert Reid-Pharr, "Violent Ambiguity: Martin Delany, Bourgeois Sadomasochism, and the Production of a Black National Masculinity," in *Representing Black Men*, ed. Marcellus Blount and George P. Cunningham (New York: Routledge, 1996), 75–76. For Dick's appearance, see Mellick, *Story of an Old Farm*, 604.

18. Mellick, *Story of an Old Farm*, 606, 607. Writers who have used *The Story of an Old Farm* to argue that New Jersey slavery was essentially paternalistic include: Henry Scofield Cooley, *A Study of Slavery in New Jersey* (Baltimore: Johns Hopkins University Press, 1896), 57; Irving S. Kull, "Slavery in New Jersey," in *New Jersey: A*

History, ed.-in-chief Irving S. Kull, 6 vols. (New York: American Historical Society, 1930–32), 2:729; and Zilversmit, *First Emancipation*, 28–31, esp. 30.

19. Clement Alexander Price, ed. and comp., *Freedom Not Far Distant: A Documentary History of Afro-Americans in New Jersey* (Newark: New Jersey Historical Society, 1980), 318.

20. James Oliver Horton and Lois E. Horton, *In Hope of Liberty: Culture, Community and Protest among Northern Free Blacks, 1700–1860* (New York: Oxford University Press, 1997), 26–27.

21. Zilversmit, *First Emancipation*, 21–22, 225–26; Earnest Lyght, *Path of Freedom: The Black Presence in New Jersey's Burlington County, 1659–1900* (Cherry Hill, NJ: E. and E. Publishing House, 1978), 30.

22. Zilversmit, *First Emancipation*, 32; W. E. B. Du Bois, *The Philadelphia Negro: A Social Study* (1899; repr., New York: Schocken, 1967), 15; Lorenzo Johnston Greene, *The Negro in Colonial New England* (1942; repr., New York: Atheneum, 1969), 218–19; Winthrop D. Jordan, *White over Black: American Attitudes toward the Negro, 1550–1812* (Chapel Hill: University of North Carolina Press, 1968), 105; Ira Berlin, "Time, Space, and the Evolution of Afro-American Society on British Mainland North America," *American Historical Review* 85 (1980): 45–54; Nash, *Forging Freedom*, 11; William D. Piersen, *Black Yankees: The Development of an Afro-American Subculture in Eighteenth-Century New England* (Amherst: University of Massachusetts Press, 1988), 146. For a critique of William Piersen's paternalism thesis in *Black Yankees*, see Robert K. Fitts, "The Landscapes of Northern Bondage," *Historical Archaeology* 30 (1996): 54–73.

23. Gary B. Nash and Jean R. Soderlund, *Freedom by Degrees: Emancipation in Pennsylvania and Its Aftermath* (New York: Oxford University Press, 1991), esp. 9, 27–29, 38–40, 76, 127; Shane White, *Somewhat More Independent: The End of Slavery in New York City, 1770–1810* (Athens: University of Georgia Press, 1991), 87–93; Susan E. Klepp, "Seasoning and Society: Racial Differences in Mortality in Eighteenth-Century Philadelphia," *William and Mary Quarterly*, 3rd ser., 51 (1994): 473–506; Hodges, *Slavery and Freedom in the Rural North*, 16–18, 59, 60, 122–23, 155–56, 177, 178; Graham Russell Hodges, *Root and Branch: African Americans in New York and East Jersey, 1613–1863* (Chapel Hill: University of North Carolina Press, 1999), 17, 52–53, 63–68, 116, 179–80, 208–9; Kenneth E. Marshall, "Work, Family and Day-to-Day Survival on an Old Farm: Nance Melick, a Rural Late Eighteenth- and Early Nineteenth-Century New Jersey Slave Woman," *Slavery and Abolition* 19 (1998): 22–45; Harris, *Shadow of Slavery*, 21, 33, 62; Ira Berlin, *Many Thousands Gone: The First Two Centuries of Slavery in North America* (Cambridge, MA: Harvard University Press, 1998), 184–87, 188. On the difficulties facing the black family under Northern slavery, see also Vivienne L. Kruger, "Born to Run: The Slave Family in Early New York, 1626–1827" (PhD diss., Columbia University, 1985), 16, 21, passim.

24. Allinson, *Memoir*, 4–5.

25. Andrews, *To Tell a Free Story*, 7.

26. Hodges, *Slavery and Freedom in the Rural North*, esp. chap. 2; Hodges, *Root and Branch*, esp. 64–65, 134–36.

27. See, for example, Noel V. Cazenave, "Black Men in America: The Quest for Manhood," in *Black Families*, ed. Harriet Pipes McAdoo (Beverly Hills, CA: Sage, 1981), 176–86; Robert Staples, *Black Masculinity: The Black Man's Role in American Society* (San Francisco, CA: Black Scholar Press, 1982); Richard Majors and Janet

Mancini Billson, *Cool Pose: The Dilemmas of Black Manhood in America* (New York: Lexington Books, 1992); Lawrence E. Gary, Christopher B. Booker, and Abeba Fekade, *African American Males: An Analysis of Contemporary Values, Attitudes, and Perceptions of Manhood* (Washington, DC: Howard University School of Social Work, 1993); Christopher B. Booker, *"I Will Wear No Chain!": A Social History of African American Males* (Westport, CT: Praeger, 2000); and Demico Boothe, *Why Are So Many Black Men in Prison?* (Memphis, TN: Full Surface Publishing, 2007).

28. Majors and Billson, *Cool Pose*, esp. 2, 4–5, 57–58, 105.

29. Stanley M. Elkins, *Slavery: A Problem in American Institutional and Intellectual Life*, 2nd ed. (Chicago: University of Chicago Press, 1968), 81–89. Even prior to Elkins, there were scholars who maintained that bondpeople were essentially docile and content with slavery. See especially Ulrich B. Phillips, *American Negro Slavery: A Survey of the Supply, Employment, and Control of Negro Labor as Determined by the Plantation Regime* (1918; repr., Baton Rouge: Louisiana State University Press, 1969), 341–42. Those works which initially contested this interpretation include: Joseph Cephas Carroll, *Slave Insurrections in the United States, 1800–1865* (1938; repr., New York: Negro Universities Press, 1968); Herbert Aptheker, *American Negro Slave Revolts* (1943; repr., New York: International Publishers, 1969); and Kenneth M. Stampp, *The Peculiar Institution: Slavery in the Ante-Bellum South* (1956; repr., New York: Vintage, 1989), chap. 3.

30. On male courtship, see Blassingame, *Slave Community*, 156–61. On the status of male occupations, see Robert William Fogel and Stanley L. Engerman, *Time on the Cross: The Economics of American Negro Slavery* (Boston: Little, Brown, 1974), 141. On men providing for women and children, see Blassingame, *Slave Community*, 92, and Genovese, *Roll, Jordan, Roll*, 486. On male protection and the naming of offspring, see Herbert G. Gutman, *The Black Family in Slavery and Freedom, 1750–1925* (New York: Pantheon, 1976), 188–91, 385–87. See also Genovese, *Roll, Jordan, Roll*, 422–23, 484–86, 491, regarding the protection of women. A great deal has been written on the resistance of enslaved males. See, for example, Blassingame, *Slave Community*, 284, passim; Genovese, *Roll, Jordan, Roll*, 491, passim; Gerald W. Mullin, *Flight and Rebellion: Slave Resistance in Eighteenth-Century Virginia* (New York: Oxford University Press, 1972), 145–47, passim; Robert S. Starobin, *Industrial Slavery in the Old South* (New York: Oxford University Press, 1970), 75–91; and George P. Rawick, *From Sundown to Sunup: The Making of the Black Community* (Westport, CT: Greenwood, 1972), 95–119. For a good selection of the critics of Stanley Elkins's "Sambo" thesis, see Ann J. Lane, ed., *The Debate over Slavery: Stanley Elkins and His Critics* (Urbana: University of Illinois Press, 1971), 23–75, 245–68.

31. See, for example, Daniel P. Black, *Dismantling Black Manhood: An Historical and Literary Analysis of the Legacy of Slavery* (New York: Garland, 1997), chaps. 2–3; Baptist, "Absent Subject," 147–52, 158–59; and the essays in Darlene Clark Hine and Earnestine Jenkins, eds., *A Question of Manhood: A Reader in U.S. Black Men's History and Masculinity*, vol. 1, *"Manhood Rights": The Construction of Black Male History and Manhood, 1750–1870* (Bloomington: Indiana University Press, 1999), esp. Robert E. Desrochers Jr., "'Not Fade Away': The Narrative of Venture Smith, an African-American in the Early Republic," 61–89; John K. Thornton, "African Dimensions of the Stono Rebellion," 115–29; and James Oliver Horton and Lois E. Horton, "Violence, Protest, and Identity: Black Manhood in Antebellum America," 382–98.

32. My thinking here draws from Heather Andrea Williams, "'Commenced to Think Like a Man': Literacy and Manhood in African American Civil War Regiments," in Friend and Glover, *Southern Manhood*, 197. On the fluidity of manhood over time, see Gail Bederman, *Manliness and Civilization: A Cultural History of Gender and Race in the United States, 1880–1917* (Chicago: University of Chicago Press, 1995), 5–23; Michael S. Kimmel, *Manhood in America: A Cultural History*, 2nd ed. (New York: Oxford University Press, 2006), 1–10; Booker, *"I Will Wear No Chain!,"* viii–xii; and Darlene Clark Hine and Earnestine Jenkins, "Black Men's History: Toward a Gendered Perspective," in Hine and Jenkins, *Question of Manhood*, 1–58.

33. For the basis of this summary, see Jack P. Greene, *All Men Are Created Equal: Some Reflections on the Character of the American Revolution* (Oxford: Clarendon Press, 1976); Kimmel, *Manhood in America*, 11–16, esp. 14; Bruce Dorsey, *Reforming Men and Women: Gender in the Antebellum City* (Ithaca, NY: Cornell University Press, 2002), 14–20, esp. 18, 20; and Harris, *Shadow of Slavery*, 97–99.

34. Kimmel, *Manhood in America*, 3, writes: "Manhood is not the manifestation of an inner essence; it's socially constructed. Manhood does not bubble up to consciousness from our biological constitution; it is created in our culture." On gender dynamics in Africa, see Claire Robertson, "Africa into the Americas? Slavery and Women, the Family, and the Gender Division of Labor," in *More than Chattel: Black Women and Slavery in the Americas*, ed. David Barry Gaspar and Darlene Clark Hine (Bloomington: Indiana University Press, 1996), 12.

35. Desrochers, "'Not Fade Away,'" 77.

36. US Census Bureau, *A Century of Population Growth from the First Census of the United States to the Twelfth, 1790–1900* (Washington, DC: Government Printing Office, 1909), 195–96.

37. *Second Census of the United States*, 34.

38. New Jersey is situated within five physiographic regions: (1) the Ridge and Valley, or Valley; (2) the Highlands; (3) the Piedmont; (4) the Inner Coastal Plain; and (5) the Outer Coastal Plain. For a detailed description, see Peter O. Wacker, *Land and People: A Cultural Geography of Preindustrial New Jersey: Origins and Settlement Patterns* (New Brunswick, NJ: Rutgers University Press, 1975), 2–8. The Raritan River is meticulously described in Thomas F. Gordon, *Gazetteer of the State of New Jersey* (1834; repr., Cottonport, LA: Polyanthos, 1973), 224–25.

39. For an excellent summary, see William B. Brahms, *Franklin Township, Somerset County, NJ: A History* (Franklin, NJ: Commissioned by the Franklin Township Public Library, 1998), 22–24, 29–30.

40. Wacker, *Land and People*, 133, 165–66, 189–90. Many "Dutch" people "were not from Holland but were of Flemish, Huguenot, Walloon, German, Scandinavian, Polish, and even Hungarian and Italian origin" (164).

41. Brahms, *Franklin Township*, 100–101, 102; Steven B. Frakt, "Patterns of Slave-Holding in Somerset County, N.J." (unpublished seminar paper, Special Collections, Alexander Library, Rutgers University, 1967), 12–17, 21–26. For additional evidence of the correlation between large landholdings and slave ownership, see "Hillsborough Township 'Census' of 1784," *Somerset County Genealogical Quarterly* 2 (1984): 101–6, 130–33; and Tax Ratables, Bridgewater, Somerset County, 1784, and Eastern Precinct, Somerset County, 1784, 1786, 1788 (New Jersey State Archives).

42. Ralph Voorhees, "Franklin Township Historical Notes," *Somerset County Historical Quarterly* 5–6 (1916–17): 5:28, 6:91–92.

43. "Hillsborough Township 'Census' of 1784," 132; Bridgewater, Somerset County, Tax Ratable, 1784.

44. Andrew D. Mellick Jr. Papers, MG 53, box 6, folder 1, New Jersey Historical Society (hereafter Mellick Papers). According to Mellick, his ancestors, the Malick family, owned "a fine Tan yard of about 40 Vats," and "this business was carried on until the supply of bark in that section of [the] country was exhausted."

45. Hubert G. Schmidt, "Slavery and Attitudes on Slavery, Hunterdon County, New Jersey," *Proceedings of the New Jersey Historical Society* 58 (1940): 151.

46. On slaveholding in the New York hinterland, see especially White, *Somewhat More Independent*, 88–93, and Hodges, *Slavery and Freedom in the Rural North*, 16–21, 155–56. According to Hubert Schmidt, regarding slavery in Hunterdon County, "both tradition and documentary evidence show that there were a great many masters who owned one, two, or three slaves" ("Slavery and Attitudes on Slavery," 151). Moreover, a 1784 tax ratable-turned-census for Hillsborough Township lists 326 slaves living in 322 households, which translates into 1.4 slaves per household. See "Hillsborough Township 'Census' of 1784," 101–6, 130–33. The nature of small slaveholdings in central New Jersey is also born out in the tax ratables listed in note 41.

47. For the actual law, see *Acts of the Twenty-Eighth General Assembly of the State of New Jersey* (Trenton, NJ: Wilson and Blackwell, 1804), 251–54. For discussion, see Marion Thompson Wright, "New Jersey Laws and the Negro," *Journal of Negro History* 28 (1943): 171–78; Arthur Zilversmit, "Liberty and Property: New Jersey and the Abolition of Slavery," *New Jersey History* 88 (1970): 215–26; and Hodges, *Slavery and Freedom in the Rural North*, 135–36.

48. Hodges, *Slavery and Freedom in the Rural North*, 136.

49. Zilversmit, "Liberty and Property," 221.

50. Allinson, *Memoir*, 12–15. "William Griffith was not only an eminent lawyer, but a philanthropist, and bore a prominent part in originating and conducting the New Jersey Abolition Society," writes William Allinson (13).

51. William Paterson, *Laws of the State of New Jersey* (Newark, NJ: Mattias Day, 1800), 311. The document manumitting Quamino uses almost exactly the same language.

52. Allinson, *Memoir*, 15.

53. "Manumissions of Slaves in Somerset County," *Somerset County Historical Society* 1–2 (1912–13): 1:275–79, 2:46–51. Nance was manumitted in 1821 (1:278).

54. Hodges, *Slavery and Freedom in the Rural North*, 136.

55. The censuses are conveniently located in Giles R. Wright, *Afro-Americans in New Jersey*, 85–87.

56. Henry Louis Gates Jr., *Thirteen Ways of Looking at a Black Man* (New York: Random House, 1997).

Chapter One

1. In 1982, a group of South Asian historians led by Ranajit Guha formed subaltern studies, which sought to restore the agency stripped from subaltern (sub-

ordinate) peoples by colonialist, Marxist, and nationalist versions of history. Appropriating the term "subaltern" from Antonio Gramsci's work, subaltern scholars have influenced studies in Latin American, European, and African history by advocating that elite texts be read "against the grain" to make the subaltern speak. See, for example, Ranajit Guha, "The Prose of Counter-Insurgency," in *Selected Subaltern Studies*, ed. Ranajit Guha and Gayatri Chakravorty Spivak (New York: Oxford University Press, 1988), 45–84; Gayatri Chakravorty Spivak, "Can the Subaltern Speak?" in *Marxism and the Interpretation of Culture*, ed. Carry Nelson and Lawrence Grossberg (Urbana: University of Illinois Press, 1988), 271–313; and the December 1994 issue of the *American Historical Review* (vol. 99), specifically Gyan Prakash, "Subaltern Studies as Postcolonial Criticism," 1475–90; Florence E. Mallon, "The Promise and Dilemma of Subaltern Studies: Perspectives from Latin American History," 1491–515; and Frederick Cooper, "Conflict and Connection: Rethinking Colonial African History," 1516–45. For a more recent use of subaltern studies within the context of late nineteenth-century American history, see Gunja Sengupta, "Elites, Subalterns, and American Identities: A Case Study of African-American Benevolence," *American Historical Review* 109 (2004): 1104–39.

2. John H. Hageman, "Memorial of Samuel Allinson, 'The Philanthropist of New Jersey,'" *Proceedings of the New Jersey Historical Society*, 2nd ser., 8 (1884): 72.

3. For an excellent overview, see Zilversmit, *First Emancipation*, 61–83.

4. On the life of Samuel Allinson, see Hageman, "Memorial of Samuel Allinson," 10, and William Nelson, *New Jersey Biographical and Genealogical Notes* (1916; repr., Baltimore: Clearfield, 1992), 7–8.

5. "Sundry Letters between Samuel Allinson and Some of his most intimate Friends. Between the Years 1764 and 1790," Samuel Allinson Papers, Special Collections, Alexander Library, Rutgers University, New Brunswick, NJ; cited in George Fishman, "The Struggle for Freedom and Equality: African Americans in New Jersey, 1624–1849/50" (PhD diss., Temple University, 1990), 187–89.

6. On Quakerism and the Golden Rule with regard to slavery, see Jean R. Soderlund, *Quakers and Slavery: A Divided Spirit* (Princeton, NJ: Princeton University Press, 1985), 18 and passim.

7. Samuel Allinson to Richard Hartstone, "Sundry Letters," 26/12M/1772.

8. Soderlund, *Divided Spirit*, 182. By a 1769 law, slaveowners in New Jersey were required to post a substantial bond in the sum of £200 or instruct their estates to pay £20 annually to insure that former slaves were not burdens on the towns and townships where they lived. Needless to say, this was a difficult financial undertaking for many owners wishing to liberate their bondpeople. See Marion Thompson Wright, "New Jersey Laws and the Negro," 170, and Hodges, *Slavery and Freedom in the Rural North*, 24–25.

9. Just prior to the War for Independence, a half million blacks—a few free, the rest enslaved—lived in the rebellious colonies, according to Sidney Kaplan and Emma Nogrady Kaplan, "Bearers of Arms: Patriot and Tory," in Hine and Jenkins, *Question of Manhood*, 165.

10. Samuel Allinson to William Livingston, "Sundry Letters," 13/7M/1778.

11. William Livingston to Samuel Allinson, "Sundry Letters," 25/7M/1778. For further discussion on Livingston's antislavery sentiment, see Hodges, *Slavery and Freedom in the Rural North*, 115–16.

12. Soderlund, *Divided Spirit*, 182.

13. [Samuel Allinson], "Reasons in favor of a Law, 'for the more equitable Manumission of Slaves in New Jersey &c.,'" 24/12M/1773, Abolition Collection, MSS, box 1, folder 8, Burlington County (NJ) Historical Society.

14. On the colonial hierarchical structure, see Soderlund, *Divided Spirit*, 18; Horton and Horton, *In Hope of Liberty*, 39–40; and esp. Gordon S. Wood, *The Radicalism of the American Revolution* (New York: Knopf, 1992).

15. On segregation in Quaker meetinghouses, see Litwack, *North of Slavery*, 206–7; Thomas E. Drake, *Quakers and Slavery in America* (New Haven, CT: Yale University Press, 1950), 120, 177–78; and esp. Ryan P. Jordan, *Slavery and the Meeting House: The Quakers and the Abolitionist Dilemma, 1820–1865* (Bloomington: Indiana University Press, 2007), chap. 3.

16. James Oakes, *The Ruling Race: A History of American Slaveholders* (New York: Knopf, 1982), xi, in conjunction with Drake, *Quakers and Slavery*, 17, and Soderlund, *Divided Spirit*, 181–86. Oakes adds that "a liberal espouses a far different social fiction: 'All men are created equal'" (xi).

17. Soderlund, *Divided Spirit*, 184.

18. This William Allinson was the uncle of Quamino's biographer. For a brief comment on his life, see Nelson, *Biographical and Genealogical Notes*, 8.

19. William Allinson Journal, entry for 17/2M/1805, Manuscripts Division, Clements Library, University of Michigan, Ann Arbor.

20. Allinson, *Memoir*, 3, 16, 29.

21. William Allinson Journal, entry for 17/2M/1805.

22. William Allinson Journal, entry for 18/2M/1805.

23. William Allinson Journal, entry for 30/10M/1804.

24. William Allinson Journal, entry for 10/6M/1806.

25. Allinson believed that "we are all Brethren by Creation," and thus it was his "incumbent Duty" to help "him who hath no helper." See William Allinson Journal, entry for 9/2M/1805.

26. Horton and Horton, "Violence, Protest, and Identity," 387.

27. See ibid., 382–83. Michael Kimmel refers to the "masculine achiever" model as the "self made man," an ideal he argues spanned the postrevolutionary and antebellum era, in *Manhood in America*, 13–16.

28. Hageman, "Memorial of Samuel Allinson," 72–73.

29. "William J. Allinson" (n.p., n.d. [c. 1873]), Allinson Family Papers, MSS, Coll. 968, box 5, folder 35B, Special Collections, Magill Library, Haverford College, Haverford, PA. Despite its anonymity, the piece was obviously written by a fellow Friend. The close relationship between the Allinson brothers, also indicative of the Christian gentleman, is conveyed through their frequent and sentimental correspondence. In 1847, for example, William communicated to Samuel, "Few brothers I flatter myself, have loved each other so entirely; and we are far approaching the season when a survivor will doat upon the pleasant memories . . ." See William J. Allinson to Samuel Allinson, 12/9M/1847, Allinson Family Papers, box 5, folder 35C.

30. Correspondingly, "a central theme in the abolitionists' attacks on slavery was that it robbed [black] men of their manhood," write Horton and Horton, "Violence, Protest, and Identity," 384.

31. Both the Seven Years' and Revolutionary wars brought many problems to pacifist Friends. See Drake, *Quakers and Slavery*, 55, 90, and Soderlund, *Divided Spirit*, 7.

32. Nelson, *Biographical and Genealogical Notes*, 10–11.

33. Hageman, "Memorial of Samuel Allinson," 75–76, 78.

34. Nelson, *Biographical and Genealogical Notes*, 10, reports that William Allinson "established himself in Burlington as a druggist, but subsequently devoted himself to literary pursuits, compiled one or more school books, and for a number of years was editor of the *Friends' Review*." See also "William J. Allinson," 2, 5–6, 7–8.

35. The "free produce movement" had a long history dating back to the mid eighteenth century, when Quaker John Woolman advocated such a tactic when opposing slavery. This tactic, however, was not seriously employed by Quakers until the 1780s, during the public outcry against the African slave trade. The free produce campaign was given new life in the 1810s and 1820s by Elias Hicks, a staunch critic of Quaker orthodoxy. Hicks exacerbated the conflict over the rightful theological understanding of Quakerism, culminating in the Hicksite Separation of 1827–28. I have found no evidence that the Allinson family played a direct role in the schism. (See, for example, Drake, *Quakers and Slavery*, 115–17, and Jordan, *Slavery and the Meetinghouse*, 8–13.) All the founders of the PFPAF, we are told, "were old-line Quaker abolitionists, Orthodox Friends, and members of the evangelical or 'Gurneyite' wing of their Yearly Meeting"—the highest Quaker authority among Philadelphia–New Jersey Friends. Joseph John Gurney and other English Quakers introduced evangelicalism to American Quakers during the late 1830s. See Drake, *Quakers and Slavery*, 163, 172–73.

36. *Friends' Review: A Religious, Literary, and Miscellaneous Journal*, September 4, 1847. See also Drake, *Quakers and Slavery*, 173.

37. "An Old Slave Set Free," *Friends' Review*, October, 16, 1847. Zilversmit, *First Emancipation*, 77, writes: "Isaac Jackson, a member of a committee to visit slaveholders, reported that in one year he had visited the masters of over 1,100 slaves, all members of a quarterly meeting near Philadelphia."

38. "An Old Slave Set Free." Similarly, upon learning his owner would manumit him, Quamino reportedly responded, "You give me free, master!" See Allinson, *Memoir*, 13.

39. "An Old Slave Set Free."

40. *Non-Slaveholder* (January 1846): 1–2.

41. Drake, *Quakers and Slavery*, 181–82.

42. Ibid., 174.

43. William J. Allinson, *Poems* (Philadelphia: Claxton, Remsen, and Haffelfinger, 1873), 30–31.

44. Dorsey, *Reforming Men and Women*, 187–91.

45. Allinson, *Memoir* 3, 17. The phrase "treasure in heaven" (p. 30) is from Matthew 19:16–24 and Luke 12:32–34.

46. Luke 16:22, as quoted in Allinson, *Memoir*, 30.

47. Luke 12:35–36, 46, as quoted in Allinson, *Memoir*, 20.

48. Allinson, *Memoir*, 4, 6–7.

49. Melish, *Disowning Slavery*, 184n33.

50. F. W. H. Migeod, "Personal Names among Some West African Tribes," *Journal of the African Society* 17 (1917): 39–40; Lorenzo Dow Turner, *Africanisms in the Gullah Dialect* (1949; repr., Columbia: University of South Carolina Press, 2002), 304n15; J. L. Dillard, *Black English: Its History and Usage in the United States* (New York: Vintage, 1973), 124; Newbell Niles Puckett, collector, *Black Names in America: Origins and Usage*, ed. Murray Heller (Boston: Hall, 1975), 434.

51. Allinson, *Memoir*, 6, 9, mentions that Quamino lived with his enslaved parents and four siblings under the Buccau family. For informative discussions on naming in slave communities, see Peter H. Wood, *Black Majority: Negroes in Colonial South Carolina from 1670 through the Stono Rebellion* (New York: Knopf, 1974), 181–85, and Gutman, *Black Family*, 185–201.

52. John S. Mbiti, *African Religions and Philosophy* (1969; repr., London: Heinemann, 1988), 118.

53. For the definitive statement on the "double consciousness" of American blacks, see W. E. B. Du Bois, *The Souls of Black Folk* (1903; repr., Millwood, NY: Vintage, 1990), 3.

54. Allinson, *Memoir*, 9, 16.

55. Dorsey, *Reforming Men and Women*, 187.

56. For reactions to Uncle Tom, see Andrews, *To Tell a Free Story*, 179–81.

57. Fredrickson, *Black Image in the White Mind*, 111–12. See also Dorsey, *Reforming Men and Women*, 192–93.

58. Allinson, *Memoir*, 6, 10, 13.

59. Dorsey, *Reforming Men and Women*, 187, 193.

60. Allinson, *Memoir*, 3.

61. To this point, Frederick Douglass, the fugitive slave turned famous abolitionist, believed that white artists were incapable of painting blacks impartially "because of their preconceived notions of what blacks looked like." See John Stauffer, "Creating an Image in Black: The Power of Abolition Pictures," in *Prophets of Protest: Reconsidering the History of American Abolitionism*, ed. Timothy Patrick McCarthy and John Stauffer (New York: Free Press, 2006), 258.

62. Allinson, *Memoir*, 16, 23, 29.

63. James Sidbury, *Becoming African in America: Race and Nation in the Early Black Atlantic* (New York: Oxford University Press, 2007), 159, 160.

64. Nelson, *Biographical and Genealogical Notes*, 8, mentions that Allinson inherited his deceased uncle's home. See also "William J. Allinson," 2. Allinson points out in the *Memoir* that Quamino and his wife, Sarah, "had regular prayer-meetings and class-meetings in their house" (16).

65. Allinson, *Memoir*, 27.

66. Ibid., 23.

67. Ibid., 29.

68. Ibid., 28.

69. Mellick Papers, "Scrap Book," MG 53, box 7.

70. On Mellick's life, see "The Son Follows Father, Death of Andrew D. Mellick, Jr., This Morning," *Daily Press* (Plainfield), November 6, 1895; "Andrew D. Mellick, Obituary of a Man Who Has Made Somerset County Famous by His Pen—A Beautiful Character," *Unionist Gazette* (Somerville), November 14, 1895 (hereafter

"Andrew D. Mellick, Obituary"); A. Van Doren Honeyman, "The Author of 'The Story of an Old Farm,'" *Somerset County Historical Quarterly* 1 (1912): 23–34; and Andrew D. Mellick Jr., *Lesser Crossroads*, ed. Hubert G. Schmidt (New Brunswick, NJ: Rutgers University Press, 1948), v–xii.

71. Bederman, *Manliness and Civilization*, 12.

72. "Andrew D. Mellick, Obituary."

73. Honeyman, "Author of 'The Story of an Old Farm,'" 25.

74. Bederman, *Manliness and Civilization*, 12.

75. See note 70.

76. "Andrew D. Mellick, Obituary."

77. Hubert Schmidt wrote that Mellick "shared the moral code and some of the prejudices of his own day" (*Lesser Crossroads*, ix).

78. Mellick, *Story of an Old Farm*, 56, 98, 100, 169, 215, 224, 607, 608.

79. Ibid., 604–5, 608.

80. Rayford W. Logan, *The Betrayal of the Negro from Rutherford B. Hayes to Woodrow Wilson* (New York: Da Capo, 1997), 168, originally published as *The Negro in American Life and Thought: The Nadir, 1877–1901* (New York: Dial, 1954).

81. "Andrew D. Mellick, Obituary"; Honeyman, "Author of 'The Story of an Old Farm,'" 32.

82. Quoted in Logan, *Betrayal of the Negro*, 162.

83. Ibid., 266.

84. Ibid., 217–18.

85. Ibid., chap. 13.

86. "Andrew D. Mellick, Obituary"; Honeyman, "Author of 'The Story of an Old Farm,'" 28.

87. For the standard account of Larison's life, see Harry B. Weiss, *Country Doctor: Cornelius Wilson Larison of Ringoes, Hunterdon County, New Jersey, 1837–1910: Physician, Farmer, Educator, Author, Editor, Publisher and Exponent of Phonetic Spelling* (Trenton: New Jersey Agricultural Society, 1953).

88. Larison, who had difficulty with pronunciation early in life, developed a great interest in spelling reform, a passion which led him to purchase a printing press, with which he printed his own works in his own orthography. See ibid., 29, 155–56, 158; see also 217, for a listing of Larison's published works.

89. On hegemony, see Michael C. Berthold, "'The peals of her terrific language': The Control of Representation in *Silvia Dubois, a Biografy of the Slav Who Whipt Her Mistres and Gand Her Fredom*," *MELUS: Journal of the Society for the Study of the Multi-Ethnic Literature of the United States* 20 (1995): 4.

90. Larison, *Silvia Dubois*, 35–47, esp. 39.

91. See Edward W. Said, *Orientalism* (1978; repr., New York: Vintage, 1994), 2–9, 35–36, and Eric J. Hobsbawm, *The Age of Empire, 1875–1914* (1987; repr., New York: Vintage, 1989), 80–81.

92. "Andrew D. Mellick, Obituary"; Honeyman, "Author of 'The Story of an Old Farm,'" 32.

93. Judith R. Walkowitz, *City of Dreadful Delight: Narratives of Sexual Danger in Late-Victorian London* (Chicago: University of Chicago Press, 1992), 38–41, 206–7.

94. Quoted in "Andrew D. Mellick, Obituary"; and Honeyman, "Author of 'The Story of an Old Farm,'" 28.

95. "Andrew D. Mellick, Obituary"; Honeyman, "Author of 'The Story of an Old Farm,'" 30.

96. William O. McDowell to Andrew D. Mellick Jr., March 28, 1889, Mellick Papers, MG 53, box 2, folder 12.

97. Thomas N. McCarter to Andrew D. Mellick Jr., January 28, 1890, Mellick Papers, MG 53, box 2, folder 12.

98. Honeyman, "Author of 'The Story of an Old Farm,'" 30.

99. Mellick, *Story of an Old Farm,* 225, 608.

100. Ibid., 225.

101. Ibid., 221.

102. Dorsey, *Reforming Men and Women,* 149.

103. See William L. Van Deburg, *Slavery and Race in American Popular Culture* (Madison: University of Wisconsin Press, 1984), 69–76; Nell Irvin Painter, *Sojourner Truth: A Life, A Symbol* (New York: Norton, 1996), 8–10; Logan, *Betrayal of the Negro,* 224; and Melish, *Disowning Slavery,* xiv, 3, 214–15, 220–21, 224–25. In 1894 a New Jersey minister gave an address in which he stated that "slavery in New Jersey was not so bitter as it was elsewhere [i.e., in the South]." See John Bodine Thompson, "Readington Negroes," *Unionist Gazette* (Somerville), October 25, 1894, courtesy of Fred Sisser III.

104. Abraham Messler, *Centennial History of Somerset County* (Somerville, NJ: Jameson, 1878), 41.

105. Ibid., chap. 10, esp. pp. 127–28.

106. See, for example, "Died," *New Brunswick Fredonian,* April 21, 1864; "Died," *Unionist Gazette* (Somerville), February 19, 1885; "Death of an Aged Slave," *Unionist Gazette* (Somerville), March 1, 1888; and "New Jersey's Last Slave Dead," *Unionist Gazette* (Somerville), August 7, 1887. These and subsequent newspapers are courtesy of Fred Sisser III.

107. *Hunterdon Republican* (Flemington), n.d. Attached to this account is an obituary, dated 1868, of a former enslaved woman who resided at Potterstown, Hunterdon County.

108. "New Jersey's Last Slave Dead."

109. "Blawenburg," *Unionist Gazette* (Somerville), September 3, 1885.

110. See, for example, "Henry Schenck Dies," *Hunterdon Democrat* (Flemington), May 8, 1883; "Death of Aged Negro," *Unionist Gazette* (Somerville), July 18, 1901; and "Death of an Old Somerset Slave," *Unionist Gazette* (Somerville), October 9, 1902.

111. "A Centenarian," *Somerset Messenger* (Somerville), n.d.

112. Mellick, *Story of an Old Farm,* 222, 224, 225, 608–11.

113. Margaret Nevius Van Dyke Malcolm, "As I Remember Scenes from My Childhood," *The Princeton Recollector* 4 (1979): 1, 6.

114. Melish, *Disowning Slavery,* xiii, 3.

115. This insight draws from Michel-Rolph Trouillot, *Silencing the Past: Power and the Production of History* (Boston: Beacon, 1995).

116. Allinson, *Memoir,* 12–15.

117. Quarles, *Black Abolitionists,* 47–49.

118. Andrew D. Mellick Jr. to Edmund Randolph, January 8, 1889, Mellick Papers, MG 53, box 2, folder 11.

Chapter Two

1. Mellick, *Story of an Old Farm*, 225–26, 602–12.

2. Thompson, "Readington Negroes." The history of the Reformed Dutch Church of Readington is discussed in James P. Snell, comp., *History of Hunterdon and Somerset Counties, New Jersey, with Illustrations and Biographical Sketches of its Prominent Men and Pioneers* (Philadelphia: Everts and Peck, 1881), 496–97.

3. William D. Piersen, "White Cannibals, Black Martyrs: Fear, Depression, and Religious Faith as Causes of Suicide among New Slaves," *Journal of Negro History* 62 (1977): 147–59, esp. 151.

4. Michael A. Gomez, *Exchanging Our Country Marks: The Transformation of African Identities in the Colonial and Antebellum South* (Chapel Hill: University of North Carolina Press, 1998), 158–67.

5. Hodges, *Root and Branch*, 38–40, 80, 134–36.

6. On Africans' participation in the slave trade, see Patrick Manning, *Slavery and African Life: Occidental, Oriental, and African Slave Trades* (Cambridge: Cambridge University Press, 1990), chap. 5; John Thornton, *Africa and Africans in the Making of the Atlantic World, 1400–1800*, 2nd ed. (Cambridge: Cambridge University Press, 1998), chaps. 3–4; and Stephanie E. Smallwood, *Saltwater Slavery: A Middle Passage from Africa to American Diaspora* (Cambridge, MA: Harvard University Press, 2007), 20–32. For recent interpretative analyses of the Middle Passage, see Smallwood, *Saltwater Slavery*, chap. 6; Marcus Rediker, *The Slave Ship: A Human History* (New York: Viking Penguin, 2007), chap. 4; Sowande' Mustakeem, "'I Never Have Such a Sickly Ship Before': Diet, Disease, and Mortality in 18th-Century Atlantic Slaving Voyages," *Journal of African American History* 93 (2008): 474–96; and Jerome S. Handler, "The Middle Passage and Material Culture of Captive Africans," *Slavery and Abolition* 30 (2009): 1–26. On the association of Africans with unrestrained sexuality, see Jordan, *White over Black*, 32–40.

7. For Phillis's story, see Snell, *Hunterdon and Somerset*, 104, and Voorhees, "Franklin Township Historical Notes," 5:28. For similar commentary regarding a New England bondwoman, Belinda, captured in Africa, see Sharon M. Harris, ed., *American Women Writers to 1800* (New York: Oxford University Press, 1996), 253–54. DeHart's death is verified in Albert L. Stokes, "The DeHart Family," *Genealogical Magazine of New Jersey* 60 (1965): 6.

8. For a brief discussion of the experiences of black women aboard slave ships, see Deborah Gray White, *Ar'n't I a Woman?*, 63–64. For a gendered analysis of the transatlantic slave trade with an emphasis on female captives, see Morgan, *Laboring Women*, chap. 2. On Africans' fear of white cannibalism, see Piersen, "White Cannibals," 148.

9. The landmark book regarding the overall volume of the transatlantic traffic in enslaved Africans is Philip D. Curtin, *The Atlantic Slave Trade: A Census* (Madison: University of Wisconsin Press, 1969). Curtin estimates that 9,566,100 Africans arrived in the Americas from 1451 to 1870 (268). His contention has elicited two

types of critical responses from scholars: upward revision of different sectors of the slave trade by some, and complete rejection by others—notably J. E. Inikori and James Rawley—who argue that his global calculation for African imports is exceedingly low. For reviews of the debates, see Paul E. Lovejoy, "The Volume of the Atlantic Slave Trade: A Synthesis," *Journal of African History* 23 (1982): 473–501, and Lovejoy, "The Impact of the Atlantic Slave Trade on Africa: A Review of the Literature," *Journal of African History* 30 (1989): 365–94. According to a recent reassessment of the Atlantic slave trade, approximately 10.7 million total African captives were forced over to the Americas, of which 3.6 million were brought alive to the United States. See David Eltis, "The U.S. Transatlantic Slave Trade, 1644–1867: An Assessment," *Civil War History* 54 (2008): 354.

10. Cedric J. Robinson, *Black Marxism: The Making of the Black Radical Tradition* (1983; repr., Chapel Hill: University of North Carolina Press, 2000), 121–22.

11. The literature on West African religious beliefs and practices is vast and complex. For critical general studies, see, for example, Geoffrey Parrinder, *West African Religion: A Study of the Beliefs and Practices of Akan, Ewe, Yoruba, Ibo, and Kindred Peoples* (London: Epworth, 1969); Parrinder, *African Traditional Religion*, 3rd ed. (Westport, CT: Greenwood, 1970); Mbiti, *African Religions and Philosophy*; John S. Mbiti, *Concepts of God in Africa* (London: S.P.C.K. Holy Trinity Church, 1970); Dominique Zahan, *The Religion, Spirituality, and Thought of Traditional Africa*, trans. Kate Ezra Martin and Lawrence M. Martin (1970; repr., Chicago: University of Chicago Press, 1979); and Benjamin C. Ray, *African Religions: Symbol, Ritual, and Community* (Englewood Cliffs, NJ: Prentice-Hall, 1976). See also Albert J. Raboteau, *Slave Religion: The "Invisible Institution" in the Antebellum South* (New York: Oxford University Press, 1978). I also profited from the following brief discussions: Jessie Gaston Mulira, "The Case of Voodoo in New Orleans," in *Africanisms in American Culture*, ed. Joseph E. Holloway (Bloomington: Indiana University Press, 1990), 37, and Morgan, *Laboring Women*, 64.

12. Regarding the African influence on slave religion in North America, see especially Raboteau, *Slave Religion*; Mechal Sobel, *Trabelin' On: The Slave Journey to an Afro-Baptist Faith* (Westport, CT: Greenwood, 1979); Sobel, *The World They Made Together: Black and White Values in Eighteenth-Century Virginia* (Princeton, NJ: Princeton University Press, 1987); and Margaret Washington Creel, *"A Peculiar People": Slave Religion and Community-Culture Among the Gullahs* (New York: New York University Press, 1988). See also Piersen, *Black Yankees*, chap. 9, and Thornton, *Africa and Africans*, chap. 9.

13. See Hodges, *Root and Branch*, 139n1; Leon F. Litwack, *Been in the Storm So Long: The Aftermath of Slavery* (New York: Knopf, 1979), 56; Nell Irvin Painter, *Exodusters: Black Migration to Kansas after Reconstruction* (New York: Knopf, 1977), chap. 15; and Milton C. Sernett, *Bound for the Promised Land: African American Religion and the Great Migration* (Durham, NC: Duke University Press, 1997), chap. 3.

14. Blassingame, *Slave Community*, 7–11, 17–18, 20.

15. Nathan Irvin Huggins, *Black Odyssey: The African-American Ordeal in Slavery* (1977; repr., New York: Vintage, 1990), 38–54. For the phrase, see Daniel C. Littlefield, *Rice and Slaves: Ethnicity and the Slave Trade in Colonial South Carolina* (1981; repr., Urbana: University of Illinois Press, 1991), 75n4.

16. Smallwood, *Saltwater Slavery*, 124, 126–27.

17. Equiano claims that he was born in Igbo land in present-day Nigeria. See Olaudah Equiano, *The Interesting Narrative of the Life of Olaudah Equiano, or Gustavus Vassa, the African. Written by Himself* [1789], reprinted in *Pioneers of the Black Atlantic: Five Slave Narratives from the Enlightenment, 1772–1815*, ed. Henry Louis Gates Jr. and William L. Andrews (Washington, DC: Counterpoint, 1998), 217–22. The validity of Equiano's famous and frequently cited narrative is challenged in Vincent Carretta, "Olaudah Equiano or Gustavus Vassa? New Light on an Eighteenth-Century Question of Identity," *Slavery and Abolition* 20 (1999): 96–105. Carretta suggests that Equiano was a native of South Carolina rather than of Africa. Equiano's "rhetorical ethos," writes Carretta, "his authority to speak as a victim and eye-witness of slavery in Africa, the West Indies, North America, Europe and the Middle East was dependent on the African nativity he claimed" (97). For works confirming Equiano's native African origins, see Alexander X. Byrd, "Eboe, Country, Nation, and Gustavus Vassa's *Interesting Narrative*," *William and Mary Quarterly*, 3rd ser., 63 (2006): 123–48, and Paul E. Lovejoy, "Autobiography and Memory: Gustavus Vassa, alias Olaudah Equiano, the African," *Slavery and Abolition* 27 (2006): 317–47. Marcus Rediker provides perhaps the best resolution to this controversy. He argues that if Equiano "was born in South Carolina, he could have known what he knew only by gathering the lore and experience of people who had been born in Africa and made the dreaded Middle Passage aboard the slave ship. He thus becomes the oral historian, the keeper of the common story, the griot of sorts, of the slave trade, which means that his account is no less faithful to the original experience, only different in its sources and genesis. All who have studied Equiano—on both sides of the debate—agree that he spoke for millions" (*Slave Ship*, 109).

18. Raboteau, *Slave Religion*, 7.

19. Mellick, *Story of an Old Farm*, 602–3, 632, 648.

20. Aaron Malick Record Book.

21. Mellick, *Story of an Old Farm*, 224.

22. Thompson, "Readington Negroes."

23. Mellick, *Story of an Old Farm*, 611.

24. Ibid., 223, 603. On Yombo's physicality, see also Aaron Malick Record Book, and Mellick Papers, "Correspondence Book," MG 53, box 7, folder 1. On rites-of-passage ceremonies, see Merran McCulloch, *The Peoples of Sierra Leone Protectorate* (London: International African Institute, 1950), 29–35; Kenneth Little, *The Mende of Sierra Leone: A West African People in Transition* (London: Routledge and Kegan Paul, 1951), 119–30; Arnold van Gennep, *The Rites of Passage*, trans. Monika B. Vizedom and Gabrielle L. Caffee (1909; repr., Chicago: University of Chicago Press, 1961), 80–82, 85–87; Mbiti, *African Religions and Philosophy*, chap. 12; and Ray, *African Religions*, 91–95. See also Mullin, *Flight and Rebellion*, 40–42.

25. Hodges, *Root and Branch*, 77; Elizabeth Donnan, ed., *Documents Illustrative of the History of the Slave Trade to America*, 5 vols. (Washington, DC: Carnegie Institute of Washington, 1932), 3:510–12.

26. Mellick, *Story of an Old Farm*, 75–76, 631, 648–49; Snell, *Hunterdon and Somerset*, 506; Recorded Wills, West Jersey, no. 522730 (1789–95), pp. 15–19, New Jersey State Archives. The last reference is Jacob Kline's 1789 will, which attests that he was the father of five sons, whereas Andrew Mellick's *Story of an Old Farm* (648–49) lists only four.

27. For a summary of the importance of black labor in the eighteenth-century North, see Berlin, *Many Thousands Gone*, 55–57, 182–83.

28. Evarts B. Greene and Virginia Harrington, *American Population before the Federal Census of 1790* (New York: Columbia University Press, 1932), 111, 112. Hunterdon's white population was 8,691 and 14,510 in 1745 and 1772, respectively. For 1745 census, see also US Census Bureau, *Century of Population Growth*, 184.

29. Mellick, *Story of an Old Farm*, 156, 216, 220, 223, 648.

30. William A. Whitehead, *Contributions to the Early History of Perth Amboy and the Adjoining Country, with Sketches of Men and Events in New Jersey during the Provincial Era* (New York: Appleton, 1856), 317. See also Mellick, *Story of an Old Farm*, 224.

31. Donnan, *Documents*, 3:510–12; James G. Lydon, "New York and the Slave Trade, 1770 to 1774," *William and Mary Quarterly*, 3rd ser., 35 (1978): 382 (table 4).

32. This definition is based upon Anthony Benezet, *Some Historical Account of Guinea, Its Situation, Produce, and the General Disposition of Its Inhabitants: With an Inquiry into the Rise and Progress of the Slave Trade, Its Nature, and Lamentable Effects* (1771; repr., London: Frank Cass, 1968), 1, and James Pope-Hennessy, *Sins of the Father: A Study of the Atlantic Slave Traders, 1441–1807* (London: Weidenfeld and Nicolson, 1967), 38.

33. Puckett, *Black Names*, 463.

34. Christopher Fyfe, *A History of Sierra Leone* (Oxford: Oxford University Press, 1962), 2, 3. On the politicization of women during the colonial era, see Carol P. Hoffer, "Mende and Sherbro Women in High Office," *Canadian Journal of African Studies* 6 (1972): 151–64.

35. Gomez, *Country Marks*, 88.

36. On trade and conflict, see Walter Rodney, *A History of the Upper Guinea Coast, 1545–1800* (1970; repr., New York: Monthly Review, 1982), 103 and passim. See also Gomez, *Country Marks*, 88–92. One of several general regions in Africa from which slaves were imported, Sierra Leone included present-day Guinea-Bissau, Guinea, Sierra Leone, Liberia, and the Ivory Coast. See Gomez, *Country Marks*, 27n45.

37. Hodges, *Root and Branch*, 80–81n48.

38. Lucia McMahon and Deborah Schriver, eds., *To Read My Heart: The Journal of Rachel Van Dyke, 1810–1811* (Philadelphia: University of Pennsylvania Press, 2000), 44. The journal makes no mention of the bondwoman's transatlantic experience.

39. Mellick, *Story of an Old Farm*, 224.

40. William Snelgrave, *A New Account of Some Parts of Guinea and the Slave-Trade* (1743; repr., London: Frank Cass, 1971), 163, 165–67. See also John Newton, *The Journal of a Slave Trader, 1750–1754*, ed. Bernard Martin and Mark Spurrell (London: Epworth, 1962), 80, 103, 105, and Alexander Falconbridge, *An Account of the Slave Trade on the Coast of Africa* (1788; repr., New York: AMS, 1973), 19–20, 24–25, 27–28.

41. Zahan, *Religion, Spirituality*, 31; Little, *Mende of Sierra Leone*, 219; Mbiti, *African Religions and Philosophy*, 15–16.

42. Olaudah Equiano explains that, after he was brought aboard his slaver, "I was immediately handled, and tossed up, to see if I were sound, by some of the crew; and I was now persuaded that I had got into a world of bad spirits, and that they were going to kill me" (*Interesting Narrative*, 218).

43. For works that argue against "fetishism" as representing the core of African religious beliefs, see, for example, Parrinder, *West African Religion*, 8–10, and Parrinder *African Traditional Religion*, 15–17.

44. William Smith, *A New Voyage to Guinea: Describing the Customs, Manners, Soil, Climate, Habits, Buildings, Education, Manual Arts, Agriculture, Trade, Employments, Languages, Ranks of Distinction, Habitations, Diversions, Marriages, and whatever else is memorable among the Inhabitants* (1744; repr., London: Frank Cass, 1967), 26–27.

45. Newton, *Journal of a Slave Trader*, 56. For a parallel account, see John Atkins, *A Voyage to Guinea, Brasil, and the West Indies; In His Majesty's Ships, the Swallow and Weymouth* (1735; repr., London: Frank Cass, 1970), 57–58.

46. Joseph Corry, *Observations upon the Windward Coast of Africa, the Religion, Character, Customs, &c. of the Natives; with a System upon which they may be Civilized, and a Knowledge Attained of the Interior of this Extraordinary Quarter of the Globe; and upon the Natural and Commercial Resources of the Country, made in the years 1805 and 1806* (1807; repr., London: Frank Cass, 1968), 61, 63.

47. Morgan, *Laboring Women*, 50. But, as Morgan also emphasizes, "women were never the majority of the transports."

48. Ibid.

49. Zahan, *Religion, Spirituality*, 31.

50. For mediums and diviners, see M. J. Field, *Religion and Medicine of the Ga People* (London: Clarendon Press, 1937), 100–109; Parrinder, *African Traditional Religion*, 100–104; Mbiti, *African Religions and Philosophy*, 171–78; Ray, *African Religions*, 103–11; and Zahan, *Religion, Spirituality*, 83–85. On secret societies, see Parrinder, *West African Religion*, chap. 12; McCulloch, *Peoples of Sierra Leone*, 29–34; Little, *Mende of Sierra Leone*, 12–14; Fyfe, *History of Sierra Leone*, 10–11; and Gomez, *Country Marks*, 94–99n31.

51. Gomez, *Country Marks*, 96.

52. Quoted in Donnan, *Documents*, 2:266.

53. Atkins, *Voyage to Guinea*, 71–73. Captain Harding struck Tomba several times with a "Hand-spike," laying him out on deck. Afterward, "Captain Harding, weighing the Stoutness and Worth of the two [male] Slaves, did, as in other Countries they do by Rogues of Dignity, whip and scarify them only." Conversely, Harding sentenced "three others, Abettors, but not Actors . . . to cruel Deaths; making them first eat the Heart and Liver of one of them killed" (73).

54. Ottobah Cugoano, *Thoughts and Sentiments on the Evil and Wicked Traffic of the Slavery and Commerce of the Human Species, Humbly Submitted to the Inhabitants of Great-Britain, by Ottobah Cugoano, A Native of Africa* [1787], reprinted in Gates and Andrews, *Pioneers of the Black Atlantic*, 94.

55. See Gomez, *Country Marks*, 166. Yet the seeds of this militant consciousness, as Jennifer Morgan insinuates, were often planted on the West African coast in slave castles and forts, where "slavers treated sexual difference as a way of organizing captives." Hence, "women at slave forts forged connections with one another even before they left the coast." See, Morgan, *Laboring Women*, 55.

56. For example, David Barry Gaspar has effectively shown how Akan religious ceremonies emboldened bondmen to rebel in eighteenth-century Antigua. Similarly, according to Carolyn Fick, voodoo empowered slaves to resist in Saint Domingue by serving as both a unifying and spiritual force in their daily lives. Joao

Reis likewise discusses the role that Allah or Yoruba Gods, *orisha*, played in inspiring the resistance of slaves in Bahia. Islam, Reis contends, united slaves across ethnic and legal boundaries, as well as across the rural/urban divide that was imperative to the success of their 1835 revolt. See David Barry Gaspar, *Bondmen and Rebels: A Study of Master–Slave Relations in Antigua* (Baltimore: Johns Hopkins University Press, 1985), 244–46; Carolyn E. Fick, *The Making of Haiti: The Saint Domingue Revolution from Below* (Knoxville: University of Tennessee Press, 1990), 44–45, 94, 137, 244; and Joao Jose Reis, *Slave Rebellion in Brazil: The Muslim Uprising of 1835 in Bahia* (Baltimore: Johns Hopkins University Press, 1993), 112–15, 118–28.

57. Equiano, *Interesting Narrative*, 219.

58. Snelgrave, *Guinea and the Slave-Trade*, 168.

59. For the basis of this idea, see Elisabeth Kubler-Ross, *On Death and Dying* (New York: Macmillan, 1969), 38–138.

60. John Matthews, *A Voyage to the River Sierra Leone, on the Coast of Africa, Containing an Account of the Trade and Productions of the Country, and of the Civil and Religious Customs and Manners of the People; in a Series of Letters to a Friend in England* (1788; repr., London: Frank Cass, 1966), 65.

61. [John Lequear?], *Traditions of Hunterdon*, ed. D. H. Moreau (Flemington, NJ: Moreau, 1957), 79, originally published as a series of articles entitled "Traditions of Our Ancestors," *Hunterdon Republican* (Flemington), 1869–70.

62. Mullin, *Flight and Rebellion*, 17; Piersen, "White Cannibals," 151–52; Bertram Wyatt-Brown, "The Mask of Obedience: Male Slave Psychology in the Old South," *American Historical Review* 93 (1988): 1228–29.

63. Wyatt-Brown, "Mask of Obedience," 1229.

64. Jordan, *White over Black*, 24–28, 32–40, 109–10, 150–63.

65. For slave codes, see Marion Thompson Wright, "New Jersey Laws and the Negro," 165–66, 167–68, 171; James C. Connolly, "Slavery in Colonial New Jersey and the Causes Operating against its Extension," *Proceedings of the New Jersey Historical Society*, n.s., 14 (1929): 196, 199; and Hodges, *Slavery and Freedom in the Rural North*, 22–25. For the best discussion of the slave uprising in 1712, in which twenty-three captives were convicted of killing nine whites and wounding several others, see Kenneth Scott, "The Slave Insurrection in New York in 1712," *New York Historical Society Quarterly* 45 (1961): 43–74.

66. See Jordan, *White over Black*, in conjunction with David Brion Davis, *The Problem of Slavery in Western Culture* (Ithaca, NY: Cornell University Press, 1966), 447–49, and Anne McClintock, *Imperial Leather: Race, Gender, and Sexuality in the Colonial Conquest* (New York: Routledge, 1995), 56–60.

67. *New York Gazette*, March 25, 1734. For executions, see *Weekly Rehearsal* (Philadelphia), February 11, 1734. See also Hodges, *Root and Branch*, 68–73, 89–90. On power relations, see James C. Scott, *Domination and the Arts of Resistance: Hidden Transcripts* (New Haven, CT: Yale University Press, 1990), 8.

68. *Boston Weekly News Letter*, January 18–25, 1739. See also Hodges, *Root and Branch*, 90–91.

69. Alex Bontemps, *The Punished Self: Surviving Slavery in the Colonial South* (Ithaca, NY: Cornell University Press, 2001), 88.

70. With regard to the murder and public burning, see, respectively, *New York Gazette and Weekly Post Boy*, December 25, 1752, and *Pennsylvania Gazette* (Philadel-

phia), January 9, 1753. See also Messler, *Centennial History*, 128–29; Snell, *Hunterdon and Somerset*, 759; Mellick, *Story of an Old Farm*, 226; and Hodges, *Root and Branch*, 134–36.

71. Whitehead, *Early History of Perth Amboy*, 318–19; Mellick, *Story of an Old Farm*, 225–26.

72. Graham Russell Hodges, *Slavery, Freedom, and Culture among Early American Workers* (Armonk, NY: Sharpe, 1998), 42.

73. Bontemps, *Punished Self*, ix; see also chaps. 5–9.

74. Black, *Dismantling Black Manhood*, chaps. 2–3.

75. For a cogent statement on the reality of patriarchal communities in Africa, see Robertson, "Africa into the Americas?," 12.

76. See especially Raymond A. Bauer and Alice H. Bauer, "Day to Day Resistance to Slavery," *Journal of Negro History* 27 (1942): 388–419; Darlene Clark Hine and Kate Wittenstein, "Female Slave Resistance: The Economics of Sex," in *The Black Woman Cross-Culturally*, ed. Filomina Chioma Steady (Cambridge, MA: Harvard University Press, 1981), 289–300; Elizabeth Fox-Genovese, "Strategies and Forms of Resistance: Focus on Slave Women in the United States," in *In Resistance: Studies in African, Caribbean, and Afro-American History*, ed. Gary Y. Okihiro (Amherst: University of Massachusetts Press, 1986), 144–65; Fox-Genovese, *Within the Plantation Household*, chap. 6; Betty Wood, "Some Aspects of Female Resistance to Chattel Slavery in Low Country Georgia, 1763–1815," *Historical Journal* 30 (1987): 603–22; and Stephanie M. H. Camp, *Closer to Freedom: Enslaved Women and Everyday Resistance in the Plantation South* (Chapel Hill: University of North Carolina Press, 2004), chap. 2.

77. *New York Gazette*, March 25, 1734.

78. By using the arts of resistance paradigm outlined by anthropologist James C. Scott, we can read the couple's suicide as a public declaration of the "hidden transcript," which Scott defines as those acts, plots, and so on that take place outside the sphere of the power holders, represented here by Jacob Kline (*Arts of Resistance*, 4–5, 202, 203, 206–12).

79. Mellick, *Story of an Old Farm*, 224.

80. On the ethnicity of New Jersey slaves, see Hodges, *Root and Branch*, 80n46.

81. William Dunlap, *History of the Rise and Progress of the Arts of Design in the United States*, ed. Alexander Wyckoff, rev. ed., 3 vols. (New York: Blom, 1965), 1:299.

82. Piersen, "White Cannibals," 151.

83. See note 5.

84. For suicides, see Inquisitions on the Dead (1688–1798), 4 vols., 3:372, 380, New Jersey State Archives. The names "Jeane" and "Dine" are both present in the Mende lexicon of names. "Jeane" is a probable English corruption of "Jena" (pronounced "Jen"), meaning "a small bird," and "Dine" an altered form of "Dinna," meaning "a broad-leaved plant that grows in swamps." See Puckett, *Black Names*, 379, 398. Nash, *Forging Freedom*, 81, indicates that enslaved blacks were frequently given English names "in a shortened or diminutive form, as if to connote [their] half-person status" under bondage.

85. Piersen, "White Cannibals," 151; Piersen, *Black Yankees*, 74–75; Gomez, *Country Marks*, 116–20; Michael Mullin, *Africa in America: Slave Acculturation and Resistance in the American South and the British Caribbean, 1736–1831* (Urbana: University of Illinois Press, 1992), 69.

86. Gomez, *Country Marks*, 94n28.

87. McCulloch, *Peoples of Sierra Leone*, 39–40; Little, *Mende of Sierra Leone*, 217–18, 227; Gomez, *Country Marks*, 94, 320n28; W. T. Harris and Harry Sawyerr, *The Springs of Mende Belief and Conduct: A Discussion of the Influence of the Belief in the Supernatural among the Mende* (Freetown: Sierra Leone University Press, 1968), 65 and passim.

88. Mbiti, *Concepts of God*, 54.

89. Harris and Sawyerr, *Mende Belief and Conduct*, 30, 31, 32, 89, 136–37. Conversely, "the wicked go to the place where they till the soil with their elbows and so suffer extreme hunger" (i.e., *ngombi-me-hun*, "the place of eating knees," which is obviously equivalent to the Christian notion of hell) (89). See also Sobel, *World They Made Together*, 171–77.

90. Gomez, *Country Marks*, 94, provides a brief summary of Mende spirits.

91. Zahan, *Religion, Spirituality*, 4, 27–28; Harris and Sawyerr, *Mende Belief and Conduct*, 47–48. See also Raboteau, *Slave Religion*, 82–83.

92. Zahan, *Religion, Spirituality*, 21.

93. James Albert Ukawsaw Gronniosaw, *A Narrative of the Most Remarkable Particulars in the Life of James Albert Ukawsaw Gronniosaw, an African Prince, as Related by Himself* [1772], reprinted in Gates and Andrews, *Pioneers of the Black Atlantic*, 35, 39, 41, 42, 45. See also Hodges, *Root and Branch*, 123. On the life and ministry of Reverend Frelinghuysen, see, for example, F. J. Schrag, "Theodorus Jacobus Frelinghuysen: The Father of American Pietism," *Church History* 14 (1945): 201–16, esp. 204.

94. Gronniosaw, *Narrative of the Most Remarkable Particulars*, 34–35.

95. Ibid., 42–43, 45–46. See also Hodges, *Root and Branch*, 123–24.

96. See Harris and Sawyerr, *Mende Belief and Conduct*, chap. 2; McCulloch, *Peoples of Sierra Leone*, 39–42; Little, *Mende of Sierra Leone*, 218–21; Parrinder, *West African Religion*, chap. 11; Parrinder, *African Traditional Religion*, chap. 5 and passim; and Mbiti, *African Religions and Philosophy*, 83–91.

97. Harris and Sawyerr, *Mende Belief and Conduct*, 13, 14.

98. On spirits having personalities, see Sobel, *Trabelin' On*, 17. Gomez, *Country Marks*, 94, emphasizes the transhuman existence of spirits in Mende culture.

99. Sobel, *Trabelin' On*, 41.

100. [Lequear?], *Traditions of Hunterdon*, 80.

101. Mellick, *Story of an Old Farm*, 603. "The experience of acculturation," writes Gerald Mullin, "means that as slaves came to know varieties of whites and their ways, they acquired occupational skills, fluent English, and a distinctive, 'sensible' manner in speaking situations," a description we cannot apply firmly to Yombo (*Flight and Rebellion*, 37). See also Gomez, *Country Marks*, 8–11, and Bontemps, *Punished Self*, chaps. 5–7. For a statement on Northern captives' adoption of white cultural norms, see Zilversmit, *First Emancipation*, 28. On earrings, see chapter 3 of this study.

102. Recorded Wills, no. 522730, p. 15, New Jersey State Archives.

103. "Bedminster Township Ratable of 1785," *Somerset County Genealogical Quarterly* 4 (1986): 264, shows that Aaron Malick owned one bondperson, who was undoubtedly Yombo.

104. For example, the New Jersey slave code of 1713 prohibited free blacks from owning property, and thus virtually nullified their economic opportunities. See Marion Thompson Wright, "New Jersey Laws and the Negro," 167, and Hodges, *Root and Branch*, 67, 70.

105. Piersen, "White Cannibals," 151–53; Mullin, *Flight and Rebellion*, chap. 2; Mullin, *Africa in America*, 14, 31, 33, 69, 86–87; Kenneth Scott, "Slave Insurrection in New York," 46–49; Gomez, *Country Marks*, 116–24, 127–28, 131; Berlin, "Time, Space," 52–53.

106. Mellick, *Story of an Old Farm*, 605.

107. For religious institutions' views on slavery, see Hodges, *Slavery and Freedom in the Rural North*, xiii–xiv, 25–32, 67–80.

108. [Lequear?], *Traditions of Hunterdon*, 79.

109. Mellick, *Story of an Old Farm*, 602–3.

Chapter Three

1. Mellick, *Story of an Old Farm*, 611–12.

2. Mellick Papers, "Scrap Book," MG 53, box 7.

3. Mellick, *Story of an Old Farm*, 603.

4. Genovese, *Roll, Jordan, Roll*, 626–27, discusses the contradictory views that Southern bondpeople had of the putative "bad" or mean men in their communities who fought whites yet bullied fellow blacks. There are numerous studies of day-to-day slave resistance. See, for example, the pioneering work by Bauer and Bauer, "Day to Day Resistance to Slavery," 388–419.

5. Hodges, *Root and Branch*, 140.

6. Ibid.

7. Gary B. Nash, *Race and Revolution* (Madison, WI: Madison House, 1990), 58.

8. Ibid., 57. This literature includes: Nash, *Forging Freedom*, 43–52, 54–59; Benjamin Quarles, *The Negro in the American Revolution* (1961; repr., New York: Norton, 1973), chap. 3; Quarles, "The Revolutionary War as a Black Declaration of Independence," in *Slavery and Freedom in the Age of the American Revolution*, ed. Ira Berlin and Ronald Hoffman (Charlottesville: University Press of Virginia, 1983), 283–301; Mullin, *Flight and Rebellion*, chap. 5; Sylvia R. Frey, *Water from the Rock: Black Resistance in a Revolutionary Age* (Princeton, NJ: Princeton University Press, 1991), 49–53, 224–32; Harry Reed, *Platform for Change: The Foundations of the Northern Free Black Community, 1775–1865* (East Lansing: Michigan State University Press, 1994), 3, 6, 11–12, 61–63; Hodges, *Slavery and Freedom in the Rural North*, chap. 3; Hodges, *Root and Branch*, chap. 5; and Cassandra Pybus, *Epic Journeys of Freedom: Runaway Slaves of the American Revolution and their Global Quest for Liberty* (Boston: Beacon, 2006), chaps. 1–4.

9. That is to say, Mellick (*Story of an Old Farm*, 602–3) did not dispute William Sutphen's original account, found in Mellick Papers, "Scrap Book."

10. Aaron Malick Record Book.

11. Mellick, *Story of an Old Farm*, 603. Prasenjit Duara, *Rescuing History from the Nation* (Chicago: University of Chicago Press, 1995), 22–23, argues that European imperialists historically have depicted the putative backward and primitive dark-skinned peoples as having no history to justify their colonization. Similarly, according to Paul Gilroy, *"There Ain't No Black in the Union Jack": The Cultural Politics of Race and Nation* (Chicago: University of Chicago Press, 1987), 5–8, the power of racism

is based on the ability to embed blacks in the present, while erasing and denying the past.

12. Mellick, *Story of an Old Farm*, 608. On the dynamism of slave resistance, see James C. Scott, *Arts of Resistance*, 188–89.

13. Scholars of subaltern studies would classify such phraseology as "an occasional outbreak" as "the prose of counter-insurgency," meaning any elite language that implicitly strips the actions of subaltern groups of political or moral validity. See Guha, "Prose of Counter-Insurgency," 45–84, esp. 46.

14. For a vast compilation of eighteenth-century fugitive slave advertisements, see Graham Russell Hodges and Alan Edward Brown, eds., *"Pretends to Be Free": Runaway Slave Advertisements from Colonial and Revolutionary New York and New Jersey* (New York: Garland, 1994). The editors point out that the 662 notices listed in *"Pretends to Be Free"* "describe 753 fugitive slaves, an average of more than eleven per year between 1716 and 1783." They caution, however, that these advertisements "do not constitute all the fugitive bondpeople of early New York and New Jersey" (vx). I have been able to locate a number of the notices found in their book and have incorporated them into this discussion. Some of the notices found in *"Pretends to Be Free"* also appear in Billy G. Smith and Richard Wojtowicz, eds., *Blacks Who Stole Themselves: Advertisements for Runaways in the Pennsylvania Gazette, 1728–1790* (Philadelphia: University of Pennsylvania Press, 1989).

15. Mellick Papers, "Scrap Book."

16. *Parker's New York Gazette or Weekly Post-Boy*, June 21, 1759; *New York Gazette or Weekly Post-Boy*, May 26, 1763, and December 25, 1766.

17. *New York Gazette or Weekly Post-Boy*, July 3, 1766; *Pennsylvania Chronicle* (Philadelphia), June 13, 1768.

18. *Pennsylvania Gazette* (Philadelphia), June 19, 1776, and July 9, 1777; *Pennsylvania Journal* (Philadelphia), October 30, 1776. Mellick, *Story of an Old Farm*, 603–4, indicates that General John Taylor was an associate of Aaron Malick's.

19. Snell, *Hunterdon and Somerset Counties*, 104; Voorhees, "Franklin Township Historical Notes," 5:28–29.

20. Mellick, *Story of an Old Farm*, 602–3.

21. Graham Hodges, while discussing the various labor roles of bondpeople in eighteenth-century rural New Jersey, comments that "any enslaved black on a reasonably large farm had to perform a variety of tasks" (*Slavery and Freedom in the Rural North*, 47; see also 44–50). Accordingly, Roluff Van Dike of Somerset County advertised the sale of "a Likely hearty Negro Man, about 26 or 27 years of age, and understands all sorts of farming business, and is a very good tanner" for £130. See *Archives of the State of New Jersey*, 2nd ser., vol. 5 (Newark: State of New Jersey, 1917), 83.

22. Larison, *Silvia Dubois*, 67, 76. The real name of Silvia's owner was Dominicus ("Minna") Dubois, but Silvia refers to him as "Minical" in her reminiscence (9). I have substituted "Minna" for "Minical" in the quotation.

23. Abraham Van Doren Honeyman, ed., "The Revolutionary War Record of Samuel Sutphin [*sic*], Slave," *Somerset County Historical Quarterly* 3 (1914): 186–90, reprinted in *New Jersey in the American Revolution, 1763–1783: A Documentary History*, ed. Larry R. Gerlach (Trenton: New Jersey Historical Commission, 1975), 355, 356. Gerlach's reprint is heavily footnoted. The original testimonial is located in Pen-

sion Records for Samuel Sutphen, 10321, Military Pensions (Revolutionary War), National Archives, Washington, DC (hereafter Pension Records for Samuel Sutphen). I discovered the pension application at the David Library of the American Revolution, Washington Crossing, PA.

24. Sobel, *World They Made Together*, 30.

25. Quoted in Voorhees, "Franklin Township Historical Notes," 6:27.

26. This analysis is indebted to Katherine Verdery, *What was Socialism, and What Comes Next?* (Princeton, NJ: Princeton University Press, 1996), chap. 2, which creatively explores the struggles between the "people" and the "state" in Romania during the 1980s.

27. Similarly, Genovese, *Roll, Jordan, Roll*, 597–98, contends that resistance and accommodation were part of a single process of slave survival.

28. This analysis draws from Paul E. Lovejoy, "Fugitive Slaves: Resistance to Slavery in the Sokoto Caliphate," in Okihiro, *In Resistance*, 71–74.

29. Quoted in Schmidt, "Slavery and Attitudes on Slavery," 165–66.

30. Demarest's account is quoted in Kull, "Slavery in New Jersey," 2:731. For the date, see Francis Bazley Lee, *Genealogical and Memorial History of the State of New Jersey*, 4 vols. (New York: Lewis Historical Publishing, 1910), 1:149. On David Demarest, a New Jersey minister, see John P. Wall, *The Chronicles of New Brunswick, New Jersey* (New Brunswick, NJ: Thatcher-Anderson, 1931), 103.

31. Mullin, *Flight and Rebellion*, 56. For other critical discussions, see Genovese, *Roll, Jordan, Roll*, 648–57; Peter H. Wood, *Black Majority*, 241, 263–68; Deborah Gray White, *Ar'n't I a Woman?*, 74–77; Fox-Genovese, *Within the Plantation Household*, 319–20; Shane White, *Somewhat More Independent*, 125; John Hope Franklin and Loren Schweninger, *Runaway Slaves: Rebels on the Plantation* (New York: Oxford University Press, 1999), 98–99; and Camp, *Closer to Freedom*, chap. 2.

32. Kull, "Slavery in New Jersey," 731; Franklin and Schweninger, *Runaway Slaves*, 98.

33. For an overview of geography in New Jersey, see Wacker, *Land and People*, 2–8.

34. *Rivington's New York Gazetteer*, August 5, 1773. For additional property advertisements with respect to central New Jersey, see, for example, *New Jersey Journal* (Chatham), April 30, 1783; *Political Intelligencer* (New Brunswick), January 20, 1784; *New Jersey Gazette* (Trenton), March 30, 1784; and *Federal Post* (Trenton), October 21, 1788. New Brunswick was located partly in Somerset and Middlesex counties.

35. *Pennsylvania Chronicle* (Philadelphia), October 8, 1770.

36. On the timing of flight, see Smith and Wojtowicz, *Blacks Who Stole Themselves*, 11n30, and Hodges and Brown, *"Pretends to Be Free,"* xxxiii (Appendix 1, Table 5). For the phrase "weapon of the weak," see James C. Scott, *Weapons of the Weak*. The crux of Scott's argument, which has implications for enslaved blacks, is that open, collective rebellion represents only one form of peasant political action. Everyday acts of resistance (i.e., "weapons of the weak") constitute peasants' safest, most effective, and hence primary means of resistance.

37. On the high turnover rate, see Shane White, *Somewhat More Independent*, 88–93, and Hodges, *Slavery and Freedom in the Rural North*, 16–21, 155–56. On gender and slave labor, see Cooley, *Study of Slavery in New Jersey*, 55, and Hodges, *Slavery and Freedom in the Rural North*, 44–50. Stephanie Camp, writing on antebel-

lum Southern slavery, notes that "the geography of containment was somewhat more elastic for men than it was for women, in large measure because the work that provided opportunities to leave the plantation was generally reserved for men" (*Closer To Freedom*, 28). Camp's astute observation also holds true for the rural North.

38. *Pennsylvania Gazette* (Philadelphia), September 10, 1761.

39. *Pennsylvania Journal* (Philadelphia), October 13, 1763. "High Dutch" was an eighteenth-century term for German.

40. For the containment concept, see Camp, *Closer to Freedom*, 28.

41. Mellick, *Story of an Old Farm*, 603.

42. Ibid.

43. Susan E. Klepp and Billy G. Smith, eds., *The Infortunate: The Voyage and Adventures of William Moraley, an Indentured Servant* (1743; repr., University Park: Pennsylvania State University Press, 1992), 94. See also Shane White, *Somewhat More Independent*, 106–13.

44. Larison, *Silvia Dubois*, 54. This "law" was not mandated in New Jersey.

45. Mellick Papers, "Scrap Book."

46. Leonard Lundin, *Cockpit of the Revolution: The War for Independence in New Jersey* (Princeton, NJ: Princeton University Press, 1940). British forces occupied New Brunswick from 1776 to 1777, and New York City from 1776 to 1783.

47. Jacob Magill, "Somerset Traditions Gathered Forty Years Ago," *Somerset County Historical Quarterly* 2 (1913): 25.

48. [Eliza Susan Quincy], "Basking Ridge in Revolutionary Days: Extracts from a Lady's Published Recollections," *Somerset County Historical Quarterly* 1 (1912): 35.

49. Magill, "Somerset Traditions," 25.

50. Thompson, "Readington Negroes."

51. *Archives of the State of New Jersey*, 2nd ser., vol. 4 (1914), 406.

52. On living space, see Stephanie B. Stevens, *Outcast: A Story of Slavery in Readington Township, Hunterdon County, New Jersey* (White House Station, NJ: Merck, 2003), 29, and Hodges, *Slavery and Freedom in the Rural North*, 53–54. "No one," wrote a racist Hunterdon County historian, "had more receptive ears for local gossip than did the average darky or was more generous in sharing it with others" (see Schmidt, "Slavery and Attitudes," 160).

53. "Somerset Patriotism Preceding the Revolutionary War: From Minutes of Meetings of Citizens and Committees," *Somerset County Historical Quarterly* 5 (1916): 242, 245, 246.

54. Dorothy A. Stratford, "The Docket of Jacob Van Noorstrand," *Genealogical Magazine of New Jersey* 43 (1968): 65–66. Stratford's work on Van Noorstrand was published in several installments in the *Genealogical Magazine of New Jersey* from 1967 to 1969, in issues 42 through 44. Further references to Stratford's work (hereafter cited as "Jacob Van Noorstrand") will give the issue and page numbers only.

55. Honeyman, "Revolutionary War Record of Samuel Sutphin," 355n1; "Hillsborough Township 'Census' of 1784," 102.

56. Greene, *All Men Are Created Equal*.

57. E. Alfred Jones, *The Loyalists of New Jersey: Their Memorials, Petitions, Claims, Etc., from English Records* (Newark: New Jersey Historical Society, 1927), 15–16.

58. George Fishman, "Taking a Stand for Freedom in Revolutionary New Jersey: Prime's Petition of 1786," *Science and Society* 56 (1992): 353.

59. Ibid., 355.

60. Ibid., 354.

61. Ibid., 354–55.

62. See Zilversmit, *First Emancipation*, 24–28, 159, 188–89; Marion Thompson Wright, *Education of Negroes in New Jersey*, 20–21, 23–25, 34, 56, 63, 71–76; and Hodges, *Slavery and Freedom in the Rural North*, 60, 61, 70, 71, 116, 156.

63. Letter written by Nicholas C. Jobs, May 26, 1834, in Pension Records for Samuel Sutphen.

64. Stratford, "Jacob Van Noorstrand," 42:99; 43:17, 20, 62, 63, 67; 44:43, 44, 84.

65. Hodges, *Slavery and Freedom in the Rural North*, 95. See also Shane White, *Somewhat More Independent*, 127, 130–31.

66. Quoted in Hodges, *Slavery and Freedom in the Rural North*, 95. Every able-bodied male between the ages of sixteen and sixty, including free blacks, was required to serve in the Patriot military. See Robert J. Gough, "Black Men and the Early New Jersey Militia," *New Jersey History* 88 (1970): 227–37, esp. 228–29.

67. *New York Gazette and Weekly Mercury*, July 24, 1775; William S. Stryker, comp., *Official Register of the Officers and Men of New Jersey in the Revolutionary War* (1872; repr., Baltimore: Genealogical Publishing, 1967), 427.

68. Mellick, *Story of an Old Farm*, 603; Stryker, *Official Register*, 343.

69. *New Jersey Gazette* (Trenton), September 8, 1779; Stryker, *Official Register*, 799.

70. *New Jersey Gazette* (Trenton), February 16, 1780; Stryker, *Official Register*, 581.

71. Klepp and Smith, *Infortunate*, 96.

72. Stryker, *Official Register*, 656.

73. See Mellick, *Story of an Old Farm*, 611, 648.

74. Ibid., 554; Mellick Papers, "Scrap Book."

75. Mellick, *Story of an Old Farm*, 602–3.

76. Mellick Papers, "Scrap Book."

77. *Archives of the State of New Jersey*, 2nd ser., vol. 5 (1917), 154.

78. Klepp and Smith, *Infortunate*, 94.

79. Connolly, "Slavery in Colonial New Jersey," 196–97.

80. Klepp and Smith, *Infortunate*, 94.

81. Marion Thompson Wright, "New Jersey Laws and the Negro," 174–75.

82. Larison, *Silvia Dubois*, 69.

83. Ibid., 70. As Thomas P. Slaughter writes in *Bloody Dawn: The Christiana Riot and Racial Violence in the Antebellum North* (New York: Oxford University Press, 1991), "We can only imagine with horror what it must have been like for a free black to be imprisoned on suspicion of being a slave, to languish in jail while advertisements were placed to see if any 'master' came forward to claim his 'property,' and if no 'master' showed up, to be sold into bondage, nonetheless, until the 'free' black worked off the costs of his incarceration" (23).

84. *Pennsylvania Packet* (Philadelphia), November 9, 1779.

85. *Pennsylvania Packet* (Philadelphia), December 22, 1779. Trenton is now located in Mercer County in South Jersey.

86. *New Jersey Gazette* (Trenton), February 16, 1780.

87. *New Jersey Journal* (Chatham), May 7, 1780.

88. *New York Gazette or Weekly Post-Boy*, May 26, 1763. For another "smooth-tongu'd Fellow," see *New York Gazette or Weekly Post-Boy*, June 14, 1756.

89. See *New York Gazette or Weekly Post-Boy*, December 25, 1752; *Pennsylvania Gazette* (Philadelphia), January 9, 1753; Mellick, *Story of an Old Farm*, 226; Hodges, *Root and Branch*, 134–35; and Snell, *Hunterdon and Somerset*, 759.

90. As a correlation to their possibly (accentuated) imposing stature, enslaved blacks tended to pay great attention to their physical appearance. For example, Dick, who ran away from his Woodbridge owner, was described as "a well-looking, well built fellow" who "takes uncommon Pains with his short wooly Hair"; see *New York Gazette or Weekly Post-Boy*, June 18, 1770. For additional examples of style consciousness among central New Jersey bondpeople, see *Pennsylvania Journal and Weekly Advertiser* (Philadelphia), October 13, 1763; *Pennsylvania Chronicle* (Philadelphia), October 8, 1770; and *New Jersey Gazette* (Trenton), May 12, 1779. For further discussion on slave style, see note 107.

91. Larison, *Silvia Dubois*, 30, 94.

92. *Unionist Gazette* (Somerville), July 18, 1901, courtesy of Fred Sisser III.

93. See note 37.

94. Klepp and Smith, *Infortunate*, 95.

95. For physical description, see Mellick, *Story of an Old Farm*, 603.

96. See Alex Lichtenstein, "'That Disposition to Theft, with which they have been Branded': Moral Economy, Slave Management, and the Law," *Journal of Social History* 21 (1988): 413–40. See also Booker, *"I Will Wear No Chain!,"* 26.

97. Mellick Papers, "Scrap Book."

98. Booker, *"I Will Wear No Chain!,"* 29.

99. *New York Gazette and Weekly Mercury*, May 24, 1773.

100. *New Jersey Gazette* (Trenton), November 13, 1782.

101. *Hunterdon Gazette* (Flemington), November 21, 1838.

102. Mellick, *Story of an Old Farm*, 603.

103. In addition to Jordan, *White over Black*, see Davis, *Problem of Slavery in Western Culture*, 447–49, and McClintock, *Imperial Leather*, 56–60.

104. *New Jersey Journal* (Chatham), May 7, 1780.

105. Quoted in Schmidt, "Slavery and Attitudes," 153.

106. Mellick, *Story of an Old Farm*, 603.

107. Shane White and Graham White, *Stylin': African American Expressive Culture from its Beginnings to the Zoot Suit* (Ithaca, NY: Cornell University Press, 1998), chaps. 1–2. See also Shane White, *Somewhat More Independent*, 194–200, 203–5, and Hodges, *Slavery and Freedom in the Rural North*, 59–60, 152–53, 154.

108. Thomas Winterbottom, *An Account of the Native Africans in the Neighbourhood of Sierra Leone, to which is added An Account of the Present State of Medicine among them*, vol. 1 (1803; repr., London: Frank Cass, 1969), 104.

109. Aaron Malick Record Book; Mellick, *Story of an Old Farm*, 602.

110. See White and White, *Stylin'*, 48n30, and chapter 1 of this study, which connects Yombo to the Mende of West Africa.

111. Smith, *New Voyage to Guinea*, 203.

112. Dunlap, *Arts of Design*, 1:288.

113. Graham Russell Hodges, ed., *Black Itinerants of the Gospel: The Narratives of John Jea and George White* (Madison, WI: Madison House, 1993), 3.

114. Malcolm, "Scenes from My Childhood," 1, 11. For further discussion of the religiosity of New Jersey captives, see Messler, *Centennial History*, 130–31; A. W. McDowell, "Pluckamin One Hundred Years Ago," *Our Home: A Monthly Magazine . . . Mostly by Somerset and Hunterdon County Writers, and Largely Pertaining to These Counties* 1 (1873): 532; Abraham Van Doren Honeyman, ed., "A Former Lamington 'Black Saint,'" *Somerset County Historical Quarterly* 8 (1919): 321; Schmidt, "Slavery and Attitudes," 161–63; and Allinson, *Memoir*, 6–8.

115. Stratford, "Jacob Van Noorstrand," 44:84.

116. Allinson, *Memoir*, 6.

117. On the Christianization of putatively backwards captives in Somerset County, see Messler, *Centennial History*, 130–31.

118. See Bontemps, *Punished Self*, chaps. 5–7, and Rawick, *From Sunup to Sundown*, 6.

119. Mellick, *Story of an Old Farm*, 612.

120. Larison, *Silvia Dubois*, 80.

121. Dunlap, *Arts of Design*, 1:288.

122. Majors and Billson, *Cool Pose*, 40.

Chapter Four

1. US Census Bureau, *Century of Population Growth*, 195.

2. Ibid., 183, 194. Albany, Columbia, Dutchess, Orange, Ulster, Westchester, and Rensselaer counties comprised the Hudson River Valley.

3. Allinson, *Memoir*, 4. "Being extremely illiterate, his [Quamino's] language was often incoherent; and he not unfrequently laboured in vain to find fitting phrases fully to convey the thoughts he was anxious to express" (22).

4. Marshall, "'Ain't No Account,'" 31–33.

5. Allinson, *Memoir*, 4.

6. Ibid., 4, 5, 6, 9, 15. On the high turnover rate and rural isolation, see, for example, Shane White, *Somewhat More Independent*, 88–93, and Hodges, *Slavery and Freedom in the Rural North*, 16–21, 155–56.

7. See note 38.

8. Frederick Douglass, *Narrative of the Life of Frederick Douglass, An American Slave, Written by Himself* [1845], ed. Benjamin Quarles (Cambridge, MA: Harvard University Press, 1960), 24–25; Harriet A. Jacobs, *Incidents in the Life of a Slave Girl, Written by Herself* [1861], ed. Jean Fagan Yellin (Cambridge, MA: Harvard University Press, 1987), 5–6, 13–14; Henry Bibb, *Narrative of the Life and Adventures of Henry Bibb, An American Slave* [1849], in *Puttin' on Ole Massa: The Slave Narratives of Henry Bibb, William Wells Brown, and Solomon Northup*, ed. Gilbert Osofsky (New York: Harper and Row, 1969), 64–65; William Wells Brown, *Narrative of William Wells Brown, A Fugitive Slave, Written by Himself* [1847], in Osofsky, *Puttin' on Ole Massa*, 185.

9. Important works on enslaved Southern children include: Thomas L. Webber, *Deep Like the Rivers: Education in the Slave Quarter Community, 1831–1865* (New York: Norton, 1978); Wilma King, *Stolen Childhood: Slave Youth in Nineteenth-Century Amer-

ica (Bloomington: Indiana University Press, 1995); and Marie Jenkins Schwartz, *Born in Bondage: Growing up Enslaved in the Antebellum South* (Cambridge, MA: Harvard University Press, 2000). There are no studies that focus specifically on enslaved youth in the North; however, Painter, *Sojourner Truth*, 11–18, provides an insightful discussion of the childhood of former upstate New York slave Sojourner Truth. For the enslaved childhood of Silvia Dubois in Somerset County and present-day Susquehanna, Pennsylvania, see Larison, *Silvia Dubois*, 53–56.

10. Thompson, "Readington Negroes." See also John B. Thompson Papers, Special Collections, Alexander Library, Rutgers University, New Brunswick, NJ. Phillis was probably hired out by Henry Post sometime between 1809 and 1829. These dates reflect when Henry and Martha were married, and the year Martha died. See Snell, *Hunterdon and Somerset Counties*, 489.

11. Allinson, *Memoir*, 4. The probable identity of Schenk is discussed in Marshall, "'Ain't No Account,'" 17–18.

12. A. J. Williams-Myers, *Long Hammering: Essays on the Forging of an African American Presence in the Hudson River Valley to the Early Twentieth Century* (Trenton, NJ: Africa World Press, 1994), 5.

13. Larison, *Silvia Dubois*, 53–56, 65–66.

14. For further evidence of these tensions, see Shane White, *Somewhat More Independent*, 125.

15. For a related comment on the "slave community," see Nell Irvin Painter, "Soul Murder and Slavery: Toward a Fully Loaded Cost Accounting," in *Southern History across the Color Line* (Chapel Hill: University of North Carolina Press, 2002), 30. The average slaveholder in Dutchess County at the time of the 1790 federal census owned 2.8 slaves. See Michael E. Groth, "The African American Struggle against Slavery in the Mid-Hudson Valley, 1785–1827," *Hudson Valley Regional Review* 11 (1994): 76n14.

16. See Painter, *Sojourner Truth*, 17.

17. Allinson, *Memoir*, 19–30.

18. Ibid., 4–5.

19. Henry Noble MacCracken, *Old Dutchess Forever!: The Story of an American County* (New York: Hastings House, 1956), 125, maintains that in Dutchess County there was an "absence of riots, insurrection, and violence" among the enslaved. For crime and ensuing burning, see Williams-Myers, *Long Hammering*, 46.

20. Genovese, *Roll, Jordan, Roll*, 615.

21. Allinson, *Memoir*, 5.

22. Messler, *Centennial History*, 128–29.

23. Mellick, *Story of an Old Farm*, 226.

24. For an interesting and relevant discussion on "slave mentality," see Painter, *Sojourner Truth*, 17.

25. Orlando Patterson, *Slavery and Social Death: A Comparative Study* (Cambridge, MA: Harvard University Press, 1982), 2.

26. *New York Gazette or Weekly Post-Boy*, October 15, 1753.

27. *New York Gazette* (*Weyman's*), September 6, 1763.

28. Mellick, *Story of an Old Farm*, 225, 604.

29. Allinson, *Memoir*, 5. While in exile in Poughkeepsie, "Quamino was several times taken to see his old master; and once Buccau [Brokaw] . . . came to see him" (4).

30. Quoted in MacCracken, *Old Dutchess*, 352; see also 362–63.

31. Groth, "African American Struggle against Slavery," 65 (table A).

32. Hodges, *Root and Branch*, 145.

33. Quarles, *Negro in the American Revolution*, 116.

34. Williams-Myers, *Long Hammering*, 56–57, 174.

35. Edgar J. McManus, *Black Bondage in the North* (Syracuse, NY: Syracuse University Press, 1973), 141.

36. Allinson, *Memoir*, 5.

37. Ibid., 6.

38. Painter, "Soul Murder and Slavery," 12–13. Painter's use of the term "soul murder"—meaning the violation of one's inner being, or the extinguishing of one's identity—to explore American slavery's legacy of violence relies partly on the book written by Leonard Shengold, *Soul Murder: The Effects of Child Abuse and Deprivation* (New Haven, CT: Yale University Press, 1989). As Painter explains, "the 'abuse' in the subtitle can be violent and/or sexual, which presents children with too much sensation to bear," whereas "'deprivation' . . . refers to neglect that deprives children of enough attention to meet their psychic needs" (17n4).

39. Silvia Dubois was enslaved from around 1788/9 to 1807/8, and Sojourner Truth from about 1797 to 1826. See, respectively, Larison, *Silvia Dubois*, 12, and Painter, *Sojourner Truth*, 3, 24.

40. Painter, *Sojourner Truth*, 16–17.

41. Ibid., 15–16.

42. Larison, *Silvia Dubois*, 67.

43. Ibid., 60, 75.

44. In the words of Silvia Dubois's amanuensis, Cornelius Larison, "Her love of freedom is boundless. To be free is the all-important thing with Sylvia. Bondage, or even restraint, is near akin to death for Sylvia. Freedom is the goal—freedom of speech, freedom of labor, freedom of the passions, freedom of the appetite—unrestrained in all things" (ibid., 45). And yet, it is clear that slavery had a lasting and negative impact on her mind.

45. For a forthright and succinct analysis of the difficulties under which enslaved women attempted to forge gender conventions, see Fox-Genovese, *Within the Plantation Household*, 290–302. See also Deborah Gray White, *Ar'n't I a Woman?*; Jones, *Labor of Love*, chap. 1; Brenda E. Stevenson, "Gender Convention, Ideals, and Identity among Antebellum Virginia Slave Women," in Gaspar and Hine, *More Than Chattel*, 169–90; and Marli F. Weiner, *Mistresses and Slaves: Plantation Women in South Carolina, 1830–1880* (Urbana: University of Illinois Press, 1998). Like the historiography on enslaved women, that on enslaved men focuses primarily on the plantation South (see, for example, note 77). On the forging of gender conventions among Northern bondpeople and the difficulties thereof, see James Oliver Horton, "Freedom's Yoke: Gender Conventions among Antebellum Free Blacks," *Feminist Studies* 12 (1986): 51, 52–53.

46. Allinson, *Memoir*, 6.

47. Ibid.

48. The fact that at least eight of Isaac Brokaw's ten children were baptized in the Reformed Dutch Church suggests that this was his religious home. See Elsie Foster, *Our Brokaw-Bragaw Heritage* (n.p., n.d. [c. 1970]), 15, courtesy of Fred Sisser III.

49. "The Brokaw-Bragaw Family," *New York Genealogical and Biographical Record* 87 (1956): 12–13, 15, 16–17.

50. Theodore Thayer, *As We Were: The Story of Old Elizabethtown* (Elizabeth: New Jersey Historical Society, 1964), 131.

51. Allinson, *Memoir*, 8.

52. *Pennsylvania Gazette* (Philadelphia), September 11, 1740.

53. *New Jersey Gazette* (Trenton), August 7, 1786.

54. For the respect accorded Barnet, see McDowell, "Pluckamin," 532. For the year of Barnet's death, see Honeyman, "'Black Saint,'" 321. This account also mentions that Barnet and his wife, Amber, were freed in 1825.

55. Quoted in Honeyman, "'Black Saint,'" 321.

56. Allinson, *Memoir*, 6–7.

57. Ibid., 7.

58. Parallel to Quamino's experience, Nell Irvin Painter, *Sojourner Truth*, 22, explains that the slave Isabella (Sojourner Truth) had "freed herself from fear through the discovery of Jesus' love."

59. *Anecdotes and Memoirs of William Boen, A Coloured Man, Who Lived and Died Near Mount Holly, New Jersey, To Which is Added, The Testimony of Friends of Mount Holly Monthly Meeting Concerning Him* (Philadelphia: John Richards, 1834), 4.

60. Ibid., 5.

61. Clifton Johnson, ed., *God Struck Me Dead: Religious Conversion Experiences and Autobiographies of Ex-slaves* (New York: Pilgrim, 1987), 56. See also Raboteau, *Slave Religion*, 266–75.

62. This analysis is greatly indebted to Hodges, *Root and Branch*, 123–24. On racism in the Dutch Reformed Church, see Zilversmit, *First Emancipation*, 25, and Gerald F. De Jong, *The Dutch Reformed Church in the American Colonies* (Grand Rapids, MI: Eerdmans, 1978), 138.

63. Sobel, *World They Made Together*, 13; David Northrup, *Africa's Discovery of Europe, 1450–1850* (New York: Oxford University Press, 2002), 28–29.

64. Allinson, *Memoir*, 16.

65. On the emergence and decline of the Methodist commitment to black abolition, see Donald D. Mathews, *Slavery and Methodism: A Chapter in American Morality, 1780–1845* (Princeton, NJ: Princeton University Press, 1965), chap. 1. On Methodism's appeal to African Americans, see Nathan O. Hatch, *The Democratization of American Christianity* (New Haven, CT: Yale University Press, 1989), 102–13. These issues are also discussed in Hodges, *Root and Branch*, 182–83.

66. Hodges, *Root and Branch*, 181.

67. Quoted in Hodges, *Slavery and Freedom in the Rural North*, 77.

68. *Newark Sunday News*, April 14, 1901. For Woodward's death, see *Unionist Gazette* (Somerville), July 18, 1901. Both sources are courtesy of Fred Sisser III.

69. Hatch, *Democratization of American Christianity*, 106–8; Hodges, *Root and Branch*, 182–83.

70. Allinson, *Memoir*, 7–8.

71. Ibid., 8.

72. Ibid.

73. Blassingame, *Slave Community*, 147. See also Raboteau, *Slave Religion*, 305–8.

74. This analysis draws from Baptist, "Absent Subject," 151.

75. Allinson, *Memoir*, 9.

76. Ibid., 16.

77. Black, *Dismantling Black Manhood*, chaps. 2–3. For more optimistic portrayals of the manhood of enslaved (Southern) males, see, for example, Blassingame, *Slave Community*, 92, 156–61, 284; Gutman, *Black Family*, 188–91, 385–87; and Genovese, *Roll, Jordan, Roll*, 423–24, 484–86, 491.

78. Baptist, "Absent Subject," 147–52, 158–59.

79. Allinson, *Memoir*, 14.

80. See, for example, Blassingame, *Slave Community*, 146–47; Raboteau, *Slave Religion*, 304–11; Gaspar, *Bondmen and Rebels*, 244–46; Fick, *Making of Haiti*, 44–45, 94, 137, 244; and Reis, *Slave Rebellion in Brazil*, 112–15, 118–28.

81. James C. Scott, *Arts of Resistance*, 8.

82. Allinson, *Memoir*, 9. Spelled in various forms, the word "Guinea," according to *The Oxford English Dictionary*, 2nd ed., vol. 4 (Oxford: Clarendon Press, 1989), "is used loosely for West Africa or for some far-off or unknown country."

83. Allinson, *Memoir*, 9. Apparently, the ability of the enslaved to choose their owners upon their previous owner's death was a common practice in Somerset County. In his 1791 will, for example, Jacob Van Nostrand of Raritan bequeathed his "Negro man, Tom, and the rest of my blacks to choose their masters." See *Archives of the State of New Jersey*, 1st ser., vol. 37 (1942), 376. Similarly, the 1803 will of Bridgewater Township resident John Brokaw (Isaac Brokaw's third son) granted the "Negro wench, Hannah, to have choice to live where she pleases." See *Archives of the State of New Jersey*, 1st ser., vol. 39 (1946), 57.

84. Allinson, *Memoir*, 9–10. On the probable identity of Smock, see Marshall, "'Ain't No Account,'" 35.

85. See Genovese's pioneering analysis of paternalism, in *Roll, Jordan, Roll*, 3–7, 658–60, and passim. His essential argument is that enslaved people used the tradition of paternalism among slaveholders to find a measure of humanity in an otherwise inhumane system.

86. Larison, *Silvia Dubois*, 54.

87. Honeyman, "'Black Saint,'" 321, 322. McDowell, "Pluckamin," 532, mentions that Dr. Oliver Barnet was a deist.

88. McDowell, "Pluckamin," 532; cited in Honeyman, "'Black Saint,'" 322. For a slightly different version of the exchange between Cuffy and Dr. Oliver Barnet, see Stephen Wickes, *History of Medicine in New Jersey and of its Medical Men, From the Settlement of the Province to A. D. 1800* (Newark, NJ: Dennis, 1879), 137.

89. *Anecdotes and Memoirs of William Boen*, 8.

90. Quoted in William Alexander Linn, "Slavery in Bergen County, N.J.," *Papers and Proceedings of the Bergen County Historical Society* 4 (1907–8): 36, 37. See also J. M. Van Valen, *History of Bergen County, New Jersey* (New York: New Jersey Publishing and Engraving, 1900), 51; also 49–50. For additional discussion, see Hodges, *Early American Workers*, 42.

91. Van Valen, *History of Bergen County*, 52.

92. See Baptist, "Absent Subject," 137, 142–43.

93. *Anecdotes and Memoirs of William Boen*, 6.

94. Allinson, *Memoir*, 8–9.

95. Ibid., 10. For Griffith's amenable disposition, see Wickes, *Medicine in New Jersey*, 271.

96. Allinson, *Memoir*, 11. For discussion of the gradual emancipation law of 1804, see Marion Thompson Wright, "New Jersey Laws and the Negro," 171–78; Zilversmit, "Liberty and Property," 215–26; and Hodges, *Slavery and Freedom in the Rural North*, 135–36.

97. Allinson, *Memoir*, 13.

98. Ibid., 12.

99. Vincent Harding, *There Is a River: The Black Struggle for Freedom in America* (New York: Harcourt Brace Jovanovich, 1981), 148. Conversely, Harding argues that Douglass's religious convictions "also had held the possibility of blinding him to the ultimate harshness of those realities [in his life], decreasing the sense of need to face them and organize against them with more than hope and faith, without losing either."

100. Allinson, *Memoir*, 13.

101. Ibid., 13–14.

102. Wyatt-Brown, "Mask of Obedience," 1242.

103. Allinson, *Memoir*, 14.

104. Ibid.

105. Ibid.

106. The phrase is borrowed from Dwight A. McBride's *Impossible Witnesses: Truth, Abolitionism, and Slave Testimony* (New York: New York University Press, 2001).

Chapter Five

1. Mellick, *Story of an Old Farm*, 603–4.

2. Ibid., 604–5.

3. Mellick's comment on Nance's "zone" does not appear in the original account of Aaron Malick's slaves (see below, note 8), and suggests that he was uncomfortable with the "black" body. His racialization of Dick and Nance, however, is most grossly reflected in one of the subheadings in his book, "Black Dick and Nance" (*Story of an Old Farm*, 605). Mellick could easily have chosen a subheading devoid of any sexual innuendoes. Instead, he reinforces Dick's blackness by reducing him to a sexual object—that is, as a black "dick" or penis. For a fascinating discussion of the tendency among Europeans to reduce non-European colonial subjects and the lands that they inhabited to genitalia, see McClintock, *Imperial Leather*, 1–4, 40–44, 52–56, 108–14. Similarly, according to Mary Louise Pratt, *Imperial Eyes: Travel Writing and Transculturation* (London: Routledge, 1992), esp. 51–53, European travel writers often "produced" the various nonwhite peoples whom they encountered as bodies and appendages, if not genitalia.

4. Mellick, *Story of an Old Farm*, 604.

5. Shane White, *Somewhat More Independent*, 151.

6. Mellick, *Story of an Old Farm*, 603.

7. In 1782, for example, Samuel Minor of Middlesex County advertised the sale of a twenty-six-year-old bondwoman and her boy of eight and girl of two, "either together or separate, as best suit the purchasers"; see *New Jersey Gazette* (Trenton), November 20, 1782. Two years later, Nathaniel Hunt, also of Middlesex, publicized the sale of his twenty-five-year-old bondwoman "with or without a male child"; see *New Jersey Gazette* (Trenton), February 24, 1784.

8. Aaron Melick Record Book.

9. For the name "Ballod," see Mellick, *Story of an Old Farm*, 602. The name "Balla" is found in Puckett, *Black Names*, 356–57.

10. Mellick, *Story of an Old Farm*, 605, 608, 610, 611. The birth dates of Dick and Nance's five children appear in Aaron Malick's will. See *Archives of the State of New Jersey*, 1st ser., vol. 40 (1947), 228. There is a discrepancy between Malick's will and Andrew Mellick's book regarding the name of one of the male children. The book (p. 605) mentions a "Ben" (b. 1796) but the will does not. This Ben was born the same year as Nance's son Dick, which suggests that Mellick confused the boy's name. Indeed, upon the enslaved family's break-up in 1809, Mellick does not mention that a Ben was sold (p. 611). For the name "Deon," see Aaron Melick Record Book.

11. "Manumissions of Slaves in Somerset County," 1:278.

12. For young Dick, see ibid., 1:279. For Diana (Dinah/Deon), see Stevens, *Outcast*, 74, 77. For Sam, see Mellick Papers, "Notebook," MG 53, box 4, folder 2.

13. For quotations, see Mellick Papers, "Notebook," MG 53, box 4, folder 2. The residency of Dr. Henry Van De Veer is confirmed in "Manumissions of Slaves in Somerset County," 1:279.

14. Shane White, *Somewhat More Independent*, 88–93; Hodges, *Slavery and Freedom in the Rural North*, 16–21, 155–56.

15. Nash and Soderlund, *Freedom by Degrees*, 9, 27–29, 38–40, 76, 127.

16. Shane White, *Somewhat More Independent*, 134–38, esp. 93.

17. Hodges, *Slavery and Freedom in the Rural North*, 43–44, 77–79, 187, esp. 17.

18. US Census Bureau, *Century of Population Growth*, 195; US Census Bureau, *Third Census of the United States, 1810* (Washington, DC: Government Printing Office, 1811), 30. The census of 1800 was damaged in a fire. It was not until 1820 that federal censuses began differentiating enslaved blacks by either age or gender. Tewksbury was (and is) 31.80 square miles. See Frank S. Kelland and Marylin C. Kelland, *New Jersey: Garden or Suburb? A Geography of New Jersey* (Dubuque, IA: Kendall/Hunt, 1978), 213.

19. US Census Bureau, *Century of Population Growth*, 196; US Census Bureau, *Third Census*, 29a. Bedminster was 32.50 square miles. See Kelland and Kelland, *Garden or Suburb?*, 219. This figure includes present-day Peapack-Gladstone Borough.

20. Wacker, *Land and People*, 195.

21. US Census Bureau, *Century of Population Growth*, 195, 196; Kelland and Kelland, *Garden or Suburb?*, 209, 211, 219, 220. Sussex County in 1790 included present-day Warren County. It is important to note that not all of West Jersey was characterized by low density in the black population during this time period. For example, as pointed out by Wacker, *Land and People*, 195, a "cluster of blacks [resided] in western Salem County."

22. US Census Bureau, *Third Census*, 32.

23. Deborah Gray White, *Ar'n't I a Woman?*, chap. 4, esp. p. 119.

24. Malcolm, "Scenes from My Childhood," 12.

25. Deborah Gray White, *Ar'n't I a Woman?*, 122.

26. Andrew Mellick, in *The Story of an Old Farm*, refers to Aaron and Charlotte by the surname "Malick" and their children by the surname "Melick." Given Mellick's authority on the lives of his ancestors, I have adopted these name designations in this study.

27. Mellick, *Story of an Old Farm*, 606–7.

28. For the basis of this analysis, see Webber, *Deep Like the Rivers*, 66; Norrece T. Jones Jr., *Born a Child of Freedom, Yet a Slave: Mechanisms of Control and Strategies of Resistance in Antebellum South Carolina* (Hanover, NH: University Press of New England, 1990), 115–16; and Fitts, "Landscapes of Northern Bondage," 55–58.

29. On underground black culture, see Shane White, *Somewhat More Independent*, 179, 180–81, and Hodges, *Root and Branch*, 48–49, 52, 89, 93–96, 115–16. See also Jessica Kross, "'If you will not drink with me, you must fight with me': The Sociology of Drinking in the Middle Colonies," *Pennsylvania History* 64 (1997): 41. According to W. J. Rorabaugh, *The Alcoholic Republic: An American Tradition* (New York: Oxford University Press, 1979), 14–16, "The male drinking cult pervaded all social and occupational groups."

30. Nicolas W. Proctor, *Bathed in Blood: Hunting and Mastery in the Old South* (Charlottesville: University Press of Virginia, 2002), chap. 6.

31. Ibid., chap. 7, esp. 144.

32. Ibid., 157–58.

33. Kenneth S. Greenberg, *Honor and Slavery: Lies, Duels, Noses, Masks, Dressing as a Woman, Gifts, Strangers, Humanitarianism, Death, Slave Rebellions, the Proslavery Argument, Baseball, Hunting, and Gambling in the Old South* (Princeton, NJ: Princeton University Press, 1996), 124–35, esp. 133.

34. Malcolm, "Scenes from My Childhood," 10.

35. See especially Jones Jr., *Born a Child of Freedom*, chap. 4.

36. Stratford, "Jacob Van Noorstrand," 43:65–66.

37. Ibid., 43:16–17.

38. [Lequear?], *Traditions of Hunterdon*, 75.

39. Larison, *Silvia Dubois*, 67.

40. Mellick, *Story of an Old Farm*, 602–3, 605, 611–12.

41. Ibid., 225.

42. Ibid., 606.

43. Malcolm, "Scenes from My Childhood," 13.

44. *Archives of the State of New Jersey*, 1st ser., vol. 26 (1904), 526–27.

45. Mellick, *Story of an Old Farm*, 605–6.

46. Fox-Genovese, *Within the Plantation Household*, 142.

47. Mellick, *Story of an Old Farm*, 602, 604, esp. 605.

48. Daniel Melick was the second oldest son among Aaron and Charlotte Malick's five children. He was the only sibling still living at home during the time of Dick and Nance's purchase in 1798 (ibid., 564–65).

49. Ibid., 608.

50. Ibid., 605, 632. With regard to the plantation South, John Blassingame, *Slave Community*, 93, remarks that "an overwhelming majority of the slaves throughout

the antebellum period attended church with their masters. Then, after the regular services ended, the ministers held special services for the slaves." On slaves' attendance of white church services in New Jersey, see chapter 3 of this study.

51. Mellick, *Story of an Old Farm*, 606. See also Kull, "Slavery in New Jersey," 2:729.

52. Chloe Spear recalled that, as a slave in Boston, she and her friends would pass the time in the church gallery "playing, eating nuts, and enjoying other diversions" (quoted in Piersen, *Black Yankees*, 51).

53. Raboteau, *Slave Religion*, 222–23.

54. Klepp and Smith, *Infortunate*, 96.

55. For firsthand commentary on geography in New Jersey and Pennsylvania in the late eighteenth century, see Rayner Wickersham Kelsey, ed., *Cazenove Journal, 1794: A Record of the Journey of Theophile Cazenove through New Jersey and Pennsylvania* (Haverford: Pennsylvania History Press, 1922), passim.

56. Larison, *Silvia Dubois*, 96. Camp meetings were part of the revivalist movement following the Revolutionary War. Dubois recalled that camp meetings were interracial affairs, attended by a great number of people, from far and near. She stated that, at one camp meeting, "there were four pulpits, a good way apart, and four preachers [probably of different denominations] were preaching all the time. And they hollered, and the folks hollered—good God, how they hollered"; the meeting lasted about a week (96–97). For historical corroboration, see Frey, *Water from the Rock*, 252, 262.

57. Klepp and Smith, *Infortunate*, 96.

58. Mellick, *Story of an Old Farm*, 606.

59. Ibid.

60. Proctor, *Bathed in Blood*, 2.

61. Mellick, *Story of an Old Farm*, 606–7.

62. Shane White, *Somewhat More Independent*, 194–200; Hodges, *Slavery and Freedom in the Rural North*, 59–60, 152–53, 154.

63. Mellick, *Story of an Old Farm*, 607.

64. Equiano, *Interesting Narrative*, 219.

65. Berlin, "Time, Space," 48.

66. Ibid., 54.

67. Mellick, *Story of an Old Farm*, 606.

68. Paterson, *Laws of the State of New Jersey*, 238. For further discussion on white anxiety regarding slaves' alcohol consumption, see Rorabaugh, *Alcoholic Republic*, 13–14, and Kross, "If you will not drink with me," 34–35.

69. For Quick, see Voorhees, "Franklin Township Historical Notes," 6:91–92.

70. For Tom, see Inquisitions on the Dead, vol. 3 (1688–1798), p. 401, and for Betty Ryder, see Somerset County Court of Common Pleas, Inquisitions, box 2, New Jersey State Archives.

71. *Rivington's New York Gazetteer*, March 31, 1774.

72. *Political Intelligencer and New Jersey Advertiser* (Trenton), November 11, 1783.

73. For Linden, see *Pennsylvania Gazette* (Philadelphia), May 21, 1767; see also *New York Gazette*, December 25, 1766. For Peter, see *Pennsylvania Journal* (Philadelphia), September 13, 1776.

74. Stratford, "Jacob Van Noorstrand," 44:43.

75. *William Veghte v. Enoch Johnson* (c. 1820), courtesy of Fred Sisser III. Veghte's residency in Franklin Township is confirmed in Donald A. Sinclair, "Somerset County Gravestones: Pleasant Plains Cemetery, Franklin Township," *Genealogical Magazine of New Jersey* 26 (1951): 85.

76. *Anecdotes and Memoirs of William Boen*, 3.

77. Indeed, advertisements for the sale of enslaved blacks frequently equated their honesty with sobriety. See, for example, *New York Mercury*, March 1, 1756; *New York Journal or General Advertiser*, February 4, 1768; and *New Jersey Journal* (Chatham), July 26, 1780.

78. Mellick, *Story of an Old Farm*, 578.

79. Charles S. Boyer, *Old Inns and Taverns in West Jersey* (Camden, NJ: Camden County Historical Society, 1962), 82.

80. Mellick, *Story of an Old Farm*, 578.

81. Shane White, "'It Was a Proud Day': African Americans, Festivals, and Parades in the North, 1741–1834," *Journal of American History* 81 (1994): 16.

82. Mellick, *Story of an Old Farm*, 607.

83. Larison, *Silvia Dubois*, 67.

84. Mellick, *Story of an Old Farm*, 605.

85. Cooley, *Study of Slavery in New Jersey*, 55. There were, however, exceptions to this rule. For example, Silvia Dubois said that she did all types of slave labor (she could drive a wagon, manage a boat, and worked in a bar). See Larison, *Silvia Dubois*, 56–57, 58–59, 65, in conjunction with Hodges, *Slavery and Freedom in the Rural North*, 49–50, 152.

86. Quoted in Kull, "Slavery in New Jersey," 730.

87. For Margaret Melick, see Mellick, *Story of an Old Farm*, 604. Plenty of evidence exists for New Jersey with regard to enslaved children and domestic work. In 1765, for example, Cornelius Polhamus of Hopewell, Hunterdon (now Mercer) County, wanted to sell his "Negro Wench, this Country born, about 15 Years of Age, and understands all Kinds of House-work"; see *Archives of the State of New Jersey*, 1st ser., vol. 24 (1902), 507. In 1778 a Mrs. Ross at Brunswick Landing in Middlesex County advertised for sale "a Likely, handy Negro Boy, about fourteen or fifteen years of age," who was "an excellent house servant, and would suit any gentlemen that wants a waiting-boy"; see *Archives of the State of New Jersey*, 2nd ser., vol. 2 (1903), 188.

88. According to Margaret Malcolm, "Scenes from My Childhood," 12, she could, as a small child, "milk, make butter, spin flax into thread as fine as we could sew with, and fine woolen yarn for stockings. Nearly all this knowledge I stole from Mammy." See also the 1778 newspaper advertisement placed by innkeeper Henry Worly of Somerset County for the sale of his female slaves, found in *Archives of the State of New Jersey*, 2nd ser., vol. 2 (1903), 127–28.

89. Mellick, *Story of an Old Farm*, 240, 242. See also Rosalie Fellows Bailey, *Pre-Revolutionary Dutch Houses and Families in Northern New Jersey and Southern New York* (1936; repr., New York: Dover, 1968), 24–26.

90. Mellick, *Story of an Old Farm*, 17, 605.

91. Klepp, "Seasoning and Society," 486.

92. Mellick, *Story of an Old Farm*, 240, 635.

93. Kelsey, *Cazenove Journal*, 16.

94. Mellick, *Story of an Old Farm*, 243.

95. Jones, *Labor of Love*, 22, reminds us that agricultural labor in the South "represented the chief lot of all slaves, female and male," and adds that, "although women predominated as household workers, few devoted their energies full time to this kind of labor." Debra L. Newman, "Black Women in the Era of the American Revolution in Pennsylvania," *Journal of Negro History* 61 (1976): 284, argues that most black women in early Pennsylvania were employed as laundresses, seamstresses, and domestic workers. And, as indicated by Shane White, *Somewhat More Independent*, 164, "washer" was the major occupation of free black women in New York City in 1810. No doubt black women in New Jersey suffered the same occupational fate.

96. See Jones Jr., *Born a Child of Freedom*, chap. 2.

97. Zilversmit, *First Emancipation*, 28.

98. Mellick Papers, "Notebook," MG 53, box 4, folder 1.

99. *New Jersey Journal*, June 20, 1792. See also Shane White, *Somewhat More Independent*, 87.

100. Quoted in Billy G. Smith, "Black Women Who Stole Themselves in Eighteenth-Century America," in *Inequality in Early America*, ed. Carla Gardina Pestana and Sharon V. Salinger (Hanover, NH: University Press of New England, 1999), 134.

101. Larison, *Silvia Dubois*, 64.

102. Ibid., 66.

103. Ibid., 74–75.

104. Mellick, *Story of an Old Farm*, 600.

105. *Federal Post* (Trenton), October 21, 1788.

106. Ibid.; David A. Bernstein, ed., *Minutes of the Governor's Privy Council, 1777–1789*, vol. 1, *New Jersey Archives*, 3rd ser. (Trenton: New Jersey State Library, Archives and History Bureau, 1974), 285.

107. Messler, *Centennial History*, 48; "That Last Hanging," *Somerset Messenger* (Somerville), January 29, 1896, courtesy of Fred Sisser III.

108. *Federal Post* (Trenton), October 21, 1788.

109. Mellick, *Story of an Old Farm*, 604.

110. The family's decision to buy Yombo caused much tension between Aaron and Charlotte. "After much urging on the part of the husband," writes Andrew Mellick, "the wife finally stifled her [Quaker-driven] scruples and acquiesced in the purchase" (ibid., 603).

111. Max Ferrand, ed., *Records of the Federal Convention of 1787*, 4 vols. (New Haven, CT: Yale University Press, 1911–37), 1:561.

112. Frances D. Pingeon, "An Abominable Business: The New Jersey Slave Trade, 1818," *New Jersey History* 109 (1991): 15–35.

113. *Archives of the State of New Jersey*, 1st ser., vol. 40 (1947), 228.

114. Mellick, *Story of an Old Farm*, 608.

115. Ibid., 610.

116. Wilma King, "'Suffer with Them Till Death': Slave Women and Their Children in Nineteenth-Century America," in Gaspar and Hine, *More Than Chattel*, 161.

117. William Dunlap, *Diary of William Dunlap*, 3 vols. (New York: New York Historical Society, 1930–32), 1:18.

118. See, for example, Blassingame, *Slave Community*, 173–74.

119. *Acts of the Thirteenth General Assembly of the State of New Jersey* (Trenton, NJ: Collins, 1788), 486–88. See also Zilversmit, "Liberty and Property," 220–21.

120. Mellick, *Story of an Old Farm*, 608.

121. Zilversmit, "Liberty and Property," 221.

122. Mellick, *Story of an Old Farm*, 610.

123. Marion Thompson Wright, "New Jersey Laws and the Negro," 24–25.

124. See note 119.

125. Mellick, *Story of an Old Farm*, 611. Diana was sold to Jonathan Dayton (Elizabethtown); Sam to Reverend John McDowell (Elizabethtown); Dick to William R. Smiley (Elizabethtown); and Joe to Jacob Kline, Aaron Malick's nephew (New Germantown/Bedminster).

126. Aaron Melick Record Book.

127. "Manumissions of Slaves in Somerset County," 1:275–79, 2:46–51.

128. Klepp and Smith, *Infortunate*, 96.

129. For examples, see Harry B. Weiss and Grace M. Weiss, *An Introduction to Crime and Punishment in Colonial New Jersey* (Trenton, NJ: Past Times Press, 1960), 71–72n6.

130. Mellick Papers, "Notebook," MG 53, box 4, folder 2.

131. Dick and Nance's children "proved to be quiet and obedient," states Andrew Mellick (*Story of an Old Farm*, 605).

132. Painter, "Soul Murder and Slavery," 12–13.

133. Robin D. G. Kelley, *Race Rebels: Culture, Politics, and the Black Working Class* (New York: Free Press, 1994), 22, makes a similar argument while examining the infra-politics of the black working class during the age of Jim Crow.

134. Frances D. Pingeon, *Blacks in the Revolutionary Era*, New Jersey's Revolutionary Experience 14 (Trenton: New Jersey Historical Commission, 1975), 10. Generally speaking, bondmen were probably more daring in their relationships with white women. Cuffy Barnet, a slave in Hunterdon County, once threatened to leave his widowed mistress if his slave wife, Amber, could not live with him. He got his request. See Honeyman, "'Black Saint,'" 321.

135. Jordan, *White over Black*, 179.

136. Blassingame, *Slave Community*, 226n5.

137. Gutman, *Black Family*, 189–91, 307, 346. Gutman writes a great deal about the significance and roles of enslaved fathers (passim). See also Blassingame, *Slave Community*, 172–73, 178–79.

138. Mellick, *Story of an Old Farm*, 607. In another display of Christian piety, in his 1802 will, Robert Aaron, a free black, left $250 to the Dutch Reformed Church in Bedminster. One of his executors was Daniel Melick. See *Archives of the State of New Jersey*, 1st ser., vol. 39 (1946), 7.

139. Robertson, "Africa into the Americas," 12.

Epilogue

1. Statements of Benjamin Bishop, David Bishop, and William Edgar, June 28, 1760, Attorney General, Papers Relating to John Blanchard's Negro, New Jersey

State Archives. It is unclear why David Bishop testified although he is not mentioned in the accounts. He may have been present but chose not to engage himself in the altercation.

2. Unruly slaves were brought to the workhouse, where they were whipped with thirty stripes on their backs. See Hodges, *Slavery and Freedom in the Rural North*, 25.

3. Blassingame, *Slave Community*, 315.

4. Marion Thompson Wright, "New Jersey Laws and the Negro," 167.

5. Hodges, *Slavery and Freedom in the Rural North*, 22.

6. Blassingame, *Slave Community*, 230.

7. Mellick, *Story of an Old Farm*, 611.

8. Statement of David Bishop, Papers Relating to John Blanchard's Negro.

9. Cornell West, *Race Matters* (Boston: Beacon, 1993), 135–36.

10. See, for example, Kimmel, *Manhood in America*, 179–80.

11. Michael Eric Dyson, *Between God and Gangsta Rap: Bearing Witness to Black Culture* (New York: Oxford University Press, 1996), 87.

12. See Richard Pryor and Todd Gold, *Pryor Convictions and Other Life Sentences* (New York: Pantheon, 1995), 119–20; Paul Mooney, *Black Is the New White: A Memoir* (New York: Simon Spotlight Entertainment, 2009), 128; and Christine Acham, *Revolution Televised: Prime Time and the Struggle for Black Power* (Minneapolis: University of Minnesota Press, 2004), 146–47.

13. Glenda R. Carpio, *Laughing Fit to Kill: Black Humor in the Fictions of Slavery* (New York: Oxford University Press, 2008), 72.

14. Quoted in ibid., 92.

15. Ibid. See also Mooney, *Black Is the New White*, 130–31.

16. bell hooks, "Killing Rage: Militant Resistance," in *Killing Rage: Ending Racism* (New York: Holt, 1995), 11.

17. bell hooks, "Beyond Black Rage: Ending Racism," in ibid., 26.

18. See 164n71.

19. On conflict among colonized subjects, see Frantz Fanon, *The Wretched of the Earth*, trans. Richard Philcox (1961; repr., New York: Grove, 2004), 15–21, esp. 17.

20. hooks, "Killing Rage," 16.

21. For the context of this argument, see ibid.

22. Genovese, *Roll, Jordan, Roll*, 436.

23. Ibid., 625–30.

24. Trouillot, *Silencing the Past*, 22.

Bibliography

Archival Collections

Alexander Library, Rutgers University, New Brunswick, NJ
    Allinson, William J. *Memoir of Quamino Buccau, A Pious Methodist.* Philadelphia: Longstreth, 1851. Microfilm.
    John B. Thompson Papers
    Samuel Allinson Papers
Burlington County Historical Society, NJ
    Abolition Collection, MSS
Clements Library, University of Michigan, Ann Arbor, MI
    William Allinson Journal
David Library of the American Revolution, Washington Crossing, PA
    Military Pensions (Revolutionary War), 10321
Library of Michigan, Lansing, MI
    US Census of the City of Burlington (NJ), 1850. Microfilm
Magill Library, Haverford College, Haverford, PA
    Allinson Family Papers, MSS
New Jersey Department of State, Records and Archives Section, Trenton, NJ
    Attorney General, Papers Relating to John Blanchard's Negro, 1760
    Inquisitions on the Dead, 1688–1798, 4 vols.
    New Jersey Vital Statistics, Vol. C., 1848–78: Burlington County Deaths, 1848–67
    Recorded Wills, West Jersey, no. 522730 (1789–95)
    Somerset County Court of Common Pleas, Inquisitions
    Somerset County Wills, no. 840
    Tax Ratables, Bridgewater, Somerset County, 1784
    Tax Ratables, Eastern Precinct, Somerset County, 1784, 1786, 1788
New Jersey Historical Society, Newark, NJ
    Aaron Melick Record Book, 1809–18
    Andrew D. Mellick Jr. Papers

Newspapers and Periodicals

Boston Weekly News Letter
Daily Press (Plainfield)
Federal Post (Trenton)
Friends' Review
Hunterdon Democrat (Flemington)

Hunterdon Republican (Flemington)
Newark Sunday News
New Brunswick Fredonian
New Jersey Gazette (Trenton)
New Jersey Journal (Chatham)
New York Gazette
New York Gazette and Weekly Mercury
New York Gazette and Weekly Post-Boy
New York Gazette (*Weyman's*)
New York Journal or General Advertiser
New York Mercury
Non-Slaveholder
Parker's New York Gazette or Weekly Post-Boy
Pennsylvania Chronicle (Philadelphia)
Pennsylvania Gazette (Philadelphia)
Pennsylvania Journal (Philadelphia)
Pennsylvania Journal and Weekly Advertiser (Philadelphia)
Pennsylvania Packet (Philadelphia)
Political Intelligencer (New Brunswick)
Political Intelligencer and New Jersey Advertiser (Trenton)
Rivington's New York Gazetteer
Somerset Messenger (Somerville)
Somerset Unionist (Somerville)
Unionist Gazette (Somerville)
Weekly Rehearsal (Philadelphia)

Printed Primary Materials

Acts of the Thirteenth General Assembly of the State of New Jersey. Trenton, NJ: Isaac Collins, 1788.

Acts of the Twenty-Eighth General Assembly of the State of New Jersey. Trenton, NJ: Wilson and Blackwell, 1804.

Allinson, William J. *Memoir of Quamino Buccau, A Pious Methodist.* Philadelphia: Longstreth, 1851. Also available online at http://docsouth.unc.edu/neh/allinson/allinson.html.

———. *Poems.* Philadelphia: Claxton, Remsen, and Haffelfinger, 1873.

Anecdotes and Memoirs of William Boen, A Coloured Man, Who Lived and Died Near Mount Holly, New Jersey, To Which is Added, The Testimony of Friends of Mount Holly Monthly Meeting Concerning Him. Philadelphia: John Richards, 1834.

Archives of the State of New Jersey. 48 vols. Newark: State of New Jersey, 1880–1949.

Atkins, John. *A Voyage to Guinea, Brasil, and the West Indies; In His Majesty's Ships, the Swallow and Weymouth.* 1735. Reprint, London: Frank Cass, 1970.

"Bedminster Township Ratable of 1785." *Somerset County Genealogical Quarterly* 3 (1986): 262–65.

Benezet, Anthony. *Some Historical Account of Guinea, Its Situation, Produce, and the General Disposition of Its Inhabitants: With an Inquiry into the Rise and Progress of the Slave Trade, Its Nature, and Lamentable Effect.* 1771. Reprint, London: Frank Cass, 1968.

Bernstein, David A., ed. *Minutes of the Governor's Privy Council, 1777–1789.* Vol. 1, *New Jersey Archives.* 3rd ser. Trenton: New Jersey State Library, Archives and History Bureau, 1974.

Corry, Joseph. *Observations upon the Windward Coast of Africa, the Religion, Character, Customs, &c. of the Natives; with a System upon which they may be Civilized, and a Knowledge Attained of the Interior of this Extraordinary Quarter of the Globe; and upon the Natural and Commercial Resources of the Country, made in the years 1805 and 1806.* 1807. Reprint, London: Frank Cass, 1968.

Donnan, Elizabeth, ed. *Documents Illustrative of the History of the Slave Trade to America.* 5 vols. Washington, DC: Carnegie Institute of Washington, 1932–35.

Douglass, Frederick. *Narrative of the Life of Frederick Douglass, An American Slave, Written by Himself.* Edited by Benjamin Quarles. Reprint, Cambridge, MA: Harvard University Press, 1960. Originally published 1845.

Dunlap, William. *Diary of William Dunlap.* 3 vols. New York: New York Historical Society, 1930–32.

———. *History of the Rise and Progress of the Arts of Design in the United States.* Edited by Alexander Wyckoff. Rev. ed. 3 vols. New York: Blom, 1965.

Falconbridge, Alexander. *An Account of the Slave Trade on the Coast of Africa.* 1788. Reprint, New York: AMS, 1973.

Ferrand, Max, ed. *Records of the Federal Convention of 1787.* 4 vols. New Haven, CT: Yale University Press, 1911–37.

Fishman, George. "Taking a Stand for Freedom in Revolutionary New Jersey: Prime's Petition of 1786." *Science and Society* 56 (1992): 353–56.

Gates Jr., Henry Louis, and William L. Andrews, eds. *Pioneers of the Black Atlantic: Five Slave Narratives from the Enlightenment.* Washington, DC: Counterpoint, 1998.

Gerlach, Larry R., ed. *New Jersey in the American Revolution, 1763–1783: A Documentary History.* Trenton: New Jersey Historical Commission, 1975.

Gordon, Thomas F. *Gazetteer of the State of New Jersey.* 1834. Reprint, Cottonport, LA: Polyanthos, 1973.

Hageman, John H. "Memorial of Samuel Allinson, 'The Philanthropist of New Jersey.'" *Proceedings of the New Jersey Historical Society,* 2nd ser., 8 (1884): 69–89.

Harris, Sharon M., ed. *American Women Writers to 1800.* New York: Oxford University Press, 1996.

"Hillsborough Township 'Census' of 1784." *Somerset County Genealogical Quarterly* 2 (1984): 101–6, 130–33.

Jacobs, Harriet A. *Incidents in the Life of a Slave Girl, Written by Herself.* Edited by Jean Fagan Yellin. Cambridge, MA: Harvard University Press, 1987. Originally published 1861.

Johnson, Clifton H., ed. *God Struck Me Dead: Religious Conversion Experiences and Autobiographies of Ex-slaves.* Philadelphia: Pilgrim, 1969.

Kelsey, Rayner Wickersham, ed. *Cazenove Journal, 1794: A Record of the Journey of Theophile Cazenove through New Jersey and Pennsylvania.* Haverford: Pennsylvania History Press, 1922.

Klepp, Susan E., and Billy G. Smith, eds. *The Infortunate: The Voyage and Adventures of William Moraley, an Indentured Servant.* University Park: Pennsylvania State University Press, 1992. Originally published 1743.

Larison, C. W. *Silvia Dubois, A Biografy of the Slav Who Whipt Her Mistres and Gand Her Freedom.* Edited and translated by Jared C. Lobdell. New York: Oxford University Press, 1988. Originally published 1883.

Malcolm, Margaret Nevius Van Dyke. "As I Remember Scenes from My Childhood." *The Princeton Recollector* 4 (1979): 1–16.

"Manumissions of Slaves in Somerset County." *Somerset County Historical Quarterly* 1–2 (1912–13): 1:275–79, 2:46–51.

Matthews, John. *A Voyage to the River Sierra Leone, on the Coast of Africa, Containing an Account of the Trade and Productions of the Country, and of the Civil and Religious Customs and Manners of the People; in a Series of Letters to a Friend in England.* 1788. Reprint, London: Frank Cass, 1966.

McMahon, Lucia, and Deborah Schriver, eds. *To Read My Heart: The Journal of Rachel Van Dyke, 1810–1811.* Philadelphia: University of Pennsylvania Press, 2000.

Mellick Jr., Andrew D. *Lesser Crossroads.* Edited by Hubert G. Schmidt. New Brunswick, NJ: Rutgers University Press, 1948. Originally published as *The Story of an Old Farm; or, Life in New Jersey in the Eighteenth Century.* Somerville, NJ: Unionist Gazette, 1889.

Newton, John. *The Journal of a Slave Trader, 1750–1754.* Edited by Bernard Martin and Mark Spurrell. London: Epworth, 1962.

Osofsky, Gilbert, ed. *Puttin' on Ole Massa: The Slave Narratives of Henry Bibb, William Wells Brown, and Solomon Northup.* New York: Harper and Row, 1969.

Paterson, William. *Laws of the State of New Jersey.* Newark, NJ: Matthias Day, 1800.

[Quincy, Eliza Susan]. "Basking Ridge in Revolutionary Days: Extracts from a Lady's Published Recollections." *Somerset County Historical Quarterly* 1 (1912): 34–43.

Second Census of the United States: 1800. New York: Norman Ross, 1990.

Smith, William. *A New Voyage to Guinea: Describing the Customs, Manners, Soil, Climate, Habits, Buildings, Education, Manual Arts, Agriculture, Trade, Employments, Languages, Ranks of Distinction, Habitations, Diversions, Marriages, and whatever else is memorable among the Inhabitants.* 1744. Reprint, London: Frank Cass, 1967.

Snelgrave, William. *A New Account of Some Parts of Guinea and the Slave-Trade.* 1734. Reprint, London: Frank Cass, 1971.

"Somerset Patriotism Preceding the Revolutionary War: From Minutes of Meetings of Citizens and Committees." *Somerset County Historical Quarterly* 5 (1916): 241–47.

Stratford, Dorothy A. "The Docket of Jacob Van Noorstrand." *Genealogical Magazine of New Jersey* 42–44 (1967–69): 42:98–104; 43:9–25, 58–67; 44:38–48, 76–85.

Stryker, William S., compiler. *Official Register of the Officers and Men of New Jersey in the Revolutionary War.* 1872. Reprint, Baltimore: Genealogical Publishing, 1967.

US Census Bureau. *A Century of Population Growth from the First Census of the United States to the Twelfth, 1790–1900.* Washington, DC: Government Printing Office, 1909.

US Census Bureau. *Third Census of the United States, 1810.* Washington, DC: Government Printing Office, 1811.

Winterbottom, Thomas. *An Account of the Native Africans in the Neighbourhood of Sierra Leone, to which is added An Account of the Present State of Medicine among them.* Vol. 1. 1803. Reprint, London: Frank Cass, 1969.

Secondary Sources

Acham, Christine. *Revolution Televised: Prime Time and the Struggle for Black Power.* Minneapolis: University of Minnesota Press, 2004.

Andrews, William L. *To Tell a Free Story: The First Century of Afro-American Autobiography, 1760–1865.* Urbana: University of Illinois Press, 1986.

Aptheker, Herbert. *American Negro Slave Revolts.* 1943. Reprint, New York: International Publishers, 1969.

Bailey, David Thomas. "A Divided Prism: Two Sources of Black Testimony on Slavery." *Journal of Southern History* 46 (1980): 381–404.

Bailey, Rosalie Fellows. *Pre-Revolutionary Dutch Houses and Families in Northern New Jersey and Southern New York.* 1936. Reprint, New York: Dover, 1968.

Baptist, Edward E. "The Absent Subject: African American Masculinity and Forced Migration to the Antebellum Plantation Frontier." In *Southern Manhood: Perspectives on Masculinity in the Old South,* edited by Craig Thompson Friend and Lorri Glover, 136–73. Athens: University of Georgia Press, 2004.

Bauer, Raymond A., and Alice H. Bauer. "Day to Day Resistance to Slavery." *Journal of Negro History* 27 (1942): 388–419.

Bay, Mia. "Remembering Racism: Rereading the Black Image in the White Mind." *Reviews in American History* 27 (1999): 646–56.

Bederman, Gail. *Manliness and Civilization: A Cultural History of Gender and Race in the United States, 1880–1917.* Chicago: University of Chicago Press, 1995.

Berlin, Ira. *Many Thousands Gone: The First Two Centuries of African American Slavery.* Cambridge, MA: Harvard University Press, 1998.

———. *Slaves Without Masters: The Free Negro in the Antebellum South.* New York: Pantheon, 1974.

———. "Time, Space, and the Evolution of Afro-American Society on British Mainland North America." *American Historical Review* 85 (1980): 44–78.

Berthold, Michael C. "'The peals of her terrific language': The Control of Representation in *Silvia Dubois, a Biografy of the Slav Who Whipt Her Mistres and Gand Her Fredom.*" *MELUS: Journal of the Society for the Study of the Multi-Ethnic Literature of the United States* 20 (1995): 3–14.

Black, Daniel P. *Dismantling Black Manhood: An Historical and Literary Analysis of the Legacy of Slavery.* New York: Garland, 1997.

Blassingame, John W. *The Slave Community: Plantation Life in the Antebellum South.* Rev. ed. New York: Oxford University Press, 1979.

———. "Using the Testimony of Ex-Slaves: Approaches and Problems." *Journal of Southern History* 41 (1975): 473–92.

Bontemps, Alex. *The Punished Self: Surviving Slavery in the Colonial South.* Ithaca, NY: Cornell University Press, 2001.

Booker, Christopher B. *"I Will Wear No Chain!": A Social History of African American Males.* Westport, CT: Praeger, 2000.

Boothe, Demico. *Why Are So Many Black Men in Prison?* Memphis, TN: Full Surface Publishers, 2007.

Boyer, Charles S. *Old Inns and Taverns in West Jersey.* Camden, NJ: Camden County Historical Society, 1962.

Brahms, William B. *Franklin Township, Somerset County, NJ: A History.* Franklin, NJ: Commissioned by the Franklin Township Public Library, 1998.

Brearley, H. C. "Ba-ad Nigger." *South Atlantic Quarterly* 38 (1939): 75–81.

"The Brokaw-Bragaw Family." *New York Genealogical and Biographical Record* 87 (1956): 12–17.

Byrd, Alexander X. "Eboe, Country, Nation, and Gustavus Vassa's *Interesting Narrative*." *William and Mary Quarterly*, 3rd ser., 63 (2006): 123–48.

Camp, Stephanie M. H. *Closer to Freedom: Enslaved Women and Everyday Resistance in the Plantation South.* Chapel Hill: University of North Carolina Press, 2004.

Carpio, Glenda R. *Laughing Fit to Kill: Black Humor in the Fictions of Slavery.* New York: Oxford University Press, 2008.

Carretta, Vincent. "Olaudah Equiano or Gustavus Vassa? New Light on an Eighteenth-Century Question of Identity." *Slavery and Abolition* 20 (1999): 96–105.

Carroll, Joseph Cephas. *Slave Insurrections in the United States, 1800–1865.* 1938. Reprint, New York: Negro Universities Press, 1968.

Cazenave, Noel V. "Black Men in America: The Quest for Manhood." In *Black Families,* edited by Harriet Pipes McAdoo, 176–86. Beverly Hills, CA: Sage, 1981.

Connolly, James C. "Slavery in Colonial New Jersey and the Causes Operating against its Extension." *Proceedings of the New Jersey Historical Society,* n.s., 14 (1929): 181–202.

Cooley, Henry Scofield. *A Study of Slavery in New Jersey.* Baltimore: Johns Hopkins University Press, 1896.

Cooper, Frederick. "Conflict and Connection: Rethinking Colonial African History." *American Historical Review* 99 (1994): 1516–45.

Creel, Margaret Washington. *"A Peculiar People": Slave Religion and Community-Culture Among the Gullahs.* New York: New York University Press, 1988.

Curry, Leonard P. *The Free Black in Urban America, 1800–1850: The Shadow of the Dream.* Chicago: University of Chicago Press, 1981.

Curtin, Philip D. *The Atlantic Slave Trade: A Census.* Madison: University of Wisconsin Press, 1969.

Davis, David Brion. *The Problem of Slavery in Western Culture.* Ithaca, NY: Cornell University Press, 1966.

De Jong, Gerald F. *The Dutch Reformed Church in the American Colonies.* Grand Rapids, MI: Eerdmans, 1978.

Desrochers Jr., Robert E. "'Not Fade Away': The Narrative of Venture Smith, an African-American in the Early Republic." In *A Question of Manhood: A Reader in U.S. Black Men's History and Masculinity.* Vol. 1, *"Manhood Rights": The Construction of Black Male History and Manhood, 1750–1870,* edited by Darlene Clark Hine and Earnestine Jenkins, 61–89. Bloomington: Indiana University Press, 1999.

Dillard, J. L. *Black English: Its History and Usage in the United States.* New York: Vintage, 1973.

Dorsey, Bruce. *Reforming Men and Women: Gender in the Antebellum City*. Ithaca, NY: Cornell University Press, 2002.

Drake, Thomas E. *Quakers and Slavery in America*. New Haven, CT: Yale University Press, 1950.

Duara, Prasenjit. *Rescuing History from the Nation*. Chicago: University of Chicago Press, 1995.

Du Bois, W. E. B. *The Philadelphia Negro: A Social Study*. 1889. Reprint, New York: Schocken, 1967.

———. *The Souls of Black Folk*. 1903. Reprint, Millwood, NY: Vintage, 1990.

Dyson, Michael Eric. *Between God and Gangsta Rap: Bearing Witness to Black Culture*. New York: Oxford University Press, 1996.

Elkins, Stanley M. *Slavery: A Problem in American Institutional and Intellectual Life*. 2nd ed. Chicago: University of Chicago Press, 1968.

Eltis, David. "The U.S. Transatlantic Slave Trade, 1644–1867: An Assessment." *Civil War History* 54 (2008): 347–78.

Fanon, Frantz. *The Wretched of the Earth*. Translated by Richard Philcox. 1961. Reprint, New York: Grove, 2004.

Feldstein, Stanley. *Once a Slave: The Slaves' View of Slavery*. New York: Morrow, 1971.

Fick, Carolyn E. *The Making of Haiti: The Saint Domingue Revolution from Below*. Knoxville: University of Tennessee Press, 1990.

Field, M. J. *Religion and Medicine of the Ga People*. London: Clarendon Press, 1937.

Fishman, George. "The Struggle for Freedom and Equality: African Americans in New Jersey, 1624–1849/50." PhD diss., Temple University, 1990.

Fitts, Robert K. "The Landscapes of Northern Bondage." *Historical Archaeology* 30 (1996): 54–73.

Fogel, Robert William, and Stanley L. Engerman. *Time on the Cross: The Economics of American Negro Slavery*. Boston: Little, Brown, 1974.

Foster, Elsie. *Our Brokaw–Bragaw Heritage*. N.p., n.d. [c. 1970].

Fox-Genovese, Elizabeth. "Strategies and Forms of Resistance: Focus on Slave Women in the United States." In *In Resistance: Studies in African, Caribbean, and Afro-American History*, edited by Gary Y. Okihiro, 144–65. Amherst: University of Massachusetts Press, 1986.

———. *Within the Plantation Household: Black and White Women of the Old South*. Chapel Hill: University of North Carolina Press, 1988.

Frakt, Steven B. "Patterns of Slave-Holding in Somerset County, N.J." Unpublished seminar paper. Special Collections, Alexander Library, Rutgers University, 1967.

Franklin, John Hope. *The Free Negro in North Carolina, 1790–1860*. 1943. Reprint, New York: Norton, 1971.

Franklin, John Hope, and Loren Schweninger. *Runaway Slaves: Rebels on the Plantation*. New York: Oxford University Press, 1999.

Fraser, Rebecca J. *Courtship and Love among the Enslaved in North Carolina*. Jackson: University of Mississippi Press, 2007.

Fredrickson, George M. *The Black Image in the White Mind: The Debate on Afro-American Character and Destiny, 1817–1914*. New York: Harper and Row, 1971.

Frey, Sylvia R. *Water from the Rock: Black Resistance in a Revolutionary Age*. Princeton, NJ: Princeton University Press, 1991.

Fyfe, Christopher. *A History of Sierra Leone.* Oxford: Oxford University Press, 1962.

Gary, Lawrence E., Christopher B. Booker, and Abeba Fekade. *African American Males: An Analysis of Contemporary Values, Attitudes, and Perceptions of Manhood.* Washington, DC: Howard University School of Social Work, 1993.

Gaspar, David Barry. *Bondmen and Rebels: A Study of Master–Slave Relations in Antigua.* Baltimore: Johns Hopkins University Press, 1985.

Gates Jr., Henry Louis. *Thirteen Ways of Looking at a Black Man.* New York: Random House, 1997.

Genovese, Eugene D. *Roll, Jordan, Roll: The World the Slaves Made.* New York: Pantheon, 1974.

Gilroy, Paul. *"There Ain't No Black in the Union Jack": The Cultural Politics of Race and Nation.* Chicago: University of Chicago Press, 1987.

Gomez, Michael A. *Exchanging Our Country Marks: The Transformation of African Identities in the Colonial and Antebellum South.* Chapel Hill: University of North Carolina Press, 1998.

Gough, Robert J. "Black Men and the Early New Jersey Militia." *New Jersey History* 88 (1970): 227–37.

Greenberg, Kenneth S. *Honor and Slavery: Lies, Duels, Noses, Masks, Dressing as a Woman, Gifts, Strangers, Humanitarianism, Death, Slave Rebellions, the Proslavery Argument, Baseball, Hunting, and Gambling in the Old South.* Princeton, NJ: Princeton University Press, 1996.

Greene, Evarts B., and Virginia Harrington. *American Population before the Federal Census of 1790.* New York: Columbia University Press, 1932.

Greene, Jack P. *All Men Are Created Equal: Some Reflections on the Character of the American Revolution.* Oxford: Clarendon Press, 1976.

Greene, Lorenzo Johnston. *The Negro in Colonial New England.* 1942. Reprint, New York: Atheneum, 1969.

Groth, Michael E. "The African American Struggle against Slavery in the Mid-Hudson Valley, 1785–1827." *Hudson Valley Regional Review* (1994): 63–79.

Guha, Ranajit. "The Prose of Counter-Insurgency." In *Selected Subaltern Studies,* edited by Ranajit Guha and Gayatri Chakravorty Spivak, 45–84. New York: Oxford University Press, 1988.

Gutman, Herbert G. *The Black Family in Slavery and Freedom, 1750–1925.* New York: Pantheon, 1976.

Handler, Jerome S. "The Middle Passage and Material Culture of Captive Africans." *Slavery and Abolition* 30 (2009): 1–26.

Harding, Vincent. *There Is a River: The Black Struggle for Freedom in America.* New York: Harcourt Brace Jovanovich, 1981.

Harris, Leslie M. *In the Shadow of Slavery: African Americans in New York City, 1626–1863.* Chicago: University of Chicago Press, 2003.

Harris, W. T., and Harry Sawyerr. *The Springs of Mende Belief and Conduct: A Discussion of the Influence of the Belief in the Supernatural among the Mende.* Freetown: Sierra Leone University Press, 1968.

Hatch, Nathan O. *The Democratization of American Christianity.* New Haven, CT: Yale University Press, 1989.

Hine, Darlene Clark, and Earnestine Jenkins. "Black Men's History: Toward a Gendered Perspective." In *A Question of Manhood: A Reader in U.S. Black Men's*

History and Masculinity. Vol. 1, *"Manhood Rights": The Construction of Black Male History and Manhood, 1750–1870,* edited by Darlene Clark Hine and Earnestine Jenkins, 1–58. Bloomington: Indiana University Press, 1999.

Hine, Darlene Clark, and Kate Wittenstein. "Female Slave Resistance: The Economics of Sex." In *The Black Woman Cross-Culturally,* edited by Filomina Chioma Steady, 289–300. Cambridge, MA: Harvard University Press, 1981.

Hobsbawm, Eric J. *The Age of Empire, 1875–1914.* 1987. Reprint, New York: Vintage, 1989.

Hodges, Graham Russell, ed. *Black Itinerants of the Gospel: The Narratives of John Jea and George White.* Madison, WI: Madison House, 1993.

———. *Root and Branch: African Americans in New York and East Jersey, 1613–1863.* Chapel Hill: University of North Carolina Press, 1999.

———. *Slavery and Freedom in the Rural North: African Americans in Monmouth County, New Jersey, 1665–1865.* Madison, WI: Madison House, 1997.

———. *Slavery, Freedom, and Culture among Early American Workers.* Armonk, NY: Sharpe, 1998.

Hodges, Graham Russell, and Alan Edward Brown, eds. *"Pretends to be Free": Runaway Slave Advertisements from Colonial and Revolutionary New York and New Jersey.* New York: Garland, 1994.

Hoffer, Carol P. "Mende and Sherbro Women in High Office." *Canadian Journal of African Studies* 6 (1972): 151–64.

Honeyman, Abraham Van Doren. "The Author of 'The Story of an Old Farm.'" *Somerset County Historical Quarterly* 1 (1912): 23–34.

———, ed. "A Former Lamington 'Black Saint.'" *Somerset County Historical Quarterly* 8 (1919): 320–22.

hooks, bell. *Killing Rage: Ending Racism.* New York: Holt, 1995.

Horton, James Oliver. "Freedom's Yoke: Gender Conventions among Antebellum Free Blacks." *Feminist Studies* 12 (1986): 51–76.

Horton, James Oliver, and Lois E. Horton. *Black Bostonians: Family Life and Community Struggle in the Antebellum North.* New York: Holmes and Meier, 1979.

———. *In Hope of Liberty: Culture, Community and Protest Among Northern Free Blacks, 1700–1860.* New York: Oxford University Press, 1997.

———. "Violence, Protest, and Identity: Black Manhood in Antebellum America." In *A Question of Manhood: A Reader in U.S. Black Men's History and Masculinity.* Vol. 1, *"Manhood Rights": The Construction of Black Male History and Manhood, 1750–1870,* edited by Darlene Clark Hine and Earnestine Jenkins, 382–98. Bloomington: Indiana University Press, 1999.

Huggins, Nathan Irvin. *Black Odyssey: The African-American Ordeal in Slavery.* 1977. Reprint, New York: Vintage, 1990.

Jones, E. Alfred. *The Loyalists of New Jersey: Their Memorials, Petitions, Claims, Etc., from English Records.* Newark: New Jersey Historical Society, 1927.

Jones, Jacqueline. *Labor of Love, Labor of Sorrow: Black Women, Work, and the Family from Slavery to the Present.* New York: Norton, 1985.

Jones Jr., Norrece T. *Born a Child of Freedom, Yet a Slave: Mechanisms of Control and Strategies of Resistance in Antebellum South Carolina.* Hanover, NH: University Press of New England, 1990.

Jordan, Ryan P. *Slavery and the Meeting House: The Quakers and the Abolitionist Dilemma, 1820–1865.* Bloomington: Indiana University Press, 2007.

Jordan, Winthrop D. *White over Black: American Attitudes Toward the Negro, 1550–1812.* Chapel Hill: University of North Carolina Press, 1968.

Kaplan, Sidney, and Emma Nogrady Kaplan. "Bearers of Arms: Patriot and Tory." In *A Question of Manhood: A Reader in U.S. Black Men's History and Masculinity.* Vol. 1, *"Manhood Rights": The Construction of Black Male History and Manhood, 1750–1870,* edited by Darlene Clark Hine and Earnestine Jenkins, 165–202. Bloomington: Indiana University Press, 1999.

Kelland, Frank S., and Marylin C. Kelland. *New Jersey: Garden or Suburb? A Geography of New Jersey.* Dubuque, IA: Kendall/Hunt, 1978.

Kelley, Robin D. G. *Race Rebels: Culture, Politics, and the Black Working Class.* New York: Free Press, 1996.

Kimmel, Michael S. *Manhood in America: A Cultural History.* 2nd ed. New York: Oxford University Press, 1994.

King, Wilma. *Stolen Childhood: Slave Youth in Nineteenth-Century America.* Bloomington: Indiana University Press, 2006.

———. "'Suffer with Them Till Death': Slave Women and Their Children in Nineteenth-Century America." In *More Than Chattel: Black Women and Slavery in the Americas,* edited by David Barry Gaspar and Darlene Clark Hine, 147–68. Bloomington: Indiana University Press, 1996.

Klepp, Susan E. "Seasoning and Society: Racial Differences in Mortality in Eighteenth-Century Philadelphia." *William and Mary Quarterly,* 3rd ser., 51 (1994): 473–506.

Kross, Jessica. "'If you will not drink with me, you must fight with me': The Sociology of Drinking in the Middle Colonies." *Pennsylvania History* 64 (1997): 28–55.

Kruger, Vivienne L. "Born to Run: The Slave Family in Early New York, 1626–1827." PhD diss., Columbia University, 1985.

Kubler-Ross, Elisabeth. *On Death and Dying.* New York: Macmillan, 1969.

Kull, Irving S. "Slavery in New Jersey." In *New Jersey: A History,* edited by Irving S. Kull, 2:720–44. 6 vols. New York: American Historical Society, 1930–32.

Lane, Ann J., ed. *The Debate over Slavery: Stanley Elkins and His Critics.* Urbana: University of Illinois Press, 1971.

Lee, Francis Bazley. *Genealogical and Memorial History of the State of New Jersey.* 4 vols. New York: Lewis Historical Publishing, 1910.

[Lequear, John?]. *Traditions of Hunterdon.* Edited by D. H. Moreau. Flemington, NJ: Moreau, 1957. Originally published as a series: "Traditions of Our Ancestors." *Hunterdon Republican* (Flemington, 1869–70).

Levine, Lawrence W. *Black Culture and Black Consciousness: Afro-American Folk Thought from Slavery to Freedom.* New York: Oxford University Press, 1977.

Lichtenstein, Alex. "'That Disposition to Theft, with which they have been Branded': Moral Economy, Slave Management, and the Law." *Journal of Social History* 21 (1988): 413–40.

Linn, William Alexander. "Slavery in Bergen County, N.J." *Papers and Proceedings of the Bergen County Historical Society* 4 (1907–8): 36–37.

Little, Kenneth. *The Mende of Sierra Leone: A West African People in Transition.* London: Routledge and Kegan Paul, 1951.

Littlefield, Daniel C. *Rice and Slaves: Ethnicity and the Slave Trade in Colonial South Carolina.* 1981. Reprint, Urbana: University of Illinois Press, 1991.

Litwack, Leon F. *Been in the Storm So Long: The Aftermath of Slavery.* New York: Knopf, 1979.

———. *North of Slavery: The Negro in the Free States, 1790–1860.* Chicago: University of Chicago Press, 1961.

Logan, Rayford W. *The Betrayal of the Negro from Rutherford B. Hayes to Woodrow Wilson.* New York: Da Capo, 1997. Originally published as *The Negro in American Life and Thought: The Nadir, 1877–1901.* New York: Dial, 1954.

Lovejoy, Paul E. "Autobiography and Memory: Gustavus Vassa, alias Olaudah Equiano, the African." *Slavery and Abolition* 27 (2006): 317–47.

———. "Fugitive Slaves: Resistance to Slavery in the Sokoto Caliphate." In *In Resistance: Studies in African, Caribbean, and Afro-American History,* edited by Gary Y. Okihiro, 71–95. Amherst: University of Massachusetts Press, 1986.

———. "The Impact of the Atlantic Slave Trade on Africa: A Review of the Literature." *Journal of African History* 30 (1989): 365–94.

———. "The Volume of the Atlantic Slave Trade: A Synthesis." *Journal of African History* 23 (1982): 473–501.

Lundin, Leonard. *Cockpit of the Revolution: The War for Independence in New Jersey.* Princeton, NJ: Princeton University Press, 1940.

Lydon, James G. "New York and the Slave Trade, 1700 to 1774." *William and Mary Quarterly,* 3rd ser., 35 (1978): 375–94.

Lyght, Earnest. *Path of Freedom: The Black Presence in New Jersey's Burlington County, 1659–1900.* Cherry Hill, NJ: E. and E. Publishing House, 1978.

MacCracken, Henry Noble. *Old Dutchess Forever! The Story of an American County.* New York: Hastings House, 1956.

Magill, Jacob. "Somerset Traditions Gathered Forty Years Ago." *Somerset County Historical Quarterly* 2 (1913): 23–29.

Major, Clarence, ed. *Juba to Jive: A Dictionary of African-American Slang.* 1970. Reprint, New York: Penguin, 1994.

Majors, Richard, and Janet Mancini Billson. *Cool Pose: The Dilemmas of Black Manhood in America.* New York: Lexington Books, 1992.

Mallon, Florence E. "The Promise and Dilemma of Subaltern Studies: Perspectives from Latin American History." *American Historical Review* 99 (1994): 1491–515.

Manning, Patrick. *Slavery and African Life: Occidental, Oriental, and African Slave Trades.* Cambridge: Cambridge University Press, 1990.

Marshall, Kenneth E. "'Ain't No Account': Issues of Manhood and Resistance among Eighteenth-Century Slaves in Nineteenth-Century Literature Pertaining to Central New Jersey." PhD diss., Michigan State University, 2003.

———. "Work, Family and Day-to-Day Survival on an Old Farm: Nance Melick, a Rural Late Eighteenth- and Early Nineteenth-Century New Jersey Slave Woman." *Slavery and Abolition* 19 (1998): 22–45.

Mathews, Donald G. *Slavery and Methodism: A Chapter in American Morality, 1780–1845.* Princeton, NJ: Princeton University Press, 1965.

Mbiti, John S. *African Religions and Philosophy.* 1969. Reprint, London: Heinemann, 1988.

———. *Concepts of God in Africa*. London: S.P.C.K. Holy Trinity Church, 1970.

McBride, Dwight A. *Impossible Witnesses: Truth, Abolitionism, and Slave Testimony*. New York: New York University Press, 2001.

McClintock, Anne. *Imperial Leather: Race, Gender, and Sexuality in the Colonial Conquest*. New York: Routledge, 1995.

McCulloch, Merran. *The Peoples of Sierra Leone Protectorate*. London: International African Institute, 1950.

McDowell, A. W. "Pluckamin One Hundred Years Ago." *Our Home: A Monthly Magazine . . . Mostly by Somerset and Hunterdon County Writers, and Largely Pertaining to These Counties* 1 (1873): 532.

McManus, Edgar J. *Black Bondage in the North*. Syracuse, NY: Syracuse University Press, 1973.

Melish, Joanne Pope. *Disowning Slavery: Gradual Emancipation and "Race" in New England, 1780–1860*. Ithaca, NY: Cornell University Press, 1998.

Messler, Abraham. *Centennial History of Somerset County*. Somerville, NJ: Jameson, 1878.

Migeod, F. W. H. "Personal Names among Some West African Tribes." *Journal of the African Society* 17 (1917): 38–45.

Mooney, Paul. *Black Is the New White: A Memoir*. New York: Simon Spotlight Entertainment, 2009.

Morgan, Jennifer L. *Laboring Women: Reproduction and Gender in New World Slavery*. Philadelphia: University of Pennsylvania Press, 2004.

Mulira, Jessie Gaston. "The Case of Voodoo in New Orleans." In *Africanisms in American Culture*, edited by Joseph E. Holloway, 34–68. Bloomington: Indiana University Press, 1990.

Mullin, Gerald W. *Flight and Rebellion: Slave Resistance in Eighteenth-Century Virginia*. New York: Oxford University Press, 1972.

Mullin, Michael. *Africa in America: Slave Acculturation and Resistance in the American South and the British Caribbean, 1736–1831*. Urbana: University of Illinois Press, 1992.

Mustakeem, Sowande'. "'I Never Have Such a Sickly Ship Before': Diet, Disease, and Mortality in 18th-Century Atlantic Slaving Voyages." *Journal of African American History* 93 (2008): 474–96.

Nash, Gary B. *Forging Freedom: The Formation of Philadelphia's Black Community, 1720–1840*. Cambridge, MA: Harvard University Press, 1988.

———. *Race and Revolution*. Madison, WI: Madison House, 1990.

Nash, Gary B., and Jean R. Soderlund. *Freedom by Degrees: Emancipation in Pennsylvania and Its Aftermath*. New York: Oxford University Press, 1991.

Nelson, William. *New Jersey Biographical and Genealogical Notes*. 1916. Reprint, Baltimore: Clearfield, 1992.

Newman, Debra L. "Black Women in the Era of the American Revolution in Pennsylvania." *Journal of Negro History* 61 (1976): 276–89.

Northup, David. *Africa's Discovery of Europe, 1450–1850*. New York: Oxford University Press, 2002.

Oakes, James. *The Ruling Race: A History of American Slaveholders*. New York: Knopf, 1982.

Painter, Nell Irvin. *Exodusters: Black Migration to Kansas after Reconstruction.* New York: Knopf, 1977.

———. *Sojourner Truth: A Life, A Symbol.* New York: Norton, 1996.

———. *Southern History across the Color Line.* Chapel Hill: University of North Carolina Press, 2002.

Parrinder, Geoffrey. *African Traditional Religion.* 3rd ed. Westport, CT: Greenwood, 1970.

———. *West African Religion: A Study of the Beliefs and Practices of Akan, Ewe, Yoruba, Ibo, and Kindred Peoples.* London: Epworth, 1969.

Patterson, Orlando. *Slavery and Social Death: A Comparative Study.* Cambridge, MA: Harvard University Press, 1982.

Phillips, Ulrich B. *American Negro Slavery: A Survey of the Supply, Employment, and Control of Negro Labor as Determined by the Plantation Regime.* 1918. Reprint, Baton Rouge: Louisiana State University Press, 1969.

Piersen, William D. *Black Yankees: The Development of an Afro-American Subculture in Eighteenth-Century New England.* Amherst: University of Massachusetts Press, 1988.

———."White Cannibals, Black Martyrs: Fear, Depression, and Religious Faith as Causes of Suicide among New Slaves." *Journal of Negro History* 62 (1977): 147–59.

Pingeon, Frances D. "An Abominable Business: The New Jersey Slave Trade, 1818." *New Jersey History* 109 (1991): 15–35.

———. *Blacks in the Revolutionary Era.* New Jersey's Revolutionary Experience 14. Trenton: New Jersey Historical Commission, 1975.

Pope-Hennessy, James. *Sins of the Father: A Study of the Atlantic Slave Traders, 1441–1807.* London: Weidenfeld and Nicolson, 1967.

Prakash, Gyan. "Subaltern Studies as Postcolonial Criticism." *American Historical Review* 99 (1994): 1475–90.

Pratt, Mary Louise. *Imperial Eyes: Travel Writing and Transculturation.* London: Routledge, 1992.

Price, Clement Alexander, ed. and comp. *Freedom Not Far Distant: A Documentary History of Afro-Americans in New Jersey.* Newark: New Jersey Historical Society, 1980.

Proctor, Nicolas W. *Bathed in Blood: Hunting and Mastery in the Old South.* Charlottesville: University Press of Virginia, 2002.

Pryor, Richard, and Todd Gold. *Pryor Convictions and Other Life Sentences.* New York: Pantheon, 1995.

Puckett, Newbell Niles, collector. *Black Names in America: Origins and Usage.* Edited by Murray Heller. Boston: Hall, 1975.

Pybus, Cassandra. *Epic Journeys of Freedom: Runaway Slaves of the American Revolution and their Global Quest for Liberty.* Boston: Beacon, 2006.

Quarles, Benjamin. *Black Abolitionists.* New York: Oxford University Press, 1969.

———. *The Negro in the American Revolution.* 1961. Reprint, New York: Norton, 1973.

———. "The Revolutionary War as a Black Declaration of Independence." In *Slavery and Freedom in the Age of the American Revolution*, edited by Ira Berlin and Ronald Hoffman, 283–302. Charlottesville: University Press of Virginia, 1983.

Raboteau, Albert J. *Slave Religion: The "Invisible Institution" in the Antebellum South.* New York: Oxford University Press, 1978.

Rael, Patrick. *Black Identity and Protest in the Antebellum North.* Chapel Hill: University of North Carolina Press, 2002.

Rawick, George P. *From Sundown to Sunup: The Making of the Black Community.* Westport, CT: Greenwood, 1972.

Ray, Benjamin C. *African Religions: Symbol, Ritual, and Community.* Englewood Cliffs, NJ: Prentice-Hall, 1976.

Rediker, Marcus. *The Slave Ship: A Human History.* New York: Viking Penguin, 2007.

Reed, Harry. *Platform for Change: The Foundations of the Northern Free Black Community, 1775–1865.* East Lansing: Michigan State University Press, 1994.

Reid-Pharr, Robert. "Violent Ambiguity: Martin Delany, Bourgeois Sadomasochism, and the Production of a Black National Masculinity." In *Representing Black Men*, edited by Marcellus Blount and George P. Cunningham, 73–94. New York: Routledge, 1996.

Reis, Joao Jose. *Slave Rebellion in Brazil: The Muslim Uprising of 1835 in Bahia.* Baltimore: Johns Hopkins University Press, 1993.

Robertson, Claire. "Africa into the Americas? Slavery and Women, the Family, and the Gender Division of Labor." In *More than Chattel: Black Women and Slavery in the Americas*, edited by David Barry Gaspar and Darlene Clark Hine, 3–40. Bloomington: Indiana University Press, 1996.

Robinson, Cedric J. *Black Marxism: The Making of the Black Radical Tradition.* 1983. Reprint, Chapel Hill: University of North Carolina Press, 2000.

Rodney, Walter. *A History of the Upper Guinea Coast, 1545–1800.* 1970. Reprint, New York: Monthly Review, 1982.

Rorabaugh, W. J. *The Alcoholic Republic: An American Tradition.* New York: Oxford University Press, 1979.

Said, Edward W. *Orientalism.* 1978. Reprint, New York: Vintage, 1994.

Schmidt, Hubert G. "Slavery and Attitudes on Slavery, Hunterdon County, New Jersey." *Proceedings of the New Jersey Historical Society* 58 (1940): 151–69, 240–53.

Schrag, F. J. "Theodorus Jacobus Frelinghuysen: The Father of American Pietism." *Church History* 14 (1945): 201–16.

Schwartz, Marie Jenkins. *Born in Bondage: Growing up Enslaved in the Antebellum South.* Cambridge, MA: Harvard University Press, 2000.

Scott, James C. *Domination and the Arts of Resistance: Hidden Transcripts.* New Haven, CT: Yale University Press, 1990.

———. *Weapons of the Weak: Everyday Forms of Peasant Resistance.* New Haven, CT: Yale University Press, 1985.

Scott, Kenneth. "The Slave Insurrection in New York in 1712." *New York Historical Society Quarterly* 45 (1961): 43–74.

Sengupta, Gunja. "Elites, Subalterns, and American Identities: A Case Study of African-American Benevolence." *American Historical Review* 109 (2004): 1104–39.

Sernett, Milton C. *Bound for the Promised Land: African American Religion and the Great Migration.* Durham, NC: Duke University Press, 1997.

Shengold, Leonard. *Soul Murder: The Effects of Child Abuse and Deprivation.* New Haven, CT: Yale University Press, 1989.

Sidbury, James. *Becoming African in America: Race and Nation in the Early Black Atlantic.* New York: Oxford University Press, 2007.

Sinclair, Donald A. "Somerset County Gravestones: Pleasant Plains Cemetery, Franklin Township." *Genealogical Magazine of New Jersey* 26 (1951): 85.

Slaughter, Thomas P. *Bloody Dawn: The Christiana Riot and Racial Violence in the Antebellum North.* New York: Oxford University Press, 1991.

Smallwood, Stephanie E. *Saltwater Slavery: A Middle Passage from Africa to American Diaspora.* Cambridge, MA: Harvard University Press, 2007.

Smith, Billy G. "Black Women Who Stole Themselves in Eighteenth-Century America." In *Inequality in Early America,* edited by Carla Gardina Pestana and Sharon V. Salinger. Hanover, NH: University Press of New England, 1999.

Smith, Billy G., and Richard Wojtowicz, eds. *Blacks Who Stole Themselves: Advertisements for Runaways in the Pennsylvania Gazette, 1728–1790.* Philadelphia: University of Pennsylvania Press, 1989.

Snell, James P., comp. *History of Hunterdon and Somerset Counties, New Jersey, with Illustrations and Biographical Sketches of its Prominent Men and Pioneers.* Philadelphia: Everts and Peck, 1881.

Sobel, Mechal. *Trabelin' On: The Slave Journey to an Afro-Baptist Faith.* Westport, CT: Greenwood, 1979.

———. *The World They Made Together: Black and White Values in Eighteenth-Century Virginia.* Princeton, NJ: Princeton University Press, 1987.

Soderlund, Jean R. "Black Women in Colonial Pennsylvania." *Pennsylvania Magazine of History and Biography* 107 (1983): 49–68.

———. *Quakers and Slavery: A Divided Spirit.* Princeton, NJ: Princeton University Press, 1985.

Spivak, Gayatri Chakravorty. "Can the Subaltern Speak?" In *Marxism and the Interpretation of Culture,* edited by Carry Nelson and Lawrence Grossberg, 271–313. Urbana: University of Illinois Press, 1988.

Stampp, Kenneth M. *The Peculiar Institution: Slavery in the Ante-Bellum South.* 1956. Reprint, New York: Vintage, 1989.

Staples, Robert. *Black Masculinity: The Black Man's Role in American Society.* San Francisco, CA: Black Scholar Press, 1982.

Starobin, Robert S. *Industrial Slavery in the Old South.* New York: Oxford University Press, 1970.

Stauffer, John. "Creating an Image in Black: The Power of Abolition Pictures." In *Prophets of Protest: Reconsidering the History of American Abolitionism,* edited by Timothy Patrick McCarthy and John Stauffer, 256–67. New York: Free Press, 2006.

Stevens, Stephanie B. *Outcast: A Story of Slavery in Readington Township, Hunterdon County, New Jersey.* White House Station, NJ: Merck, 2003.

Stevenson, Brenda E. "Gender Convention, Ideals, and Identity among Antebellum Virginia Slave Women." In *More Than Chattel: Black Women and Slavery in the Americas,* edited by David Barry Gaspar and Darlene Clark Hine, 169–90. Bloomington: Indiana University Press, 1996.

Stokes, Albert L. "The DeHart Family." *Genealogical Magazine of New Jersey* 60 (1965): 1–9.

Thayer, Theodore. *As We Were: The Story of Old Elizabethtown.* Elizabeth: New Jersey Historical Society, 1964.

Thornton, John. *Africa and Africans in the Making of the Atlantic World, 1400–1800.* 2nd ed. Cambridge: Cambridge University Press, 1998.

———. "African Dimensions of the Stono Rebellion." In *A Question of Manhood: A Reader in U.S. Black Men's History and Masculinity.* Vol. 1, *"Manhood Rights": The Construction of Black Male History and Manhood, 1750–1870,* edited by Darlene Clark Hine and Earnestine Jenkins, 115–29. Bloomington: Indiana University Press, 1999.

Trouillot, Michel-Rolph. *Silencing the Past: Power and the Production of History.* Boston: Beacon, 1995.

Turner, Lorenzo Dow. *Africanisms in the Gullah Dialect.* 1949. Reprint, Columbia: University of South Carolina Press, 2002.

Van Deburg, William L. *Slavery and Race in American Popular Culture.* Madison: University of Wisconsin Press, 1984.

van Gennep, Arnold. *The Rites of Passage.* Translated by Monika B. Vizedom and Gabrielle L. Caffee. 1909. Reprint, Chicago: University of Chicago Press, 1961.

Van Valen, J. M. *History of Bergen County, New Jersey.* New York: New Jersey Publishing and Engraving, 1900.

Verdery, Katherine. *What Was Socialism, and What Comes Next?* Princeton, NJ: Princeton University Press, 1996.

Voorhees, Ralph. "Franklin Township Historical Notes." *Somerset County Historical Quarterly* 5–6 (1916–17): 5:28–9, 6:91–92.

Wacker, Peter O. *Land and People: A Cultural Geography of Preindustrial New Jersey: Origins and Settlement Patterns.* New Brunswick, NJ: Rutgers University Press, 1975.

Walkowitz, Judith R. *City of Dreadful Delight: Narratives of Sexual Danger in Late-Victorian London.* Chicago: University of Chicago Press, 1992.

Wall, John P. *The Chronicles of New Brunswick, New Jersey.* New Brunswick, NJ: Thatcher-Anderson, 1931.

Webber, Thomas L. *Deep Like the Rivers: Education in the Slave Quarter Community, 1831–1865.* New York: Norton, 1978.

Weiner, Marli F. *Mistresses and Slaves: Plantation Women in South Carolina, 1830–1880.* Urbana: University of Illinois Press, 1998.

Weiss, Harry B. *Country Doctor: Cornelius Wilson Larison of Ringoes, Hunterdon County, New Jersey, 1837–1910: Physician, Farmer, Educator, Author, Editor, Publisher, and Exponent of Phonetic Spelling.* Trenton: New Jersey Agricultural Society, 1953.

Weiss, Harry B., and Grace M. Weiss. *An Introduction to Crime and Punishment in Colonial New Jersey.* Trenton, NJ: Past Times Press, 1960.

West, Cornell. *Race Matters.* Boston: Beacon, 1993.

West, Emily. *Chains of Love: Slave Couples in Antebellum South Carolina.* Urbana: University of Illinois Press, 2004.

White, Deborah Gray. *Ar'n't I a Woman? Female Slaves in the Plantation South.* New York: Norton, 1985.

White, Shane. "'It Was a Proud Day': African Americans, Festivals, and Parades in the North, 1741–1834." *Journal of American History* 81 (1994): 13–50.

———. *Somewhat More Independent: The End of Slavery in New York City, 1770–1810.* Athens: University of Georgia Press, 1991.

White, Shane, and Graham White. *Stylin': African American Expressive Culture from its Beginnings to the Zoot Suit.* Ithaca, NY: Cornell University Press, 1998.

Whitehead, William A. *Contributions to the Early History of Perth Amboy and the Adjoining Country, with Sketches of Men and Events in New Jersey during the Provincial Era.* New York: Appleton, 1856.

Wickes, Stephen. *History of Medicine in New Jersey and of its Medical Men, From the Settlement of the Province to A. D. 1800.* Newark, NJ: Dennis, 1879.

Williams, Heather Andrea. "'Commenced to Think Like a Man': Literacy and Manhood in African American Civil War Regiments." In *Southern Manhood: Perspectives on Masculinity in the Old South,* edited by Craig Thompson Friend and Lorri Glover, 196–219. Athens: University of Georgia Press, 2004.

Williams-Myers, A. J. *Long Hammering: Essays on the Forging of an African American Presence in the Hudson River Valley to the Early Twentieth Century.* Trenton, NJ: Africa World Press, 1994.

Wood, Betty. "Some Aspects of Female Resistance to Chattel Slavery in Low Country Georgia, 1763–1815." *Historical Journal* 30 (1987): 603–22.

Wood, Gordon S. *The Radicalism of the American Revolution.* New York: Knopf, 1992.

Wood, Peter H. *Black Majority: Negroes in Colonial South Carolina from 1670 through the Stono Rebellion.* New York: Knopf, 1974.

Woodson, Carter Godwin *The Education of the Negro Prior to 1861.* 1919. Reprint, New York: Arno, 1968.

Wright, Giles R. *Afro-Americans in New Jersey: A Short History.* Trenton: New Jersey Historical Commission, 1988.

Wright, Marion Thompson. *The Education of Negroes in New Jersey.* New York: Columbia University Teachers College, 1941.

———. "New Jersey Laws and the Negro." *Journal of Negro History* 28 (1943): 156–99.

Wyatt-Brown, Bertram. "The Mask of Obedience: Male Slave Psychology in the Old South." *American Historical Review* 93 (1988): 1228–52.

Yetman, Norman R. "Ex-Slave Interviews and the Historiography of Slavery." *American Quarterly* 36 (1984): 181–210.

Zahan, Dominique. *The Religion, Spirituality, and Thought of Traditional Africa.* Translated by Kate Ezra Martin and Lawrence M. Martin. 1970. Reprint, Chicago: University of Chicago Press, 1979.

Zilversmit, Arthur. *The First Emancipation: The Abolition of Slavery in the North.* Chicago: University of Chicago Press, 1967.

———. "Liberty and Property: New Jersey and the Abolition of Slavery." *New Jersey History* 88 (1970): 215–26.

Index

CPSIA information can be obtained at www.ICGtesting.com
Printed in the USA
BVOW010527040113

309762BV00001B/41/P